NORTH KOREA

D1569411

NORTH KOREA

PEACE?
NUCLEAR WAR?

WILLIAM H. OVERHOLT, EDITOR

ISBN 978-1-7337378-0-7
ISBN 978-1-7337378-1-4 (ebook)

Library of Congress Control Number: 2019902114

Published by The Mossavar-Rahmani Center
for Business and Government

First Edition, 2019

Publisher's Cataloging-In-Publication Data
(Prepared by The Donohue Group, Inc.)
Names: Overholt, William H., editor.
Title: North Korea : Peace? Nuclear war? / William H. Overholt, editor.
Description: [Cambridge, Massachusetts] : Mossavar-Rahmani Center for Business and Government, [2019] | Includes bibliographical references.
Identifiers: ISBN 9781733737807
ISBN 9781733737814 (ebook)
Subjects: LCSH: Korea (North)–Foreign relations–East Asia. | Korea (North)–Foreign relations–United States. | Korea (North)–Politics and government–2011- | Korea (North)–Military policy. | Nuclear weapons–Korea (North) | Kim, Chŏng-ŭn, 1984-

Classification: LCC DS935.7778 .N67 2019 (print) | LCC DS935.7778 (ebook) | DDC 951.93052–dc23

Printed in Korea

SPONSORS OF THIS BOOK

HARVARD Kennedy School
MOSSAVAR-RAHMANI CENTER
for Business and Government

HARVARD Kennedy School
ASH CENTER
for Democratic Governance
and Innovation

KOREA INSTITUTE
HARVARD UNIVERSITY

*Sponsorship of research does not imply
endorsement of any opinion or policy.*

Compliments of

PACIFIC CENTURY INSTITUTE

19850 Plummer Street. Chatsworth, CA 91311
PHONE: 818-721-5601 FAX: 818-459-7448
pci@pacificcenturyinst.org

Table of Contents

Foreword

William H. Overholt

The North Korean nuclear crisis presents the contemporary world's greatest risk, not just of major war but most importantly of nuclear war. Despite its importance the crisis is being managed in a treacherous context of public ignorance and misinformation. Most Americans could not locate Korea on a map.

On May 8, 2018, the U.S. Secretary of State, a former Director of the CIA, when engaged in a negotiation of historic consequence, referred to North Korea's leader, Kim Jong Un, as Chairman Un, roughly equivalent to a Korean referring to Donald John Trump as President John. A television commentator of such distinction that she had lead roles for both Fox and CNN, Greta von Susteren, referred to Kim Jong Un's father, Kim Jong Il (pronounced "ill"), as Kim Jong the Second. When the Trump-Kim summit in Singapore was imminent, South Korean religious leaders, members of a group I had recently addressed, called me requesting an email address for President Trump so that they could send a mass mailing with the allegation that their own President Moon is a communist. Some leading conservative South Korean commentators assert that China doesn't care about North Korea's nuclear weapons. (For the record: Kim Jong Un's family name is Kim, Moon is not a communist and China cares deeply.) Similar ignorance has been a primary source of the tragedies of the Korean War, the Vietnam War, and the interminable bloodletting in Afghanistan, Syria and Iraq. After we lost 50,000 lives in Vietnam, some prominent American leaders said they wished they had understood that the North Vietnamese saw themselves as leading a nationalist, anti-colonial fight.

This volume assembles the work of leading experts in the hope of dispelling the misinformation and lack of information. Every author here writes from career-long study of Korea and personal experience in Korea. I have encouraged them to choose their own topics and present their own views, while making an effort to cover the most vital issues.

We can overcome lack of information and dispel misinformation, but we cannot dispel disagreement. Our chapters begin with what are perhaps the most articulate opposite views of the prospects for a denuclearized peace in Korea. We make no apologies for disagreement among our authors. We try to present enough context so that readers can make their own highly informed choices.

I have also welcomed different styles of presentation. Some subjects lend themselves to careful, academic explication. Conveying the tone of relationships sometimes requires a more conversational approach. I know from personal experience that warmth and trust between negotiators can make the difference between success and failure. The reader needs to know that sometimes, properly managed, a negotiation even between old adversaries can achieve a level of trust.

This volume was funded by the Pacific Century Institute. The Institute just requested that we assemble expertise in a context of vast public ignorance of the facts, the issues and the stakes. It did not designate opinions to be followed or authors to be selected.

No opinions offered by any contributor to this volume are endorsed by Harvard University or by any of the three Harvard institutes that supported the project.

As the assembler of this collection, I have tried to provide balance and as much thoroughness as possible. When I chose experts I not only chose ones with different viewpoints – Republican and Democrat, "soft" and "hard" – but I also let them choose their topics. When I summarize the views of certain groups I try to do so objectively; hopefully my characterizations feel accurate to each viewpoint (with some inevitable complications because no group is uniform in its opinions).

But I also offer my assessments. As Editor, I am not just a dispassionate compiler of others' opinions. I care deeply about the issues and offer judgments as seem appropriate. Although I happen to be the editor, my views have no more weight than those of any of the very distinguished chapter authors.

As I have read through these essays, and as I spoke with colleagues around the world, some strong convictions gelled. We are at a turning point in Korea, a turning point in U.S. foreign policy, a turning point in U.S.-China relations, and a turning point in the chances of having a peaceful world. Syria and the Ukraine are important but not so unique. The present North Korea crisis presents a special risk, a global risk, and a special opportunity that will not recur.

I am American. Although I try very hard to listen carefully, and to integrate, other countries' viewpoints, I write as an American and in my overview chapter I use "we" and "us" to refer to Americans and their interests. Having said this, I have worked very hard to find the most authentic and persuasive Chinese voices, and I believe that Richard Samuels and Eric Heginbotham articulate the Japanese government viewpoint accurately. Sung-Yoon Lee and Chung-In Moon are the most outspoken of the conservative and liberal South Korean viewpoints.

Just as we open with the two most pessimistic and optimistic views, respectively, the volume closes with two experts of exceptional experience and insight, whose knowledge conveys the extreme difficulty and complexity of reaching an agreement, followed by three exceptional essays that convey the value of sometimes persisting through great difficulty, against high odds, in building trust and bridging divides.

— 1 —

Overview

William H. Overholt

The Korean nuclear dilemma has deep historical roots. President Eisenhower decided to accept a humiliating draw in the Korean War rather than use nuclear weapons, thereby setting a valuable precedent for nuclear restraint that would terribly (but appropriately) frustrate General Westmoreland in Vietnam.

More directly precedent to today's nuclear proliferation crisis, in the early 1970s South Korea, then less stable than North Korea and still economically and militarily inferior, authorized its Agency for Defense Development (ADD) to develop nuclear weapons. The ADD's progress was startling: within a few years it progressed from its first task, to design a screwdriver that wouldn't break fixing rusty jeeps, to imminent manufacture of sophisticated nuclear weapons.

Richard Nixon intervened decisively against the burgeoning South Korean and Taiwanese nuclear weapon programs, threatening to sever their alliance, political and economic ties to the U.S. (U.S. government-funded research on the effort to stop South Korea, to understand the regional pressures for nuclear proliferation, and to refine U.S. nuclear strategy in Asia, led me to publish the first book on these subjects, an edited 1976 collection called *Asia's Nuclear Future*.) Nixon's intervention was successful because it gave both states a choice: have nuclear weapons but be strategically helpless or, on the other hand, enjoy economic support, political support, and security ensured by alliance with the world's most powerful country in the absence of nuclear weapons.

With Taiwan the nuclear cessation was temporary; Taipei tried again in the early 1980s and we Americans stopped them again.

(Incidentally, China owes the U.S. a big one for twice stopping the Taiwan nuclear weapon program.)

South Korea not only paused; it abandoned nuclear ambitions – notwithstanding some current controversies there. The decisive reason for the firm abandonment was the argument, made initially by Americans but then widely accepted by the Korean establishment, that a nuclear exchange on the Korean peninsula would mean the end of Korean civilization. On sober reflection, risking the end of their civilization was unacceptable to South Korean leaders. The North has so far been too preoccupied with tactical survival to reflect or act on such deep thoughts.

Theory One and Theory Two

Opponents and proponents of negotiations cluster around two opposing sets of ideas about North Korea and its strategic situation. While each camp includes people with a range of views, it is useful to describe the opposing positions in terms of the central tendencies of each. Each paragraph in the sections below on Theory One and Theory Two should be understood to be prefaced by "According to this theory, . . ."

Theory One

Opponents of flexible negotiations portray North Korea and its international tactics as relatively unchanging. After all, the regime is a grandfather (Kim Il-Sung), his son, and his grandson. They are similar personalities in a similar situation. They are dangerous international tricksters. They initiate violent incidents, for instance raining artillery on innocent South Korean islanders, then make peaceful sounding noises and extract Western money in return for empty promises. The cycle is a fund-raising gambit, which naive Washingtonians (who, unlike the North Koreans are sincere and reliable) repeatedly fall for.

Periodically Pyongyang tries limited market economic reforms but these are always insincere and always fail.

North Korea is extraordinarily dangerous, a powerful tiger always threatening to escape from its cage and destroy South Korea. Its provocations periodically kill people. The implacable leadership is determined to unify Korea under its control and will use any means to achieve that goal. Nuclear weapons are a principal tool for accomplishing that goal.

At the same time, North Korea's economic weakness makes it extremely vulnerable to collapse. In this view, the U.S. might just want to adopt the George W. Bush policy of waiting until it collapses. If North Korea collapses, the assumption is that it would be absorbed by South Korea and we would have a unified democratic Korea allied with the U.S.

Tighter and tighter sanctions are the only effective path to denuclearization. If tight enough, they will be effective. Any modification of sanctions to reward North Korean good behavior communicates weak resolve and increases North Korea's resources for expanding its nuclear arsenal. North Korea must destroy its nuclear weapons and missile delivery capabilities quickly; only after this is accomplished can any sanctions can be lifted. (In the chapter that follows, Sung-Yoon Lee says that in addition all political prisoners must be released and "all international norms" for aid must be satisfied before sanctions are lifted.)

According to most proponents of Theory One, China is basically supportive of North Korea despite lip service to nuclear disarmament. Its determination to avoid North Korean collapse means that it gives enough economic support to make sanctions ineffective. If it really wanted to, China could force Kim Jong Un to give up nuclear weapons.

In this view, the idea that negotiations can lead to denuclearization is a fantasy. On the U.S. side, negotiations are a Twitter whim, poorly thought through. North Korea has never been willing to follow through on commitments to denuclearization.

North Korea will not abandon the goal of taking over South Korea and nuclear weapons provide it with a credible strategy for doing so.

North Korea will not give up its nuclear weapons. Indeed it cannot afford to. It cannot afford to give the U.S. and China the complete list of its nuclear and missile sites that would be necessary to verify any negotiated deal. A peaceful North Korea is an oxymoron. A unified Korea, one of the fantasies of the peace advocates, might well become a pawn of China and therefore is not in the U.S. interest.

North Korea is demanding denuclearization of the peninsula – in both the north and south. It not only wants U.S. nuclear weapons withdrawn from South Korea; it wants U.S. forces out. It wants an end to U.S. nuclear guarantees of South Korea. It even seems to want all U.S. nuclear forces out of the Western Pacific. That is unacceptable to the U.S. and its allies.

Negotiations have an overwhelming risk of failure. They become an excuse for relaxing sanctions and therefore just enhance the nuclear danger. They are therefore worse than a waste of time, because they undermine the sanctions regime whose tightening is the only credible path to denuclearization.

Theory Two

Proponents of negotiations believe that the past is not necessarily prologue. Kim Jong Un is not his father or his grandfather. He has a different education, different life horizon, and different priorities including especially a high priority for the economy.

Six decades after Park Chung Hee and four decades after Deng Xiaoping saved their countries with economy-first policies, Kim Jong Un has concluded that giving the economy – not just the military – priority is vital to both national success and personal survival. While he is severely constrained by the political vulnerability of his cloistered society, by implacable demands from his own military, and by the tiny economy's vulnerability to neighboring economic giants, he is nevertheless making market-oriented changes and they are working. Non-state ownership remains even fuzzier in North Korea than in China (where it is often very fuzzy), and much of the market activity remains illegal, but everywhere – Pyongyang, the coast, interior rural areas – is showing visible improvement. The statistics are arguable, the evidence of the eyeballs is not.

While one can never rule out a reversion to the past, these changes are addictive. Growth improves elite support and reduces popular resentment. Growth provides the resources to improve security. Growth reduces international contempt. Growth is essential to Kim Jong Un's long-term survival and he knows it. He has promised growth and even, against all precedent, apologized to his people when actual growth was not up to expectations. Political and economic vulnerabilities mean there is virtually no chance that he can create another Asian miracle economy, but economic distortions have been so severe that even limited, incremental openings to market forces create significant growth.

North Korea, in this view, is not a voracious tiger. It is a frightened, tiny animal, cornered by huge neighbors, its economy only about two percent the size of South Korea in purchasing power. Like a cornered animal, it knows only how to bite. Over the years it has indeed bitten, accepting no normal rules, outraging international society, but under Kim Jong Un it has not been launching attacks or killing innocent South Korean civilians. It is looking for a way out of that corner.

Nuclear weapons do not provide North Korea with a credible strategy for conquering the south. The historical precedents for a mouse eating a neighboring elephant are quite limited, even if the mouse puffs up its fur and tries to make a big noise. Nuclear weapons give North Korea the capability to commit suicide while blowing up the whole peninsula, but they do not enable the mouse to eat the elephant.

North Korea has been quite unreliable. Its desperate internal politics often require sudden adjustments. Internationally, the tiny animal is extremely skittish. Its instincts are to hedge everything, to bluff and threaten and bite. Most recently, after what was called the Leap Day agreement, suddenly it launched a missile, destroying all the credibility of the agreement.

What Theory One people, and every commentator in Washington hoping for a future government job (almost all of them) does not mention is that Washington has also been unreliable. Theory Two argues that sanctions, as a nearly exclusive tool to induce compliance, have in fact been tried. They have failed in most international situations and they have failed with North Korea. The squeeze on North Korea been severe but ineffectual. Sanctions are essential, but they can only be effective as part of a balanced set of incentives; there must be a credible path to peace and growth.

Likewise the expectations of North Korean collapse, most prominent in the George W. Bush administration, have failed. The regime survived even the Kim Jong Il famine. Threats from the U.S. and China get the adrenaline pumping, even in this tiny animal, and strengthen local nationalism. In the unlikely event that collapse did occur, the most likely result would be civil war, spreading to a much wider war, or Chinese incorporation of North Korea as a tiny new province.

China feels very strongly about denuclearization of North Korea. Each incoming U.S. president has been pleasantly surprised by the depth of Chinese feeling and of Chinese cooperation. The Chinese posture is key to any argument that negotiations can be successful.

The formula for success, in this view, is a combination of tough sanctions, calibrated economic incentives in response to good behavior, and phased confidence building to an agreed goal.

In the view of Theory Two, negotiations are risky, and implementation of any agreement will be fraught and risky for the indefinite future. But there is a chance. The risk of nuclear war compels us to take that chance.

Both sides need to back away from extreme positions. For a long time the U.S. demand was CVID: complete, verifiable, irreversible denuclearization – without a credible path to peace and development. Conversely, the North Korean definition of denuclearization was requiring the withdrawal of U.S. nuclear weapons from the whole Western Pacific. The purpose of negotiations is convergence toward an agreement that satisfies neither side's most extravagant demands. Fortunately both sides have been showing signs of flexibility.

Assessment

Adherents to both Theory One and Theory Two agree that North Korea will not simply dismantle its nuclear weapons quickly. Nuclear weapons are the only security it has.

They also converge on an understanding that the risks to any successful negotiation are enormous. If the balance of power in Pyongyang changes, if a new president from either party comes to office in the U.S., if a conservative government is elected soon in South Korea, agreed understandings may well be repudiated. The complexities of verifying any agreement create innumerable flashpoints. Flashpoints are exacerbated by profound mutual mistrust and there is currently no clear strategy for confidence building that would overcome the mistrust.

Beyond those areas of agreement, there is a fundamental divide. But there is also a factual basis for assessing the arguments over strategy. This factual basis may not, indeed will not, resolve the deeply held differences between proponents of Theory One and Theory Two, but it can force them to modify and refine their views. And it can help the engaged, informed public to decide what approach to support.

What follows is my assessment of some of the major issues. Again, although I am the editor my views are in no way superior to those of the contending analyses below. Readers must make some decisions for themselves. Note that we do not have contending views on all subjects, such as some of the economic developments, because in some areas the evidence is just overwhelming. It's appropriate to begin by looking at the actual purposes nuclear weapons serve.

Purposes of nuclear weapons

Nuclear weapons serve many purposes and have crucial limitations. In India the initiation of nuclear weapons seems to have been driven by politicians' desire for domestic prestige and that motivation may well have been crucial to the timing of key events in North Korea as Kim Jong Un sought to consolidate his leadership role.

Nuclear weapons also seem to have played a crucial role in domestic bargaining over resources. The North Korean military is accustomed to total dominance over available resources. Kim Il-Sung's "military-first" policy has been both one of the core quasi-ideological commitments of the regime and the decisive reason why North Korea has fallen so far behind South Korea, whose priority has been economic development. On one hand, North Korea's strategic haplessness in the face of a South Korea whose purchasing power GDP is 48 times North Korea's leads the North's generals to insist that they need even more. On the other hand, it is obvious to Kim Jong Un that reversing the relative economic decline is the key to long-run strategic survival. Domestically, overcoming the impoverishment and famine caused by his father is crucial to Kim Jong Un's personal ability to live a normal life span.

This dilemma is a grossly exaggerated version of President Eisenhower's domestic dilemma. Facing a Soviet threat and a Republican Congress that wanted to fund defense generously but was balking at funding an interstate highway system, Eisenhower squared the circle. He promised that nuclear weapons would provide "more bang for a buck," thereby limiting the need for additional expensive conventional weapons, and he justified the interstate highway system on military grounds, saying that in the event of a Soviet invasion it would be necessary to move forces across the country quickly. Similarly, in the desperate North Korean struggle over resource allocation, nuclear weapons can justify a shift in the direction of economic priorities. With nuclear weapons, fewer tanks are required, so some resources can be diverted to the economy.

The core value of North Korean nuclear weapons is of course military. Although the army has huge manpower and many weapons, North Korea remains a military midget in a land of giants: China, Russia, Japan, the U.S., and South Korea. North Korean artillery and tanks could devastate Seoul overnight (this is called surge power), but then its inferior technology and training would ensure rapid defeat by South Korea and the U.S. Nuclear weapons level the playing field somewhat.

Nuclear weapons also provide international stature to a midget without friends. China tries to ensure that North Korea will not collapse, and Russia provides some economic support to needle the U.S., but Chinese leaders despise their frenemy. Kim Jong Un not only represents a midget country but also he personally was initially treated as a humorous figure – too young, too pudgy, and with a funny haircut. Nuclear weapons got Kim Jong Un his meetings with Donald Trump and made people parse his statements carefully.

While they level the playing field somewhat, nuclear weapons are not useful offensively. This is even more true for North Korea than for Russia and the United States. The fantasy of North Korea using to nuclear weapons or nuclear weapon threats to absorb South Korea is plausible only to Washington right-wingers who have not studied nuclear strategy. My first boss, Herman Kahn, the right-wing founder of modern nuclear strategy, always emphasized that in a nuclear world the only value of nuclear weapons is to deter the other side from using nuclear weapons. Half an hour after any offensive use of nuclear weapons, North Korea would disappear from the map. Since both sides know that, offensive nuclear threats by Pyongyang would be futile. While they are the near-perfect defensive weapon, North Korea's nukes are offensively worthless.

Since they are exclusively useful for defense, a credible peace would theoretically be even more useful. Then the kinds of considerations that led South Korea to abandon its nuclear weapons in the 1970s might kick in. But today the obstacles to a credible peace seem to most people insurmountable.

Is this time different?

Many of the factors that have made agreements difficult in the past remain today: contending forces in Pyongyang, changing administrations in Washington, intense mutual mistrust, the complexities of defining denuclearization, the difficulties for foreigners of verifying any agreement and the risks to Pyongyang of allowing thorough verification.

But much has changed too. Kim has a Swiss education. He knows something of how the rest of the world thinks, and he knows that the economies of the rest of the world work much better than his. He knows that whereas his father, older, ill, and with a short time horizon, could survive a normal lifespan despite causing economic devastation and a horrific famine, the son has needs to survive for four or five decades. His father just needed to survive a limited number of years, but Kim Jong Un has no chance of personal survival, in office or physically, through a normal lifespan if he does not fix the economy.

As Dwight Perkins shows, political constraints limit what Kim can achieve economically, but there is room to do decisively better than his father and grandfather. And as Andrei Lankov shows, Kim Jong Un is making decisive changes in the national priorities to emphasize economic growth, he is making structural changes in the economy, and those changes are producing growth that is visible to the eye in most areas of the economy. This is a decisive departure from past performance.

His grandfather only knew Soviet socialist ideas of how to manage an economy. His father tried a few half-baked and halfhearted market initiatives, which failed miserably. Kim Jong Un has a clearer under-standing of the required direction of change and far more determina-tion to do what is needed. His model is China, but political constraints limit his emulation. China's rules about corporate ownership are fuzzy; North Korea's new rules are much fuzzier and indeed mostly comprise the government looking the other way while an emergent entrepre-neurial class does things that are technically illegal. Moreover, polit-ical vulnerabilities make it impossible for North Korea, at least for now, to encourage foreign direct investment the way China did. But the market distortions have been so severe that even a very limited move in the right direction can be – is being – transformative.

Kim Jong Un is also transforming the social ambiance of North Korea. It remains hideously oppressive, of course. But Kim has bet his job on economic improvement and has conveyed that publicly. In his 2018 New Year's Day speech he even gave an unprecedented apology to the people for not having fully achieved his economic goals. Formerly, foreign books were dangerous. In 2008 former Special Forces Colonel Denny Lane noted (in privately but widely circulated letters) that very few people would even smile. Now visitors to North Korea report that young North Korean academics are hungry for American books and their superiors are encouraging that hunger. A Chinese expert (not one of our authors) assured me that, if I visit North Korea now, younger scholars and officials will open up easily; the key to a lively conversation, he said, is to laugh heartily at their dirty jokes and have a few dirty jokes to contribute oneself. So great are the changes that a vast generation gap has opened between the new Kim Jong Un generation and the older people who can't grasp or accept the new ways. All this is new under Kim Jong Un, potentially transformative, and quite risky for him. He knows the risks and is deliberately taking them.

One of the cosmological constants of the North Korean equation has been that it is an isolated hermit kingdom, whose leaders can only retain power so long as they keep their people from knowing how poor and oppressed they are compared with most of the rest of the world an particularly compared with South Korea. As Dwight Perkins argues, this limits their economic development, since rapid development would require a lot more trade and, crucially, foreign investment. But the old cosmological constant of isolation is changing decisively. North Koreans now know how much more prosperous China is. They know that South Korea is more prosperous and freer. They don't know magnitudes and details, but they know life is much better outside North Korea. Many try desperately to escape to China and South Korea. Kim Jong Un has opened the door much wider – not at all wide, but wider – as repeat visitors from all countries attest. His imperative is to manage down the slippery slope. His moves are tentative and contradictory (remember China's "socialist market economy"), far more so than China because he cannot suddenly repudiate his father and grandfather, but the direction is clear. Most older people in his country have been successfully indoctrinated by the ideology of the socialist hermit kingdom with military-first priorities and are very skeptical of Kim Jong Un's new directions.

Nuclear weapons have made some of this shift possible by giving Kim bargaining power with his generals and with the older generation. (Some of the older generation, including some of the top generals, had to be dispatched rather unpleasantly in order to begin the shift, but that has now largely happened.) They have given him and his country the stature they sought. Having facilitated the shift, nuclear weapons are now the principal inhibitor of even more economic success, because they incur sanctions.

There is now also a new situation in South Korea – a competent liberal government that is committed to a peace initiative. The previous liberal government, under Roh Moo Hyun, was inexperienced and incompetent and faced a relatively united conservative opposition. The current government under President Moon is experienced, competent, faces a seriously fragmented conservative opposition, and has strong public support for its peace initiative. This situation, however, is fragile, because, as Carter Eckert notes, although the peace initiative is popular, poor economic performance under Moon is undermining his support and increasing the risk that he would be replaced by a conservative government that might well repudiate some of his initiatives.

Another potentially decisive change is that the Koreans, both north and south, have taken charge of their relationship. The U.S. and China (not so much Russia and Japan) still have huge influence, but there is a crucial shift of the initiative from foreigners to Koreans. The emotional momentum of the talks is decisively different when there is a pervasive feeling that the Koreans are gradually taking charge of their own destiny. At the same time this has been a bit unsettling for Washington, which is accustomed to giving orders and having them obeyed, albeit occasionally with some complaining and minor pushback.

Importantly, China and the U.S. have moved from saying that North Korea is the other country's problem to acknowledging that North Korean nuclear weapons create immense security risks for both and that both have to be fully engaged in pressing for denuclearization. They are both now fully engaged. That too is a potentially decisive new development.

China's role

Contrary to the assumptions of some Western commentators, China has long been strongly opposed to North Korea's development of nuclear weapons. Each incoming U.S. president has been surprised at how cooperative China has been with efforts to slow or stop DPRK nuclear development. China is concerned that, if turmoil occurred within North Korea, or between North and South Korea, nuclear weapons could be used, with consequences for Chinese territory and people. Moreover, North Korean-Chinese relations sometimes get very feisty. While Chinese leaders will never articulate the concern publicly, Beijing and Shanghai are just as likely nuclear targets as Los Angeles and Washington DC. Some Chinese concerns are more immediate. Key North Korean nuclear facilities are close to the Chinese border, with inadequate safety provisions; babies in that North Korean border area are being born with no arms, no legs, no genitals. China is very worried that such nefarious conditions will spill to the Chinese side of the border too. And China worries that North Korean nuclear weapons will induce South Korea, Japan and perhaps others in China's border areas to go nuclear. That would decisively shift the regional strategic balance against China.

China's opposition to DPRK nukes is not a concession to the U.S. Frequently expressed concern in U.S. media that Trump's trade war or other Sino-American tensions will reduce Chinese cooperation against North Korean nuclearization are therefore mostly misplaced (but highhanded U.S. tactics can alienate China on some issues.)

Two personal epiphanies among many can illustrate China's depth of feeling. In 1994 I was having lunch with a Chinese official in a private dining room of Bank of China tower in Hong Kong. We were interrupted by a knock on the door and a minion came in with a folded message. The official read the message and shouted in a tone of exultant triumph. What happened? I asked. He said that a senior Chinese delegation had gone to Pyongyang to confront Kim Il Sung about the nuclear weapons program. The confrontation became very severe. Kim Il Sung got up, left the room, and dropped dead. My Chinese host thought this was a wonderful result.

In 2018 I was participating in a Track 2 meeting about regional issues and we asked a leading retired Chinese general to lead the discussion of North Korea. He said the People's Liberation Army's (PLA) main concern was that President Trump would be so anxious for a deal that he would accept North Korea retaining some nuclear weapons for a long period. China could not accept that. The only number of North Korean nuclear weapons acceptable to the PLA, he said, was zero.

Tensions between China and North Korea are sometimes severe. In reaction to North Korea's nuclear development Xi Jinping long refused to meet with Kim Jong Un. He visited Seoul before meeting with North Korean leaders – a huge insult to Kim Jong Un. After 2014 North Korean official media often referred to China as an "enemy." Chinese and U.S. military leaders at one point discussed what a division of labor in bombing North Korean nuclear facilities might look like; according to Chinese analysts Kim's awareness of that is one reason why he has become more motivated to achieve a deal. Kim Jong Un killed his half brother out of fear that China was nurturing him as a potential alternative leader of North Korea. Our Chinese authors disclose that Kim Jong Un actively sought to empower South Korean conservatives to support the U.S. THAAD anti-missile system, anathema to China, in order to divide South Korea from China.

China does not have the power to force North Korean submission. As Andrei Lankov has said, China has a sledgehammer but not a lever. It can destroy North Korea, but short of destroying it China cannot force compliance. The North Koreans are tough, nationalistic and willing to endure tremendous privation.

Americans often see China's unwillingness to destabilize North Korea economically as evidence that China doesn't put a high priority on denuclearization. China itself sees denuclearization as a very high priority indeed, but for them denuclearization is one component of a policy of ensuring against problems in North Korea that might destabilize China's border region. Chinese sanctions on North Korea have in fact been very forceful, much more consequential for the DPRK economy than all other sanctions combined. On occasion China has even cut off vital energy exports. North Korean students in China are forbidden to take any science, engineering or technology courses. But China, like South Korea, believes that sanctions must be supplemented by rewards for good behavior. That sometimes stresses the relationship with members of the U.S. establishment who believe that denuclearization depends on a single-minded determination to tighten sanctions.

The most important aspect of Chinese policy appears in the paper by our Chinese authors, one of whom was long the Chinese military's top North Korea-watcher. It must not be buried toward the end of a long essay:

"If he [Kim Jong Un] breaks his promise for denuclearization once again, the leaders of these countries will conclude that 'all the moderate and peaceful measures for tackling the Korean nuclear issue have already lost effect, and only the option of military action is left.' If that is the case, there will be no stopping an external military attack on North Korea."

Kim Jong Un knows that. He knows that the PLA has shown willingness to open the discussion with the Pentagon about a division of labor for a military attack on North Korean nuclear facilities. Anyone who thinks that we are dealing with "same old, same old" in the current discussions with Kim Jong Un needs to re-read those lines again and again. The author of those sentences was a top Chinese intelligence officer for North Korea.

The Japanese role

Japan's role, by both inclination and strategic position, is to be a strong advocate of an exclusive focus on denuclearization as the goal of negotiations and on ever-stronger sanctions as the predominant strategy for denuclearization. Japan is fearful of peace between the Koreas and determined to avoid Korean reunification. It sees peace or unification as creating a more unified Korean hostility to Japan and as giving China an opportunity to increase its influence at the expense of Japan. Any extended negotiation or gradual reduction of North Korea's nuclear weapons might curtail Washington's fear of vulnerability to future North Korean ICBMs but will leave Japan vulnerable to more than 100 current ICBMs. Japan's intense concern is quite reasonable.

Both Koreas are intensely hostile to Japan. Both fear China but dislike Japan a lot more than they dislike China. The previous, very conservative South Korean governments had this attitude. For instance South Korea has territorial disputes over one substantial island each with both China and Japan but under the conservative government decided to mute its dispute with China in order to focus on its very similar dispute with Japan. The current liberal government of South Korea has escalated tensions with Japan.

Japan's geography is of course immutable. There can be no instant negotiated solution to the North Korean nuclear capability, so any negotiation leaves Japan vulnerable and opposed.

Some of the opposition, though, derives from Japan's own policy choices. Japan has always been, at least until 2018, more hostile to China than the U.S. Among other things, this has meant determined opposition to any regional security arrangements that involved China. Japan rightly sees China as key to any negotiated solution in Korea, and it (perhaps mistakenly) sees China as being advantaged by any solution. In addition, Japan rightly sees the possibility that a Korean peace could lead to a reduction or withdrawal of U.S. troops from Korea and that in turn could raise questions about the overall U.S. military posture in eastern Asia. Japan's fear of U.S. abandonment is both real and a powerful tool to get the U.S. to support every detail of Japanese policies. (The oft-repeated line is a variation on: If you Americans aren't willing to fight to the death over our claims to the Senkaku Islands and surrounding waters, we Japanese can never trust you on anything, nor can anyone else).

Many Americans find the intense hostility between Japan and its neighbors difficult to comprehend. Particularly between allies Japan and South Korea, Washington's posture is, why can't you kids just grow up and get along? To stretch the analogy only a little bit, suppose that the subject of conversation were instead the relationship between Britain and Germany. Suppose that Germany was ruled by Hitler's grandson who was denying that the Holocaust had occurred and was, contrary to the plain words of a pacifist German postwar constitution, trying to rebuild the military of a big power. Japanese politicians and Americans who rightly value Japan as our country's most valuable ally will of course cavil at all the details of that analogy, but if you want to understand the widespread feelings in both Koreas and China, that is how they feel.

Japan's geography is a fact, and, under its current government, its relationship with its neighbors is very hard to change. Japan is a vital ally and the U.S. must be very concerned about its vulnerabilities and fears. But Japan's situation will not be improved by the alternatives to extended negotiation and possible peace. The alternatives are North Korean permanent acquisition of a far more formidable nuclear force or a new war in Korea that would inevitably affect Japan. Moreover, given Sino-American tensions and the involvement of both great powers in Korea, renewed Korean conflict would risk a wider war that would, given U.S. bases in Japan, quickly engulf Japan. Hence it is crucial for every aspect of Korean negotiations to take Japanese concerns into account, but it is in everyone's interest, including Japan's, to ensure avoidance of a massive North Korean nuclear capability and of nuclear war – if such avoidance is at all possible.

The U.S. role

U.S. policy has focused narrowly on denuclearization and narrowly on sanctions as the solution to denuclearization. This approach has failed. It has not just failed with North Korea. It has failed virtually everywhere that it has been tried.

U.S. policymakers explain the failures based on the fickle, malevolent unreliability of North Korea and the refusal of China to impose sanctions of a severity that threaten to bring the regime down. Certainly the accusation that North Korea has been provocative and unreliable is accurate. A typical example is the Leap Day agreement of February 29, 2012. The U.S. agreed to provide food aid, North Korea to stop missile tests and uranium enrichment. Eventually the Six Party talks would restart. Shortly after the agreement North Korea launched a rocket with an alleged satellite and made lame arguments that the launch was consistent with the agreement. The launch effectively killed the agreement. Chinese analysts, including our authors below, note the same cycle as Western conservatives: North Korean provocations, an agreement that Pyongyang uses for fund-raising, and breakdown of the agreement.

Washington analysts tend to mirror their observation of North Korea's provocative fickleness with an unstated assumption that Washington has been reliable and consistently sincere in its dealings with North Korea. Reality is quite different. Each time a new administration comes to office in Washington it walks away from the formal agreements and informal understandings its predecessor had with North Korea. And within administrations conservatives sometimes intervene to sabotage policies and relationships that were intended to build toward peace in Korea.

The ranks of retired top diplomats who had responsibility for North Korea include many who were disillusioned by Washington's repeated failure to follow through on understandings or relationships intended to move toward peace. As the Bush 43 administration began, the U.S. had inspectors inside North Korea's main nuclear facility. Former Special Forces Colonel Denny Lane, part of the monitoring delegation, expressed his frustration in the same terms as many career diplomats:

"This is not an exercise in who is right and who is wrong. This is an exercise in taking the time to talk to one another and to engage in discovery, something that politicians and those responsible for guiding our diplomatic futures seem not to understand. One wonders from time to time if they might be the wrong people because they seldom appear to have either the time or for that matter the inclination to try to get to know and understand our North Korean colleagues.

"One has only to look back at recent foreign policy failures, the lives lost, and the dollars spent – Cuba, Indochina, Iraq, Afghanistan and what and wherever else and wonder why. The answer of course is the Bozone Layer. And what is the Bozone Layer? It is a "robust anti-intellectual aura that surrounds individuals and bureaucracies." The Layer acts to filter out and suppress ideas that challenge the conventional wisdom of political and bureaucratic elites. From my vantage point on the 21st floor of the Koryu Hotel, there is every indication that the Bozone layer is here to stay."

That was before the Bush administration torpedoed the agreement that provided for inspections. The agreement required the U.S. and its allies to provide, in return for North Korea's shutdown of the Yongbyon nuclear facilities, light water reactors for energy, fuel, diplomatic representation, and cultural exchanges. Although the North Koreans quickly did the most important thing they had promised, namely shutting down its main nuclear complex and allowing U.S. and other inspectors into it, the U.S. did none of the things it had promised. While there were some diplomatic issues connected with these failures, for instance over whether the U.S. could keep the contents of its diplomatic pouch secret, the domestic issues loomed larger. Vice President Cheney and National Security Advisor Condoleezza Rice adamantly opposed the agreement. Under Secretary of State John Bolton told colleagues his top priority was to kill the agreement. The U.S. Congress did not want to fund the agreement. Eventually the North Koreans provided them with an excuse for blowing up the whole agreement by hedging with a small uranium enrichment program – a hedge that some U.S. diplomats found understandable under the circumstances of U.S. stalling. The constructive U.S. response would have been to demand inspections of the uranium plant and to improve U.S. implementation of the agreement.

Ambassador Donald Gregg, a 40-year veteran of the CIA and former National Security Advisor to Vice President George H. W. Bush, expresses wry bitterness when he speaks of an incident when he was Ambassador to Korea during the administration of President George H. W. Bush. With the authorization of the President, the U.S.

was moving forward successfully on an understanding with North Korea that involved curtailing U.S.-South Korea Team Spirit joint military exercises. But then Secretary of Defense Cheney, without informing the State Department or the Ambassador, suddenly reinstated the Team Spirit exercise, sabotaging the efforts of his own colleagues.

The tensions and volatility of U.S. policy toward Korea were particularly vivid when South Korean President Kim Dae Jung visited Washington early in the new George W. Bush administration. Kim Dae Jung was the most pro-American of all post-World War II Korean leaders (I write from having known him very well.) He was a hero of democracy, who had remained strong in his advocacy of democracy despite two almost-successful assassination attempts, ruthless abuse of himself and his colleagues, and an official sentence to death by execution. His ability to survive decades of death threats and humiliations was sustained by a Christian faith so profound that it could look with equanimity beyond the likelihood of violent death. At the time he was the most pro-market of South Korea's political leaders, and he rescued his country from the Asian Crisis by moving it sharply away from the quasi-socialist, centrally directed economy nurtured by his predecessors. But he had a flaw in the eyes of Washington hardliners: he was pursuing a Sunshine Policy in pursuit of a more peaceful relationship with North Korea, a policy that included a personal meeting with the North Korean dictator.

Kim Dae Jung had a strong, warm relationship with Washington during the Clinton administration. When he visited Washington at the beginning of the new George W. Bush administration, Colin Powell and the State Department welcomed him as the hero of democracy that he was. Ambassador Stephen Bosworth reassured him about the continuity of American foreign policy, a reassurance that, as Christine Bosworth relates in her chapter, he later regretted. Then Kim Dae Jung went to the White House, where his frosty reception became a public humiliation. U.S. policy shifted decisively in the hours between his visits to two different parts of the U.S. government.

Anyone who writes about these things should disclose personal involvements in the issues. I always believed that Park Chung Hee, with his economics-first strategy, saved his country. But I also believed that killing the popular leader of the opposition would be catastrophic and that opposition leader Kim Dae Jung had a key role to play in South Korea's future.

In the late 1970s I was part of a Hudson Institute team that worked with Lee Hong Koo on a paper recommending that South Korea, then always in a defensive, reactive position, could grab the diplomatic initiative from North Korea by having the South Korean president, then Park Chung Hee, offer to meet the North Korean president in either capital. This idea was considered radical and soft at the time. Park Chung Hee did not act on the advice. But under President Chun Doo Hwan, Lee Hong Koo, who may well have been using Hudson to validate his own brilliant insight, became Prime Minister and persuaded President Chun to make the offer. As we had anticipated, from then on South Korea has held the diplomatic initiative. The subsequent summits by Kim Dae Jung and Moon Jae In have remained controversial among South Korean and Washington conservatives, but each has built a new level of mutual communication and willingness to take risks in dealing with the other.

While often working on projects with Park Chung Hee's colleagues, I visited Kim Dae Jung on every visit to South Korea despite intimidation by the Korean CIA. When Kim Dae Jung was sentenced to death, I risked my career as part of the successful effort to save him.

Decades later, officials and scholars in Park Chung Hee's home region decided to hold a big celebration of the hundredth anniversary of his birth. They asked me to keynote the celebration. I said I would be honored to celebrate him as the savior of his country, but I would not gloss over his human rights abuses and would give equal billing to Kim Dae Jung. To my surprise they accepted. My American colleagues warned me strongly against going ahead. Political polarization in South Korea is worse than in Trump's America, and the impeachment of Park's daughter was worsening the tensions. They said I would likely be vilified by both sides. I went ahead anyway. The text is on my website, www.theoverholtgroup.com. The local reaction was extremely positive; the country needs healing and even Park's partisans responded well to a healing effort.

This personal history has affected my views of the value of South Korean efforts to reach out to the North, the importance of taking the risk to reach across deep Korean political divides, and the risks that initiatives for peace are always vulnerable to denunciation as soft even when they are well-considered.

When I first read the Chinese chapter below I was perturbed by their argument that the U.S. is determined to avoid a peace agreement, because the constant risk of war in Korea keeps the U.S.-ROK-Japan alliance cemented. I do not believe that argument and I was surprised that these analysts, who are as knowledgeable and objective as any I have ever met, could come to this (in my view) erroneous conclusion. That surprise led me to reflect: Suppose a Martian, with no nationalistic or ideological bias, but also no direct access to the thinking of American officials, simply viewed behavior and tried to figure out what was happening. Each time there was progress toward a peace deal the Americans walked, or ran, away. The Martian might reasonably conclude that the Americans were determined to avoid a peace deal. But the evidence is also consistent with an alternative hypothesis that in the modern era each new U.S. administration dismisses its predecessor as incompetent – and in all administrations conservatives have considerable power to characterize diplomatic initiatives as unacceptably soft and to act on that characterization.

Those who want the more familiar Washington view will find it eloquently argued in several chapters below. (No serious analyst in the West, China or South Korea questions that North Korea has a long history of provocation, dishonesty and trickery. Along with everyone else, our Chinese authors are very clear about that. None of this record of North Korean trickery is contradicted by an effort to introduce a little humility into the U.S. discussion and to identify areas of common interest and potential common action.) Christine Bosworth's mini-memoir provides a window into an alternative approach of trust-building. Kathleen Stephens, who served as Peace Corps volunteer in Korea, Under Secretary of State, Ambassador to Korea, and in a key role in Belfast during the Northern Ireland peace negotiations, provides an analogy to the diplomacy over Northern Ireland, where seemingly intractable hatred, terrorism and demonization were gradually replaced by trust-building and peace.

President Eisenhower once said that, if a problem is too difficult, enlarge it. As long as the problem is narrowly defined as denuclearization, and the strategy is largely (although not exclusively) defined as imposing enough sanctions to force compliance, the problem of denu-clearization is unsolvable. That scared little animal, North Korea, has nothing else going for it, so, as long as that is the case, it is not going to eschew nuclear weapons and it is not going to provide enough information so that other countries could (a) verify a nuclear agree-ment or, if they so chose, (b) destroy all the facilities. The images of the mangled body of Qaddafi, and of the deflated, dispirited Saddam Hussein waiting for execution, haunt North Korean leaders – vivid examples of what happens to leaders who abandon their nuclear programs under Western pressure. In particular North Korean officials speak about Qaddafi frequently.

North Korea's intense concern about abandoning its nuclear arse-nal is exactly what would have been the reaction of South Korea in the early 1970s, when Nixon demanded the South abandon its nuclear program, if Park Chung Hee's choice had been (a) be misera-bly poor, diplomatically bereft, and militarily inferior, without nuclear weapons or (b) be a little more miserably poor, diplomatically bereft, and militarily inferior, with nuclear weapons. Fortunately Park had another option: a credible path to prosperity and overwhelmingly powerful foreign security guarantees, without nuclear weapons.

What Kim Jong Un is saying is that he wants the deal Park Chung Hee got. He wants diplomatic recognition, economic access and support, and security guarantees so that he won't need the nuclear weapons. The center of gravity of Washington opinion is (a) to focus narrowly on the nuclear issue, while sometimes begrudgingly promis-ing some of the other things but never delivering; and (b) to believe, firmly and sincerely, that North Korean leaders are such bad people that they can never be trusted.

The South Korean and Chinese message is different: We hate the things Kim Jong Un had his father and grandfather have done. We've learned the lesson of North Korean trickery and we're going to hold Pyongyang to much higher standards going forward. In particular we're not going to tolerate either a bigger nuclear arsenal or addi-tional vicious attacks on South Korea. But we believe Kim is different from his father and grandfather, and his situation – his need to craft a

survivable future for at least four decades ahead – is decisively different
from his father and grandfather. We, the South Koreans and Chinese,
don't really trust him, but the Chinese, now far more actively engaged
than in the past, can provide powerful incentives for good behavior
and sanctions for bad, while the South Koreans can provide strong
economic incentives and can prevent North Korea from being overwhelmed by Chinese money and power.

The risks of such a strategy everyone acknowledges. Kim Jong Un
could lose courage or be overthrown by the alienated older generation. The opening that is occurring could lead to a popular uprising
with an uncertain outcome. For all the risks it seems to them like
the only viable path to avoid war. But to make it work they need
Washington to agree to an extended process, to a flexible mix of sanctions and incentives, and to acceptance of North Korea as a state
like others that will be given firm security guarantees by some combination of China and other powers. They need a consensus that the
nuclear problem is part of the larger problem of peace. With peace,
the nuclear problem could just possibly go away. Without a broader
peace, there is no chance that the nuclear problem will go away.

The complexities of peace

The reason many analysts believe that North Korea will never agree
to abandon its nuclear weapons is that North Korea has nothing
else. Despite the huge numbers of its army, beyond an initial surge
potential it is as hapless militarily as it is economically. But if there
were a credible peace, a peace that North Korean leaders could really
believe in, then the nuclear weapons would not seem so irreplaceable.
In fact, they then become the main obstacle to development, and
hence to a normal lifespan for Kim Jong Un, because with them the
sanctions will never go away. And, as once hapless South Korea and
other Asian countries have shown, rapid economic development can
stabilize a society and provide it with international stature and with
the resources to defend itself.

♥ CVS pharmacy®

$4.00 off

$4 off CERAVE Body Wash or Cleansers!

Expires 07/05/2019 (Up to $4.00 value)

7162 5855 2400 4008

ExtraCare card required. Offer redeemable and savings applied to qualifying purchase only. N... cash back. Tax charged on pre-coupon price wh... required. Not valid in specialty centers wit... CVS. Excludes trial / travel sizes ...u beverages where applica...

♥ CVS pharmacy

$4.00 off

$4 off CERAVE Body Wash or
Cleanser(s)

North Korea wants a peace treaty, strong external security guarantees, removal of sanctions, and economic development assistance
– the package South Korea had in the 1970s. It says that it would
then no longer need its nuclear weapons. Some Western officials still
do not want to go in that direction because of residual hopes that
North Korea will collapse. It won't, at least not because of the impoverishment that has existed for decades and is now improving. After
many bad experiences with North Korean aggression and broken
promises, many Western officials and commentators do not believe
that Pyongyang is sincere. But some do. And current South Korean
leaders and Chinese leaders believe that North Korea has a different
leader, different national priorities, and a different strategic context
that make its new strategy more credible.

The road to peace, like everything else with North Korea, is tortuous and treacherous. The U.S. is unwilling to rush into a peace treaty,
because a peace treaty would logically require dismantling of the
United Nations Command, the umbrella under which the U.S maintains forces in South Korea and continues to command the South
Korean military. In principle, a force justified by the U.S.-ROK alliance could just replace the legal justification of the U.N. Command,
with negligible changes in practical arrangements, but the international arguments and the domestic politics of South Korea might
become more complicated. So progress toward peace might well begin
with a declaration of non-hostility rather than a legal peace treaty.

To make peace credible enough for North Korea to begin dismantling its nuclear weapons, further steps would be necessary. The
declaration of ˹ ˺n-hostility would not be at all credible unless the
U.S. r˹   ˺h Korea and establishes a diplomatic mission in
                  ns like a simple step but Washington conser-
                  ʌts activists have long argued that diplomatic
                  ˺ unacceptable gift to an unworthy regime.
                  ˺nts would have to be mollified, persuaded

                  ˹ North Korea has no credible means of
                  ˺ues to be surrounded by hostile giants,

so it will not abandon nuclear weapons without credible security guarantees from some combination of China and the U.S., together with satisfactory relationships with South Korea, Russia, and Japan. An appropriate arrangement is plausible. China has a security treaty already; all it needs to do is to reduce the level of political hostility, which is likely if Pyongyang begins to behave itself. Likewise, South Korea would be eager for peace, friendship and a security arrangement if North Korea's sporadic conventional attacks cease and its nuclear weapons begin to go away. The U.S. will be skeptical and divided until a great deal of progress has been made.

Finally, of course, peace would mean the removal of economic sanctions and their replacement by open trade and aid.

In short, the price that North Korea's neighbors will demand is that North Korea turn itself into a normal, non-nuclear country like, say, Ghana. The price that North Korea will demand for abandoning its nuclear weapons is that it be treated like a normal developing country, deserving of open trade, investment, aid, and security assurances. These desired endpoints are easy to state, but for each side the chicken and egg problem makes the process tortuous. How much of the normalization/security/economic package are the big powers willing to grant before most of the nukes are gone? How much can North Korea open itself up to inspections before it can be confident that Kim Jong Un won't end up as the next Gaddafi? How can trust be built when both sides have been so untrustworthy?

Unification

The ultimate assurance of peace on the Korean peninsula would be a successful unification of North and South. That outcome is indeed desired by a substantial part of the population in both pieces of the peninsula. In the 1970s passions about this were so strong that South Koran students threatened to march en masse across the demilitarized zone, in the face of North Korean firepower, to enforce unification.

North Korea and South Korea have always maintained that there is one Korean nation that should be unified, but not surprisingly they have differed strongly over what the governing structure of the unified nation should be and what process should lead to unification. In the 1970s, when North Korea was the stronger power, Pyongyang called for immediate unification, with the details to be worked out later, while Seoul demanded a gradual, incremental process. As South Korea has come to tower over the North, there has been more speculation about unification on South Korean terms, perhaps following collapse of the North Korean regime.

South Koreans have had very ambivalent feelings about the prospects for such a unification. Some studies have indicated that such a German-style unification would impose unacceptable economic costs on the south. Not only are the economies far more different than were the economies of the two Germanies, but also the societies are far more different than Germany's Osties and Westies, a difference that still troubles Germany. South Korea is a sophisticated, middle-class democratic society. North Korea is basically a peasant society with a tiny technocratic elite; it has none of East Germany's Weimar Republic-era exposure to democracy. Clearly a sudden unification, even if peaceful, would be a far more traumatic event that the unification of Germany.

The Bush 43 administration tended to assume that a North Korean collapse was likely and that it would end with North Korea being absorbed by South Korea. To the contrary, North Korea has proved quite resilient and conditions there are now much better than under Kim Jong Un's father. Moreover the optimistic assumption that a collapsing DPRK would end up incorporated into South Korea was rather like the same administration's assumption that destroying Saddam Hussein's regime in Iraq would lead to a strong, prosperous democracy; instead it led to chaos and essentially turned over much of the Middle East to Iranian influence. Collapse might well lead to a civil war that spread to into a much wider war. The Chinese military assumes that a North Korean collapse would lead to North Korea's becoming incorporated as a province of China.

The historical arguments for this are included in the chapter below on China and North Korea.

A process more satisfying to Koreans and Americans would be agreement on a confederation, with a system analogous to what China has proposed for Taiwan and implemented in Hong Kong: one nation, two systems. Such an arrangement would permit gradual, and quite possibly very profitable, economic integration and would not, at least initially, threaten the positions of either elite. The downside would be decades of potentially disruptive wrangling over the details of integration.

A condition of success for any form of unification, including confederation, would be to ensure that the top leadership of each side feels secure. That is particularly difficult for a North Korean leadership that has depended for its domestic stability on keeping the North Korean people ignorant of how much better their neighbors live than they do. Indeed for a long time, the North Korean media portrayed a South Korea that was bereft compared with the allegedly better situation of North Koreans. Times have changed, however. North Koreans have experienced the famine created by Kim Jong Un's father and they know that life is much better in China and South Korea. North Korean scholars and senior officials have rapidly increasing access to U.S. books and a wide range of foreign contacts. Kim Jong Un is going to have to manage this perilous situation regardless of what foreigners do.

The U.S. and Chinese militaries both are inclined to oppose Korean unification, due to opposite fears. The PLA fears that a unified Korea would be a U.S. ally, possibly bringing U.S. troops to the Yalu River border. The U.S. military fears on the contrary that a unified Korea might be coopted by China. To anyone with direct experience of Korean nationalism both of these fears seem overblown; Koreans are the world's most nationalistic people and, if there were any real unity, they would be determinedly independent. Top civilian leaders in China and the U.S. might well see the advantages of peace as outweighing the risks that Korea would lean to the other side.

Japan does not want to see a strong independent Korea, because it would be a very powerful state and, because of the history of Japanese colonialism, for the indefinite future it would almost certainly be quite hostile to Japan.

Despite the complications, eventual unification on a one nation, two systems basis remains a plausible outcome – plausible, not likely. The Korean inclination toward some kind of unity is strong on both sides. The alternative paths to unification seem too dangerous or too expensive. Wise civilian leaders in Washington and Beijing need to weigh the weak military arguments opposing unification against the continued risk of division. Japan needs to consider whether building its national self-esteem on historical revisionism is worth the cost of hostility with its neighbors; Germany has consigned World War II to ancient history and so could Japan. But for the time being efforts at Korean unification will meet considerable big power resistance.

Tools for denuclearization

Military

After World War II the U.S. deliberately limited the weapons available to South Korea while the Soviet Union provided a massive buildup of weaponry for North Korea. Secretary of State Acheson indicated that South Korea was outside the U.S. defense perimeter. This unintentionally enabled a North Korean invasion. The lesson that strong defense of South Korea is essential to peace has been firmly entrenched ever since, except for the first 18 months of the Carter administration. An initially very weak South Korea focused on economic growth, while the North continued to give the military exclusive priority. The resulting superior economic growth of South Korea enabled it to build gradually stronger defenses.

By the early 1980s South Korea had superior ability to win a war. But the North maintained extraordinary forces at the Demilitarized Zone (DMZ) dividing the two Koreas, and Seoul, South Korea's capital with 10 million people and a disproportionate share of the South's economy, is only 30 miles from the DMZ. North Korea's massed artillery could devastate Seoul immediately. This "surge capability" means that, even though the South would likely win a longer war, even without U.S. help, the devastation and loss of life in Seoul would render the victory Pyrrhic.

The U.S.-ROK alliance is backed by a nuclear guarantee. During some periods that nuclear guarantee has been buttressed by the presence of U.S. nuclear weapons in South Korea. From the mid-1970s analyses have shown that there is no military advantage, and considerable disadvantages, to having U.S. nuclear weapons physically in South Korea. My own study for the U.S. government, summarized in the last chapter of my 1976 collection, **Asia's Nuclear Future**, concluded that there was no military advantage in having tactical nuclear weapons in South Korea as compared with having the same weapons stored in my basement in New York. But if a U.S. unit became trapped in wartime that would potentially create a politically impossible dilemma: use the local nuclear weapons in a situation that would create a precedent we cannot afford, or face devastating criticism for not using available weapons. (That is why, analogously, it would not have been a good idea to have U.S. nuclear weapons stored in Vietnam. Sometimes it's better to lose than to create a precedent for nuclear battles in local conflicts.)

Nonetheless, even after nuclear weapons were withdrawn based on such analyses, conservative administrations have sometimes sought to reinsert them. Since their presence or absence has traditionally been treated as top secret, this creates an issue in negotiations over denuclearizing the Korean peninsula.

The U.S. has viewed the possibility of North Korea being able to strike the U.S. with nuclear weapons as absolutely unacceptable. Japan and China are already threatened in exactly the way the U.S. fears, something U.S. leaders sometimes seem to forget. In 1994, during the Clinton administration, the U.S. was ready to bomb North Korean nuclear facilities but pulled back in favor of a Framework Agreement that allowed us to inspect the main nuclear facility in return for fuel, light water reactors, diplomatic recognition and cultural exchanges.

In the Trump administration the U.S. again explored military options. The same dilemma of course recurs, and the exploration and threats shake South Koreans, who face imminent loss of their capital and millions of their citizens. As Victor Cha notes, the resulting alliance strains are exacerbated by the repeated denigration by President Trump of Korean contributions to the alliance. Conversely, conservatives in Washington feel that President Moon strains the alliance by making friendly overtures to President Kim.

Sanctions

All the countries pressing North Korea to abandon nuclear weapons agree that economic sanctions are essential. Recently the U.N. authorized more severe sanctions, China has strengthened its sanctions, and the U.S. has begun imposing secondary sanctions (sanctions on foreign companies that ignore U.S. sanctions). But serious divisions and balances remain. China believes it is dangerous to push sanctions so far that they threaten to destabilize the regime in North Korea, while many in Washington believe that destabilization wouldn't be such a bad thing. Many in Washington think an exclusive focus on sanctions is the only path to denuclearization, and can be effective, while many others, including the governments in China and South Korea, believe that sanctions alone have proven ineffective and that the only path to success is a sophisticated combination of sanctions for bad behavior and incentives for good.

How to provide rewards for good behavior without weakening the punishments for bad behavior is a difficult question. As Stephan Haggard notes, the main possible answer that has arisen so far is to allow South Korea considerable latitude in building economic ties if North Korea behaves. With difficulty and immense controversy, one could construct a ladder of good behavior and broader sanctions relief.

What is denuclearization anyway?

For the U.S., denuclearization has always meant elimination of nuclear weapons and nuclear delivery missiles from North Korea, accepting that in return the U.S. and South Korea should not have any nuclear weapons present in South Korea. Since this is a pledge already fulfilled on the U.S. side, and since the possession of nuclear weapons inside South Korea would add nothing to U.S. ability to defend South Korea and to deter North Korea, the U.S. and South Korea would have to give up nothing. That does not mean such an agreement would be inherently unfair. But it has also long been assumed by many in Washington that North Korea would have to give up all of its nuclear capability before sanctions could be removed.

As Daniel Sneider notes in his chapter, North Korea has moved to an expansive definition of denuclearization that comprises elimination of the U.S. "threat," broadly defined. It wants assurance of peace, before it gives up its only effective means of defending itself. From a North Korean point of view that seems reasonable. But in its most expansive form it can be held to require U.S. withdrawal of non-nuclear ground, air and naval forces from South Korea, renunciation of any nuclear guarantee of South Korea's security, and even removal from Japan and the western Pacific of any forces that could be used to defend South Korea or defend North Korea.

Clearly neither instant denuclearization of North Korea nor removal of U.S. forces from the western Pacific is going to happen.

The U.S. has shown admirable flexibility in willingness to discuss an timetable for dismantling North Korean nuclear devices and delivery capabilities, but it has consistently insisted on a timetable and thorough verification. These are inherently reasonable demands, particularly in light of North Korea's past behavior. But North Korea fears that providing a comprehensive list of its sites and accepting intrusive verification would make it totally vulnerable. It would.

In essence this is a chicken and egg problem. North Korea says it will give up its nuclear weapons when it has an assured peace agreement. The U.S. says it will join a peace agreement after North Korea has given up its nuclear weapons. Both sides see the issue as life and death. If North Korea gives up its nuclear weapons, it cannot defend itself. If the North Korean nuclear program remains viable, then Washington DC becomes vulnerable to attack.

Bridging the difference between these positions is excruciatingly difficult. In principle it should be possible through a phased process of mutual concessions and trust building. Kim's new economic priority, China's stronger engagement, Washington's new-found flexibility, and increasing North-South trust provide the components of a bridge. But given the high stakes involved, the level of distrust, and the technical complexity of the steps, anyone who is strongly optimistic probably has not thought deeply.

Verification

When and if there is an agreement in principle there is a need to verify that North Korea is doing what it promised. Gary Samore's chapter brilliantly dissects the multiple layers of verification. Ultimately the verification problem recapitulates the chicken and egg problem of defining denuclearization and making a deal. The requirements of verification are the same as what the U.S. would need to obliterate North Korea's nuclear program. The North Koreans want assurance of peace before they can agree to make themselves so vulnerable. The U.S. wants verification before it will make peace.

Like the peace/sanctions dilemma, the verification dilemma is difficult but not impossible. Sino-American intelligence sharing can help. Some physicists like Siegfried Hecker (cited in the chapter by Dan Sneider, who disagrees with him) believe that less-than-total disclosure and verification could be adequate for international needs.

Human rights and negotiations

There is a persistent tendency in U.S. politics that says we shouldn't talk with North Koreans (or Iranians or . . .) because they are such terrible abusers of human rights. Well, they are terrible abusers of human rights, but we don't talk with them for their reasons. We talk with them for our reasons. We talk with them because we need to understand how their positions affect issues of vital interest to us. Through negotiations we seek insights about their vulnerabilities on issues of vital interest to us. We need to understand how we could accomplish things of vital interest to us at a time when it is not within our power to change all the things we would like to change. Avoiding a nuclear exchange is always a U.S. vital interest.

Mao Zedong was the worst abuser of human rights in the history of the human race, responsible for more deaths than any other human being. But talking with him helped us defeat the Soviet Union, at the time a mortal threat to us, and the fact that we were talking to China paved the way for a subsequent Chinese economic opening that improved the lives or more people, at a faster rate, than has ever happened in human history. Likewise, the Soviet Union was one of the bloodiest, most ruthless dictatorships in world history, but our negotiations led to mutual warning systems, surveillance systems, arms control agreements, and understanding of each others' behavior that probably saved the world from nuclear annihilation. Negotiations are not a gift or concession to an adversary. They are a search for a path to achieving important national goals – *our* national goals.

The first task of anyone who truly cares about human rights is to ensure that the people remain alive – Korean people and American people. If you are dead, no other human rights matter. Moreover, a vigorous peace process may remove some of the motivations for human rights abuse and, if successful, may create the opportunity for hitherto futile human rights protests to gain more influence over a more open and confident regime. That's what happened in China, where the human rights situation remains bad, but is extraordinarily improved compared with 1972, when Nixon met Mao. Having said that, the avoidance of nuclear war is a priority goal even if broader hopes remain frustrated.

High efforts for low probability outcomes?

There are so many complications and so much distrust that reason-able people can view the probability of successful negotiations as very low. But there are times when low probability/high stakes outcomes are the key to strategic success or failure.

In Europe during the Cold War, the probability that the Soviets would come charging through the Fulda Gap in a full-scale invasion of West Germany was fairly low. But the cost to the West if such an invasion did occur was so high that it justified spending trillions of dollars, in today's terms, to make sure that it didn't happen. Similarly, the value to us and to humanity of averting the world's most serious risk of nuclear war is worth the expenditure of enormous efforts, and the acceptance of a measured degree of risk. Each successive previous peace effort has failed but each has led to a higher level of communication, a multiplication of contacts, and a greater degree of collaboration between the U.S. and China.

The level of negotiations

It is easy to dismiss today's summitry as an embarrassing Twitter whim. Like everything else concerning North Korea, the balance sheet is complicated. The chances of success are much higher when negotiations are conducted at the chief executive level. U.S. successes in negotiation with North Korea tend to occur when top-level negotiators engage – for instance, Jimmy Carter's intervention to prevent an imminent war. Being treated at the assistant secretary level leaves the North Koreans feeling insulted. Treating North Korea's Chairman with respect enhances the prospect of success, although any patriotic American cringes when President Trump says that he would be honored to meet with Chairman Kim or even that he is in love with Chairman Kim.

Clearly negotiations between a flaky U.S. President and a North Korean Chairman who may be jerked around by dangerous domestic developments carries substantial risks. There is an equal risk that the 2020 U.S. election will lead to repudiation of any agreement by any victorious president other than Donald Trump. But both the U.S. and North Korea have serious, competent support bases. Trump's chief negotiator, Stephen Biegun, is widely respected and he can build on the legacy of Stephen Bosworth, a politically independent figure who served a Democrat President. The nuclear issue is sufficiently urgent that there is a chance a sensible outcome could lead Washington to rise above stereotypes and partisanship.

What follows

Those are my judgments.

In what follows, the world's leading experts explore the complexities and difficulties, many of which they agree on, and the prospects, which they generally disagree about. The next chapter's author is the leading opponent of the peace negotiations. Prof. Lee has testified to the U.S. Congress. While President Obama never had time to meet with his own designated special envoy to North Korea, Ambassador Stephen Bosworth, he did take the time for an exceptionally long 90 minute meeting with Prof. Lee. Then we have the views of Prof. Chung-In Moon, who has been a strategy advisor to South Korean President Moon and is perhaps the most articulate of the advocates of the peace negotiations.

Succeeding chapters address the situation Kim Jong Un faces (you wouldn't want to be in his shoes); the ways his situation and he himself differ from his predecessors; the imperatives, constraints, texture and progress of his economic strategy; how South Korean politics affects negotiating prospects; pressures for Korean unification and difficulties; the views of neighbors China and Japan; the vexing technical difficulties of deciding what denuclearization means and how to verify it; some peculiarities of the U.S. negotiations and alliance management; and perspectives on the pursuit of negotiations that seem to have a low probability of success.

After sobering analyses of conflicting views of denuclearization, and of the complexities of verification, the volume closes with two very different angles. Christine Bosworth's very personal memoir of the late Stephen Bosworth's efforts at peace shows the ups and downs of being an American diplomat tossed around by domestic political tides. Bosworth, one of America's greatest diplomats, saw an agreement that had American inspectors inside the most important North Korean nuclear facility thrown out by a George W. Bush White House that hated the agreement its predecessor had made and by a Congress that did not want to fund the peace agreement. Then he labored prior to his death for a path to peace that a Democrat Secretary of State would not allow him to take forward, under a Democrat President who did not have the time to meet with his own special representative to North Korea.

The many American diplomats, and military officers and Department of Energy specialists, who have encountered similar disappointments have a sense of deja vu as they watch yet another administration labor for an agreement that, if achieved, will face nearly united establishment skepticism and may well be repudiated by a successor to President Trump from either party.

Finally, Kathleen Stephens, arguably America's longest-serving Korea watcher, from her Peace Corps service there to her ambassadorship in Korea and her service as Acting Under Secretary of State, likens the negotiations for Korean peace to the negotiations she helped bring to fruition in Northern Ireland, where the hatred and demonization were comparable. The lesson that she and the Bosworths leave us is that diplomatic success requires steadiness and empathy.

Two thoughts encapsulate the tortuous calculations required by the Korean situation. It may be imperative to negotiate even though the probability of success is low. And one South Korean quipped: If Donald Trump gets reelected it is a catastrophe for the United States, but if he does not get reelected it is a catastrophe for Korea. This is a subject and a book for minds that are comfortable with dissonant trends, dissonant goals and dissonant personalities.

2

Countering North Korea's Carrot-and-Stick Strategy

SUNG-YOON LEE

Introduction: American solipsism

A space alien with a philosophical, if not mere keen, eye, observing in 2020 or even hundreds of years thereafter the nuclearization of the political construct known as the Democratic People's Republic of Korea (DPRK), will come to wonder: By what wondrous series of unlikely circumstances did the United States of America, the world's most powerful state in the post-1945 world order, fail, in spite of efforts spanning over more than a quarter century, to prevent the methodical and defiant march toward full nuclearization by this small, backward, impoverished, despotic, aid-dependent state?

By then, many theories may already have been presented to please the political tastes of the times. But the circumspect extraterritorial life form who, by virtue of his alien status, transcends party and passions of earthly beings, may come to disinter the root cause of America's failure: American attitude, that is, the unrelenting American propensity to underestimate and patronize Pyongyang, its hyper-proactive adversary.

To Americans, the notion that Pyongyang has almost always been the party that has wielded the carrot and stick in the North Korea-U.S. bilateral relationship instead of merely reacting to American stimuli is hard to imagine. After all, measured by all indices of state power – military, economic, soft power, or political attractiveness, the size of territory and population – the United States is so much more powerful than North Korea. Moreover, the impetus to great changes in the international order since at least the Second World War had sprouted from American initiatives.

For example, it was the U.S. that had launched the two crusades in the Great War and changed the course of humanity, vanquishing fascism in Europe and Japanese imperialism in the Asia-Pacific. Furthermore, it was the U.S. that had contained the great threat of Communism during the Cold War, meanwhile setting the benchmark for science and technology the world over and laying down the rules of international finance with the sterling shimmer of the U.S. dollar. And in this history, North Korea would be nothing but a passing footnote, if not for what it has attained against odds – its emergence in world affairs as, arguably, the most influential poor, backward, regional power commensurate with its economic, soft, and political power and its pedestrian territorial and population size.

At the same time, to the alien visitor, it will be clear that beneath all the laudable attainments and abject failures in postwar U.S. foreign policy have swirled not always visible eddies of optimism and hubris, confidence and condescension, fact and fancy, pragmatism and self-hypnosis. These contradictory whirlwinds of attitudes, by dint of America's unmatched power and wealth, have variously started, exacerbated, prolonged, tempered and, occasionally, ended American involvements abroad. The common thread in America's wrought adventures abroad, the alien may discern, is that while U.S. engagement has almost always been shaped by the practical conviction that the U.S. is always right, just, to be envied, feared, and emulated by others, the experience, from beginning to end, has almost always remained mired in the myth that when America speaks, others – especially small states, both client and adversarial alike – listen. This marks the great myth in American foreign policy; that is, by virtue of U.S. power and influence, the U.S. can affect and control other, especially smaller, states and largely effect in those target states the desired manifestations of U.S. intentions. The DPRK is not only *not* the exception to this misguided presumption but is the most stunningly unequivocal affirmation of its folly.

A confounding mix of the mockable and unconventional

All policy is an extension of assumptions and ideologies – human thoughts that may be summed up as "attitudes." The attitudes of a people define the institutions they build and the policies they effect, whether it's a private enterprise of proselytization inspired by the missionary mindset or an extensive government enterprise propelled by *mission civilastrice*. Just as war is an extreme extension of diplomacy by other means, diplomacy is a conventional application of attitudes by non-lethal means.

Herein lies the problem. The United States foreign policy establishment, including both the proven experts in bureaucracies as well as top elected leaders who must learn on the job, have predominantly viewed the DPRK as an object either to be coaxed by artful diplomacy or coerced by a combination of pressure and insouciance. Seldom has it occurred to American policymakers that the U.S., in its relations with North Korea, from the Harry Truman administration's response North Korea's invasion of the South, thus starting the Korean War in June 1950, to the latest charm offensive by Kim Jong Un, has been playing catch-up and reacting to Pyongyang's stimuli.

America's patronizing attitude, on a basic level, is quite understandable. When it comes to the weird, cultish leadership of North Korea, from the purported legendary revolutionary Kim Il Sung who supposedly almost single-handedly defeated Imperial Japan and liberated Korea from the yoke of Japanese colonial rule and founded the true, legitimate Korean state called the DPRK, to his progeny, Kim Jong Il and Kim Jong Un, genetically blessed with near-equal superhuman capabilities, the defining globally-common attitudinal denominator in the eye of the beholder is derision. To ridicule and laugh at each of the Kims across three generations comes effortlessly. In fact, if there were such a contraption as an "International Mockability Index," each of the Kims, from grandfather, son, to grandson, would be a formidable contender for the top spot virtually throughout the entire duration of his rule. The three generational continuum put together renders North Korea eminently mockable. Adding to the propensity to laugh at the North Korean leadership and not take it seriously is the problem of the regime's downright weird contradictions. For example, the leadership deifies itself and revels in extravagance while systematically depriving its population of even the most basic rights and freedoms, such as the freedom of unimpeded domestic travel, access to foreign media, speech, assembly, religion and, as the United Nations Commission of Inquiry Report on Human Rights in North Korea alleges, the "right to food and related aspects of the right to life."[1] The regime approaches foreign policy with a mix of medieval mores and avant-garde criminality.[2] The nation boasts of having become a full-fledged nuclear state after firing an inter-continental ballistic missile with the range to hit every corner of the United States,[3] while it without fail secures its place among the world's top five on the list of the UN World Food and Agriculture Organization's metric, the "Prevalence of Undernourishment in the Total Population." North Korea's most recent record of 43.4 percent of the population places it in a virtual tie for third place with Haiti (45.8), Zambia (44.5), and Madagascar (43.1 percent), trailing only the Central African Republic (61.8 percent) and Zimbabwe (46.6 percent).

The great North Korea anomaly is that all the other states on the "Top 20" list are immiserated, illiterate, pre-industrial, agriculture-based economies sans nuclear weapons or ballistic missiles. North Korea stands alone as an industrialized, urbanized, literate country armed with nukes, intercontinental ballistic missiles, and a hyperinflated military of over 1.1 million men for a population of 25 million. In other words, North Korea's man-made and man-enforced

1   See "Report of the Detailed Findings of UN Commission of Inquiry Report on Human Rights in the Democratic People's Republic of Korea," February 17, 2017, 144-208. https://documents-dds-ny.un.org/doc/UNDOC/GEN/G14/108/71/PDF/G1410871.pdf?OpenElement

2   The Democratic People's Republic of Korea is the only state in the post-1945 era that, as a matter of state policy, has mass produced and exported contraband such as drugs, counterfeits, fake familiar-brand cigarettes and pharmaceuticals, all the while assiduously adhering to the norms of state-sponsors of terrorism with active proliferation and political assassinations abroad.

3   Mark Lander and Choe Sang-Hun, "North Korea Says It's Now a Nuclear State. Could that Mean It's Ready to Talk?" The New York Times, November 29, 2017. https://www.nytimes.com/2017/11/29/world/asia/north-korea-nuclear-missile-.html

food insecurity problem has world-historical moral and legal implications.[4] The Democratic People's Republic of Korea's multifaceted
and, according to the 2014 UN report above, "unparalleled" crimes
against humanity, its bellicosity, and its disregard for transparency and
the norms of the international community are the essential characteristics of the Kim dynastic regime.

Such are the unique contradictions North Korea presents – an
anti-social, belligerent, well-nourished dictator presiding over a
backward nation of hungry, isolated people – that when Pyongyang
launches missiles or threatens the U.S. and its allies with nuclear
annihilation in spite of U.S. signals for bilateral talks or even when
apparent progress in talks has been made, American responses have
ranged from bewilderment and indignation, to even a tendency to
write North Korea off as a child throwing a temper tantrum.[5] In the
meantime, North Korea has drastically advanced its own nuclear
posture review and ballistic missile programs while reaping billions
of dollars in cash, food, fuel, and other blandishments from South
Korea, the United States, Japan, and China. The U.S. alone gave
North Korea concessionary aid in excess of $1.3 during the Bill
Clinton and George W. Bush administrations, 1995 to 2008.[6] This, a
record of unrelenting failure to take North Korea seriously, is the U.S.
legacy. In other words, it is North Korea's victory.

All politics is local

What explains Pyongyang's unconventional behavior and policies?
More than "moral turpitude," "lifestyle choice" or mere "incompe-
tence," more than anything else, the answer is the systemic constraints

4   Food and Agriculture Organization of the United Nations, "The State of Food Security
and Nutrition in the World 2018," 135-138. http://www.fao.org/3/I9553EN/i9553en.pdf

5   "Clinton Likens North Korea to Unruly Children," Reuters, July 20, 2009. https://uk
.reuters.com/article/us-korea-north-clinton/clinton-likens-north-korea-to-unruly-children
-idUSTRE56J2FV20090720

6   Mark E. Manyin and Mary Beth D. Nikitin, "Foreign Assistance to North Korea,"
Congressional Research Service, April 2, 2014. https://fas.org/sgp/crs/row/R40095.pdf

in the Korean peninsula. If the dictum "all politics is local" is more or less valid, then perhaps "all international politics is local" may also be approximately valid. Yet, seldom have U.S. policymakers, even in responding to the outbreak of the Korean War, seriously considered the internal dynamic of the Korean peninsula – a two-state formulation under which either of the two Korean states may come to be absorbed by the other. From the Kim regime's point of view, the losing systemic rivalry with the far richer South is an ominous trajectory that cannot be ignored or reversed through a conventional economic game of catch-up.

In this contest for pan-Korean legitimacy, the only way for the inferior Democratic People's Republic of Korea to overturn this gloomy dynamic and one day prevail over the vastly superior Republic of Korea (ROK) is maximize its nuclear threat capability and become much better positioned to extort the democratic, risk-averse South. For the Kim regime, nuclear-armed missiles are less a "bargaining chip" or "deterrent" than the sole means to its long-term regime preservation by ultimately emerging victorious over the incomparably richer, freer South. President Donald Trump captured this dynamic when he, in an address to the ROK National Assembly on November 7, 2017, remarked, "[T]he very existence of a thriving South Korean republic threatens the very survival of the North Korean dictatorship."[7]

Yet, this keen insight and the diplomatic and financial pressure built up against Pyongyang in 2017 was squandered when Mr. Trump, on March 8, 2017, impulsively agreed to Kim Jong Un's proposition for a summit meeting the moment it was conveyed by South Korean officials on that day. Why? Because what Kim Jong Un seeks is to ensnare the Trump administration in a protracted process of negotiations for buying time and money – in non-sanctions enforcement and the resumption of large-scale unilateral aid and investment by

---

7   "Remarks by President Trump to the National Assembly of the Republic of Korea, November 7, 2017, Seoul, Republic of Korea," The White House. https://www.whitehouse.gov/briefings-statements/remarks-president-trump-national-assembly-republic-korea-seoul-republic-korea/

South Korea and China – with which to perfect his own nuclear posture review.

In this game, for Pyongyang, it always pays to provoke. And it pays even more to placate afterwards. Why? Because, since the end of the Korean War in 1953, the risk-prone, seemingly irrational North has been able to condition the risk-averse, rational United States and South Korea to accept temporary de-escalation and the possibility of talks as the preferred option to maintaining sustained pressure – even non-military diplomatic pressure – on Pyongyang. North Korea's strategy of exerting maximum pressure on its adversaries through provocations and, on occasion, even lethal attacks, followed by a period of disingenuous diplomatic outreach has bought itself invaluable time and resources with which to advance its nuclear and ballistic missile capabilities.

Kim Jong Un, through his "unexpected" diplomatic gambit throughout 2018, has successfully coaxed the U.S. and its allies into prematurely stopping the enforcement of financial measures against his regime. Sanctions enforcement, like domestic law enforcement, requires continual effort. Neither is self-executing, and when the political will to put in the time and hard work of enforcing sanctions dissipates, even the toughest sanctions on the books lose meaning. Today, with a follow-up Donald Trump-Kim Jong Un summit looming and with Russian President Vladimir Putin and Japanese Prime Minister Shinzo Abe in line for their own summit pageantry with the North Korean leader, Kim Jong Un sits in the catbird seat, better positioned to roll out his perfected nuclear policy at an opportune time. Simply by changing his tune from *molto agitato* to *placido* and sending a few hundred state cheerleaders and performers to South Korea during the Pyeongchang Olympics in February 2018, Kim Jong Un has been able to effect a dramatic self-image makeover as a reasonable, peace-seeking steward of a responsible nuclear nation. This dramatic carrot-dangling by Kim, as in stark contrast to his belligerence and reclusive lifestyle as it stands, was, like Pyongyang's previous post-provocation peace ploys, pre-planned and entirely predictable.

Pyongyang's predictable peace ploys[8]

When pundits intone that North Korea is "unpredictable," what they actually mean is that the ultra-bizarre regime is "unconventional." Isolationist, poor, nasty, brutish, and strangely buffoonish, the North Korean regime defies the conventions of the "nation state" or "rational actor." Hence, its strangely bellicose rhetoric and threatening actions come across as "unpredictable" or "irrational," while its post-provocation concessionary ploys, such as calling for talks and summit meetings in early 2018, creates various illusions of "crisis averted" and even opportunities for a "breakthrough."

Just as it is possible today approximately to predict – through intelligence, surveillance, reconnaissance, and *reading the calendar* – North Korea's next big provocation, so it is also possible approximately to predict Pyongyang's next faux peace overture. In recent years, North Korea watchers have finally caught on that Pyongyang prefers to resort to a major provocation on a major national holiday, both its own as well as American and Chinese. For example, North Korea's first nuclear test took place on October 9, 2006, on the eve of the nation's Party Founding Day, which in this year happened to be Columbus Day in the U.S. Its second nuclear test came on May 25, 2009, which was Memorial Day in the U.S. This insult was preceded by Pyongyang's first long-range missile test during the Obama administration on Sunday, April 5, just hours before President Barack Obama, on his first visit to Europe as President, was about to deliver his first major foreign policy speech on the theme of a world without nuclear weapons. Sundays are also popular days of the week for provocations, as a bang on a Sunday spikes the odds of topping the international headlines as of Monday morning, which, in turn, paints its adversaries further into a corner. Pyongyang's third nuclear test was on February 12, 2013, right in the middle of China's most important national holiday, Lunar New Year's

---

8   The main argument and some sentences in this section are taken from the author's testimony before the Subcommittee on Asia and the Pacific, Foreign Affairs Committee, U.S. House of Representatives, "North Korea's Diplomatic Gambit: Will History Repeat Itself?" April 11, 2018.

celebrations – the first for Xi Jinping as the nation's new leader. On July 4, 2017, North Korea fired its first-ever ICBM. And on America's Independence Day in 2006, Pyongyang gave the U.S. a seven-rocket salute, including a long-range missile blast.

In a similar vein, it is also quite possible to predict Pyongyang's next faux peace offensive. After a banner ballistic year in 2017, Kim Jong Un was bound to de-escalate in 2018 and use the Olympic stage to proposition South Korea, the natural first target, for inter-Korean talks and manipulate Seoul into softening up the U.S., much to the delight of China and Russia. With temporary de-escalation and a compliant Seoul by his side, Kim Jong Un was able to proposition President Trump for a summit meeting, just as his father, Kim Jong Il, had President Bill Clinton in late-2000. The effect has been to change the atmospherics in the region from tense to cordial, re-engage Seoul and Beijing for greater political and economic cover, and pave the road for re-engaging (extorting) a Japan rather nervous about being sidelined by the U.S. Any progress on the normalization of diplomatic relations between Tokyo and Pyongyang will entail money flow in the tens of billions of dollars from the former to the latter.

Why did Kim Jong Un so dramatically change his tune at the outset of 2018? Because, once again, it pays to provoke first, then placate afterwards. In descending order of implausibility, there are four plausible explanations for Kim's sudden outreach:

First, Kim Jong Un woke up on New Year's Day and, in a moment of epiphany, decided to be a nice man going forward. Second, Kim was so touched by South Korea President Moon's patience during his yearlong bluster barrage, that Kim decided to reciprocate with warm gestures and good manners. Third, Kim felt so constricted by the U.S.-led financial sanctions enforcement over the past year that he, fearful of an impending coup, made the strategic decision sometime in the two months between shooting his most powerful ICBM to date on November 29, 2017 and New Year's Day 2018 to entice President Trump into prematurely relaxing sanctions.

Fourth, all the outreach and fake smiles as of January 2018 were pre-planned in an attempt to buy time and funds with which to complete his nuclear and ICBM capabilities, so that he may leap one giant step closer to completing the "*Juche* revolution," which, in North Korean parlance, means obliterating South Korea and establishing a United Democratic People's Republic of Korea under Kim's own rule. Evicting the U.S. forces from the region through credible nuclear threat on the U.S. mainland is an essential step in actualizing this new, incomparably happier and safer alternative future.

Kim Jong Un since 2018 has simply been taking a few pages out of his father's playbook in the early-2000s. From 2000, Kim Jong Il set a new standard in international shakedown. After firing a missile over Japan (for the first time) in 1998 and following it up with a naval skirmish against South Korea in 1999, Kim Jong Il wound down his crisis-crescendo dial and called on his South Korean counterpart, Kim Dae Jung, for a summit. Like his son, Jong Un, Kim Jong Il, upon inheriting power in the wake of his father's death in July 1994, never met with a single world leader for the first six years of his rule until popping up in Beijing in late-May 2000, thus accentuating his eccentricity and mystery. The next month, in June, Kim Jong Il hosted the first-ever inter-Korean summit meeting and pocketed $500 million from his Southern counterpart.[9] The next month, Vladimir Putin visited Kim in Pyongyang. It was the first-ever visit to North Korea by a top Russian or Soviet leader. In September, Chinese President JIang Zemin reciprocated Kim's visit to China in May with a visit to Pyongyang.

Next, Kim turned to softening up Washington. In October Kim sent his senior-most military man, Vice Marshal Jo Myong-Rok, to Washington. Mr. Jo conveyed to President Bill Clinton Kim's invitation for a summit meeting in Pyongyang. President Clinton, who was keen on traveling to Pyongyang, was saved some embarrassment and much political capital thanks to the George W. Bush-Al Gore election recount problem that dragged on until Mr. Gore's concession in mid-December. But his Secretary of State Madeleine Albright

---

9   Sung-Yoon Lee, "Engaging North Korea: The Clouded Legacy of South Korea's Sunshine Policy," American Enterprise Institute Press, April 2010. http://www.aei.org/publication/engaging-north-korea-the-clouded-legacy-of-south-koreas-sunshine-policy/

was hastily dispatched to Pyongyang before the November election. Although the Clinton visit did not materialize, undeterred, Kim made another visit to China in January 2001, imitating Deng Xiaoping's 1992 "Southern Tour" of the Special Economic Zones in China's south, a reaffirmation of Deng's reform programs started a decade before. By visiting Shanghai, Shenzhen, and Zhuhai, Kim came across as a reform-minded leader.

Likewise, in March 2018 Kim Jong Un made his first foreign visit since inheriting power in December 2011. He held his first meeting with Chinese President Xi Jinping in Beijing approximately a month shy of his first meeting with South Korean President Moon Jae-In and a prospective meeting with President Trump several weeks thereafter. In view of the past seven decades of Sino-North Korean relations, an alliance veritably forged in blood, this visit to Beijing by the third-generation North Korean leader was bound to take place.

How to stop history from repeating itself?

While Kim Jong Un cannot rule out loose talk of U.S. "preemptive strike," history since the end of the Korean War shows that neither the U.S. nor South Korea has ever responded with military force even in egregious lethal attacks by the North, such as international terrorist attacks against the South Korean government and civilians or the shootdown of a U.S. spy plane in international airspace, killing all 31 U.S. servicemen on board, on April 15, 1969, regime founder Kim Il Sung's birthday. In other words, even before crossing the nuclear Rubicon, North Korea had thoroughly deterred the U.S. with conventional weapons alone. Today, armed with nukes and ICBMs, not to mention chemical, biological, and radiological weapons, would Pyongyang be truly afraid of an attack by the U.S., for which there is no precedent?

Events since mid-2017 suggest Kim has been rather undaunted by verbal threats or U.S.-ROK combined military exercises. For example, undeterred by the rhetoric of "fire and fury" that Trump made on

August 8, 2017, Kim fired a missile over Japan three weeks later on August 29 and followed up with his nation's most powerful nuclear test to date on September 3. Moreover, deterred neither by President's Trump's name calling ("Rocket Man is on a suicide mission") nor his threat of "total destruction" while speaking at the UN General Assembly on September 19, Pyongyang shot an ICBM on a lofted trajectory of 2,800 miles into space in late-November, thus showing that its missiles had the range to hit every corner of the U.S. Such acts of defiance are atypical of a frightened man.

How should the Trump administration reverse the tide and employ its own carrot-and-stick strategy?

First, don't underestimate the North Korean leader. America's inability to take North Korea seriously as a formidable foe with a sophisticated strategic playbook of its own goes back to the first days of the Korean War. Once news broke, the Truman administration immediately assumed that the North's invasion across the 38th parallel was a mere prelude to a highly coordinated Communist expansionist plan instead of Kim Il Sung's campaign to liberate the South. Edward Barrett, a senior official in the State Department, said the relationship between Josef Stalin and Kim Il Sung was "exactly the same as that between Walt Disney and Donald Duck." The Truman administration was unable to see that the 38-year-old Kim Il Sung, so dependent on both Moscow and Beijing as he presided over his backward nation, could be anything but Stalin's puppet. The Trump administration must remember that on the ledger of nuclear diplomacy over the past quarter century, North Korea has wrested away from the U.S., South Korea, and Japan billions of dollars in aid in return for false pledges of denuclearization.

Second, eschew fuzzy wordplay as well as atmospherics. What Kim seeks is a drawn-out, open-ended, non-binding, time-saving, sanctions-busting negotiations process on the "denuclearization of the Korean peninsula." Such drawn-out "denuclearization of the Korean peninsula" negotiations North Korea regards as the sine qua non to becoming completely, verifiably, and irreversibly a de facto nuclear state. While most American policymakers blithely repeat this strange formulation (the phrase made its debut in the 2005 Joint Statement of the Six-Party Talks and is enshrined in every UN Security Council Resolution on North Korea passed since 2006), to Pyongyang the phrase means the abrogation of the U.S.-ROK alliance treaty and the ultimate goal of dislodging U.S. troops and extended nuclear deterrence from the region – that is, South Korea *and* Japan. Getting Washington to halt sanctions against Pyongyang's palace economy and sign a peace agreement are necessary steps in this long-term goal.

"Peace" sounds tantalizingly pleasant, but many a historical canard has been couched under the rubric of "peace." The Soviet-German pact of 1938 and the 1973 Paris Peace Accords brought about peace only after war. Any formal peace agreement with the DPRK as it is governed by the Kim clan will set off a series of events damaging to the interests of the U.S. and allies. It will trigger the dismantlement of the UN Command, call into question the raison d'etre of U.S. troops in South Korea and Japan, likely lead to the winddown and full withdrawal of U.S. forces in Korea and, paradoxically increase the risk of war in the Korean peninsula. Today, the revisionist regime of the DPRK is closer than ever to realizing these tantalizing dreams, thanks in part to the outside world's uncompromising gullibility.

Third, don't fall for Kim Jong Un's self-effacing humor or fake "reasonable" statements. The South Korean envoys who met Kim Jong Un on March 5, 2018, upon return home, spoke glowingly of Kim as someone who is "bold and sincere," as well as having a sense of humor. President Moon, upon meeting Kim Jong Un on April 27, 2018 and in subsequent meetings, has called him "courageous and sincere." It's a time-tested trick that Kim the First, Second, and Third have all mastered and employed variously on befuddled foreign visitors. Such is the very low expectation and strong biases that the outsider brings into his rare encounter with the North Korean leader, that when the weird strongman comes across as actually knowledgeable about world affairs, confers on the guest gracious hospitality, and even makes fun of himself, the visitor is dazzled and comes away from the meeting with the conviction that he has gained new, deep insights into the Kim regime, most likely by virtue of his own charisma, empathy, and intelligence. These are clever schemes the Kims have used on South Korean and American visitors since the early-1970s – on journalists, academics, and officials – in an attempt to come across as a reasonable party with whom the outside world can conduct conventional state-to-state business; which means, turning a blind eye to the North's nukes and gulags and paying up for the sake of de-escalation and enticing Pyongyang to keep its fake promises of peace and denuclearization.

Most importantly, do something that's never been tried before: Enforce sanctions against the DPRK over time.

Enforce sanctions and negotiate from a position of strength

While both the U.S. and South Korea in recent months have been accentuating the positive, for example emphasizing Kim Jong Un's coming-out, his decommissioning, following his nation's sixth underground nuclear test, of a tired nuclear test site in May 2017, and over a year of no ballistic missile tests, the fact remains that North Korea's nuclear and ballistic missile programs, not to mention his gulag, forge ahead – Kim's smiles-flashing façade notwithstanding. The temporary lull in North Korea's bellicose rhetoric and nuclear blackmail is a mere interlude before its next big provocation. North Korea has a compelling need to show the U.S. that it can combine a thermonuclear warhead with an ICBM that can withstand the re-entry into the earth's atmosphere. Thereafter, it will bank on being a constant nuclear threat to every major U.S. city and proceed to extort and censor the U.S. and its allies with abandon. To forge the future with proactive coercive diplomacy – one that employs unremitting financial sanctions and multi-faceted information dissemination operations into the North – in tandem with conventional diplomacy and military deterrence even in the face of fake peace overtures, offers the best hope denuclearization and changing the nature of the North Korean regime.

Sanctions are a longstanding legitimate, non-lethal instrument of statecraft. Curiously, neither U.S. nor UN sanctions against North

Korea were even remotely strong until 2016 when the U.S. for the first time enacted a relatively tough North Korea-specific sanctions legislation and the UN passed less "defensive" and more targeted financial and sectoral sanctions. While many still believe that U.S. sanctions on Pyongyang are strong or even "maxed out," the history of U.S. sanctions on North Korea is illustrative mostly for its weakness. In terms of the number and type of North Korea designations, execution of secondary sanctions (penalizing third-country partners of the DPRK who willfully violate sanctions), and resources committed to enforcing sanctions, U.S. sanctions on North Korea don't even come close to those against Iran during the Obama administration or the Trump administration's sanctions against Russia, Syria, or Iran today.

It took the Obama administration five years of meaningful sanctions enforcement just to compel Iran to return to negotiations, whereas the Trump administration, despite its rhetoric that no sanctions have been lifted since the first Trump-Kim summit, has given Pyongyang free rein to carry on as usual after just one year of concerted enforcement. The Obama administration levied substantial fines on major international banks that were in blatant violation of U.S. sanctions laws on Iran (and other targets like Sudan, Cuba, Burma, cartels, etc.). The U.S. fined BNP Paribas $8.9 billion; HSBC $1.9 billion; Commerzbank $1.45 billion; Credit Agricole $787; Standard Chartered $674 million; ING $619 million; Credit Suisse AG $536 million; Lloyd's TSB $350 million; Barclay's $298 million; Royal Bank of Scotland $100 million, etc. All the banks complied, for the alternative of being blocked out of the U.S. dollar system would have been a death knell. On the other hand, the Trump administration, to date, has designated only a small regional bank in China, Bank of Dandong, and a handful of Chinese companies, while known major violators like the Bank of China (fourth in the world in assets), Agricultural Bank of China (third in the world in assets), and China Merchants Bank (top 30 in the world) have all been given a pass by the U.S. Treasury Secretary.

The contrast in sanctions between the old, clunky, one-dimensional no-trade sanctions of the Cold War and the smart, target financial sanctions of the post-9/11 era is as stark as the efficacy of communication via a message in a bottle and Twitter. Sanctions seek to deprive the target of some value or expectations and consequently disrupt the target's future planning abilities. Sanctions assume a long-term outlook, a patient strategy of enforcement by blocking the target's access to funds, thus raising the target's anxiety index. The fact that all target nations evade sanctions enforcement, adapt and adopt new evasion schemes, and diffuse pain on its population does not mean that sanctions don't work.

The despotic DPRK has an unusually high pain threshold. The regime's disregard for human life and the absence of an alternate party or would-be challenger in the form of civic groups or military cliques enable Pyongyang to withstand sanctions with a relatively high degree of impunity. At the same time, even such a monolithic entity is not entirely unencumbered by internal and external structural vulnerabilities. The Kim regime, even with, or because of, its sustained policy of extreme repression, is in theory not impervious to a "group within that may thwart the leadership." The Kim regime's excessive dependence on China and its preponderant reliance on illicit streams of revenue from proliferation, month-laundering, counterfeiting, slave labor exports, cybercrimes, etc., does make it vulnerable to targeted financial sanctions enforcement, especially against major Chinese entities, over several years. The problem is that it's never been tried before.

President Trump must be fully informed that the terms of the gradual suspension and ultimate termination of U.S. sanctions against the Kim regime are codified into law. Unless Pyongyang takes meaningful steps toward the complete dismantlement of its nuclear plants, centrifuges, and other WMD programs; stops illicit activities such as counterfeiting U.S. currency, money laundering and proliferation; releases all political prisoners and stops censoring the North Korean people in extremis; abides by international norms as an aid-recipient nation and complies with monitoring; releases all abductees and unlawfully held foreign citizens; reforms its horrific prison camps; and, ultimately, establishes an open and representative society, the U.S. is legally bound to continue to enforce sanctions.[10]

---

10   See Sections 401 and 402, North Korean Sanctions and Policy Enhancement Act of 2016.

This fact, that the U.S. is legally bound to enforce sanctions until and unless meaningful actions are taken by the North Korean government must be communicated to Kim Jong Un, even in the bonhomous moment of summit pageantry. To return to the failed North Korea policies of the past will only give Pyongyang more time and funds to perfect its nuclear arsenal with which to threaten the region and the U.S. homeland. Coddling the Kim regime at this moment when the U.S. severely lacks leverage will ensure failure and possibly more – even the probability of war with a nuclear North Korea, a tragedy which discerning future historians and even the most casual aliens will come to attribute to the abiding American attitudinal ailment of underestimating one's adversary.

3

Why These Negotiations with North Korea Could Work

CHUNG-IN MOON

After the historic breakthroughs of 2018 on the Korean Peninsula, prospects for a negotiated settlement of the North Korean nuclear issue have never looked better. Yet skepticism looms like a perma-nent dark cloud over Washington. Pessimists insist that Pyongyang is too deceptive to engage, and it is futile, if not dangerous, to nego-tiate with North Korean leader Kim Jong Un. As it has in the past, Pyongyang will inevitably cheat and chisel by employing a so-called "salami tactic," and the situation will eventually revert from bad to worse.

This Washington consensus is misguided and outdated. It is detached from changing realities and even looks, from the perspec-tive of Seoul, like a self-defeating prophecy. Successful negotiations are not only possible, that are necessary, and they can work this time. Five factors give me confidence as we return to the negotiating table with the North Koreans.

First, unlike in the past, North Korea seems genuinely committed to dialogue and negotiation this time around. Kim Jong Un has openly expressed his desire for complete denuclearization through negotia-tion on several occasions. On April 27, 2018, he told South Korean President Moon Jae-in at the Panmunjom Summit, "Why should we suffer by having nuclear weapons if we talk more frequently, build trust, and reach a non-aggression treaty with the U.S.?" His verbal commitment is now embodied in several documents: the Panmunjom Declaration, the June 12 Singapore Declaration, and the September 19 Pyongyang Declaration. On Sept. 19, 2018, he even person-ally declared, in an unprecedented statement, that "I agreed with

President Moon to turn Korea into a land of peace free of nuclear threats and weapons." In other countries, the words of a leader might be taken with a grain of salt – but in North Korea, Kim's statements and gestures are viewed as divine commandments. In contrast to his previous assertions about "North Korea as a responsible nuclear weapons state" (2016), "North Korea as a powerful country of the East with nuclear weapons" (2017), and "completion of nuclear armament capability" (2018), Kim has embraced the goal of a nuclear free Korean Peninsula.

Skeptics still doubt the sincerity of his statements and argue that such a stance is nothing but a disguised peace offensive from a position of strength. But such suspicion should not serve as the rationale for avoiding negotiations with the North. There is no reason not to engage and negotiate with Pyongyang when it is willing to pursue denuclearization through negotiations. Even if Kim does not want to denuclearize, we should engage with him and move him towards complete denuclearization through mutual compromise and confidence building. Isn't this the *raison d'etre* of diplomacy? Neither naïve skepticism nor blind pessimism should derail the path toward a negotiated settlement. North Korea's Supreme Leader has expressed a willingness to give up his nuclear weapons – we should make the most of this.

Second, negotiation could work this time because of a convergence of motives and interests of leaders in North Korea, South Korea, and the U.S. to make these negotiations a success. As Kim Jong Un's *byungjin* policy (the simultaneous pursuit of economic development and nuclear weapons) suggests, the North might want both prosperity and nuclear bombs. But Kim's April 2018 declaration of an end to the byungjin policy indicates that he realizes he cannot have both. My three-day visit to Pyongyang in September revealed that North Korea's primary concern is to achieve prosperity. Kim might be taking a risky gamble, sacrificing nuclear weapons for the sake of economic development that could secure the longevity of his regime through increased political legitimacy and popular support. Of course, abandonment of bombs will depend on what terms he can get in return. He wants political assurances through diplomatic normalization with the U.S.; military assurance through a non-aggression treaty with the U.S.; economic assurance through the lifting of economic sanctions; acceptance of North Korea as a normal member of the international community; expansion of trade and investment and admission to multilateral lending institutions; and energy assurances that would allow the peaceful use of atomic energy. If the terms are right, Kim is willing to go for a negotiated settlement. That is why he is interested in a successful outcome of negotiations.

President Moon also wants successful negotiations, because of his commitment to peace. Peace is his top priority. For him, peace precedes unification. He also believes that a peaceful Korean Peninsula is vital to economic prosperity. For his part, U.S. President Donald Trump has every reason to want to make negotiations successful. He wants to prove that he is a great leader who solved the North Korean nuclear problem without spending a single penny – something he can claim former U.S. Presidents Bill Clinton, George W. Bush, and Barack Obama all failed to do. That is the best way to satisfy his personal ego and to prepare for reelection in November 2020. Kim's emphasis on the economy, Moon's quest for peace, and Trump's preoccupation with political achievement together are likely to enhance the possibility of successful negotiations more than ever before.

Third, the setting and level of negotiations have fundamentally changed. Previous negotiations such as the Geneva Agreed Framework, the Six Party talks, and the "Leap Day Agreement" of February 2012 all took place at the level of assistant secretary of state (in the case of the U.S.) and vice foreign minister (in the case of North Korea). Although their negotiations were sincere and serious, the relative weight of negotiators was light, and negotiated outcomes were easily nullified.

But this time is different. Dialogue and negotiations have been upgraded to the summit level, and their frequency has increased. There have already been three summits between Seoul and Pyongyang and one summit between Washington and Pyongyang in the past year alone. Channels of communication have been established among the three leaders, and intimacy and trust have also been built. That makes a big difference. This is more so because of the style of deci-sion-making. Both Kim and Trump are known to have centralized decision-making power. Leadership commitment and direct interac-tion among leaders are likely to enhance the probability of successful negotiations.

Fourth, countries involved are willing to engage in negotiations. In the past, North Korea was greatly interested in having dialogue and negotiation with the U.S. But the American stance was firmly opposed to this. The Obama administration adopted a policy of "strategic patience" since April 2009 and refused to have meaning-ful negotiations with the North. South Korea under Presidents Lee Myung-bak and Park Geun-hye also advocated sanctions, isolation and containment against North Korea, while rejecting any meaning-ful dialogue and negotiations. Japan also joined the hardline camp. It was only China that wanted to resuscitate the Six Party talks, whereas Russia had very limited influence.

Since early 2018, however, the overall landscape for negotiations has begun to change. As Kim shifted his stance in favor of dialogue and negotiations, South Korea was the most supportive country. President Moon has played an active role in mediating between Pyongyang and Washington and facilitating the entire negotiation process. President Trump also responded to the new initiative by South Korea and North Korea by agreeing to hold the summit with Chairman Kim. China has also been supportive of a negotiated settlement by closely coordinat-ing with the U.S. and South Korea. Russia has also joined this school. Japan has been the only country that has been reluctant to endorse the path to a negotiated settlement. However, given the dense ties between Tokyo and Washington, Japan is also likely to follow the American lead, should the U.S. decide to go for negotiations. The alignment of national interests and political will is a driving factor for the success of the current peace and denuclearization diplomacy.

Finally, I would like to raise a straightforward question to those skeptics and pessimists of the current moves toward negotiations: Are there better, realistic alternatives to negotiations? Since 2009, South Korea and the U.S. have been pushing for sanctions and pressure on North Korea. But they have not been effective in altering North Korea's behavior. As sanctions and pressure intensified, Pyongyang, on the contrary, expedited the nuclearization process and responded with nuclear tests and missile-test launches. In fact, its recent decision to come to the negotiation table is a result more of engagement policy by the U.S. and South Korea than of sanctions and maximum pressure.

When sanctions and pressure did not work, the Trump administration considered resorting to military options such as preventive war, preemptive attack, or delivery of some kind of "bloody nose." Such options might still be on the table. However, their practical utility in degrading North Korea's nuclear capability is fundamentally limited, and the risks are extremely grave. As demonstrated by the "surgical strike" option that was considered in May 1994 by then U.S. Secretary of Defense William Perry, such options would entail enormous collateral damage, and the people and government of South Korea would ferociously oppose them. China and Russia would also be extremely critical of such actions. As Winston Churchill once argued, "jaw-jaw is far better than war-war."

In view of the arguments I have made above, negotiations are the prudent course of action. The motives and interests of the respective leaders and the overall setting for negotiations could make the difference this time around. As William Perry aptly pointed out, we need to "talk first, get tough later." The issue at stake is not whether negotiations could work this time, but how we can make the negotiations successful. I have some suggestions to both North Korea and the U.S. in this regard.

Pyongyang and Washington should discard the habit of mutual demonization and promote two-way understanding and trust building. They should not judge each other's present and future behavior by their past behavior. If they treat each other as the devil, there is no way they can make progress since the devil does not negotiate. That is the best way to narrow the trust gap that is essential for successful negotiations.

Both sides should be "realistic and practical." Goals for negotiation should be adjusted to changing circumstances. A good example is complete denuclearization. The Washington pessimists insist on "all in one, and all or nothing." If North Korea does not give up its nuclear facilities, materials, and bombs all in one, then there will be no relaxation of sanctions. We need to implement an incremental approach, not an all-in-one approach. The skeptical logic of "dismantle first, and I will reward you later" won't work. However, the North Korean approach of "you relax sanction first, then I will go for declaration, inspection, verification, and dismantling" will not work either. That is a classic example of the salami tactics that the U.S. will never accept. Moreover, North Korea should give up the illusion that it can follow the Pakistani model. No one will recognize North Korea as a nuclear weapons state.

Both sides should be more flexible. They must put all possible cards on the table, including a temporary halt to joint South Korea–U.S. military drills, replacement of armistice with a peace treaty, allowance of North Korea's peaceful use of atomic energy and space/satellite programs, and normalization of diplomatic relations between North Korea and the United States. We must not exclude these options just because they are being demanded by Pyongyang. The North should also put on the table all the options involving the complete, verifiable, and irreversible dismantling of nuclear facilities, materials, weapons, ballistic missiles, and knowledge infrastructure. While addressing issues through dialogue, both sides could probe mutual intentions and demand responsibility for any breach of faith.

They can also be flexible in the sequencing of denuclearization. Verification fundamentalists argue for the sequential stages of freezing, declaration, inspection, verification, and finally, dismantling. But they could think about other ways too: maybe, they could call for verifiable dismantling of important portions of nuclear facilities and materials first, such as the Yongbyon nuclear facilities, as well as the removal of ICBMs, and then, declaration and inspection could come later, along with verifiable dismantling of nuclear bombs. They need to have more flexible and imaginative thinking in dealing with each other rather than having a fixed and stereotypical approach.

Compromise is the most valued virtue in negotiations. Yes, the U.S. is a superpower, whereas North Korea is a small state. Asymmetry between the two seems inevitable. But subjugation of one to the other will not result in successful negotiations. There should be a compromise that is mutually acceptable. This is more so because North Korea is not a nation that has surrendered. For example, there could be a compromise between the American demand to "dismantle first, reward later" and the North Korean call for "simultaneous exchange based on the principle of action for action." If North Korea takes positive steps, such as verifiable dismantling of Yongbyon nuclear facilities and/or acceptance of declaration and inspection of nuclear materials, the U.S. needs to allow a partial relaxation of sanctions against North Korea. Such a move could further reinforce Pyongyang's denuclearization efforts.

In conclusion, the great reversal in 2018 is a small but significant stepping stone toward peace-making and denuclearization on the Korean Peninsula. We should not have false expectations. This process will be a long and treacherous odyssey. There is no such thing as a quick fix. Nevertheless, dialogue and negotiations are the surest path to a better outcome for all.

4

Kim Jong Un's Survival Strategy

Andrei Lankov

The young leader

On December 19th, 2011, a special TV broadcast told North Koreans that Kim Jong Il, the second ruler of the Kim dynasty, had died after some 17 years in full control of the country. Few people doubted that he was going to be replaced by his son, Kim Jong Un, whose personality cult had already advanced by that time.

Being born in 1984, the new North Korean leader was young – indeed, so embarrassingly young that the official media did not openly report his age. At the time of his ascent, he was the youngest chief executive in the world; he turned 28 in January 2012 when he had already inherited his father's top position.

Due to some unknown reasons, Kim Jong Il long procrastinated when it came to the appointment of a successor. The second ruler of the Kim dynasty reluctantly made the final decision on succession only in early 2009, after he suffered a massive stroke, which, obviously, reminded the aging North Korean leader of his own mortality. His choice for a successor was his third son Kim Jong Un, but it took another year before the would-be leader was presented to the public in early October 2010, that is, merely one year before he was to inherit his father's power. Only then the North Korean media began to build up the personality cult of the 'Young General,' telling the audience about the would-be leader's superhuman qualities.

Kim Jong Il obviously assumed that his son would have enough time to amass necessary political and administrative experience, for years acting as an assistant and apprentice to the dictator father – pretty much like Kim Jong Il himself who spent almost 25 years as a heir designate and political apprentice to Kim Il Sung, the founder of the dynasty. However, the sudden death of Kim Jong Il changed everything and catapulted the young successor straight to the summit of power.

When Kim Jong Un was first selected, this decision raised some eyebrows, since the successor was not merely youngest of Kim Jong Il's known children, but also the least known of them (even his name was not spelled correctly for a while). However, the subsequent events demonstrated that, in spite of his young age and seeming inexperience, Kim Jong Un was indeed made of the right stuff for a successful authoritarian leader.

To understand what Kim Jong Un wants to achieve, we have to keep in mind his major policy goals. There are two such goals: first, he wants to stay alive and in power – in other words he wants, like his father and grandfather, eventually to die a natural death at a ripe old age, not being overthrown, imprisoned or killed. Second, he wants to develop his country.

Unfortunately for him, Kim Jong Un has good reasons to believe that loss of power would likely mean the loss of life as well. North Korea is a brutal place, and Kim Jong Un, if he is removed from power, will have little opportunity to find asylum in any other country – he has been nobody's puppet and nobody's loyal ally. The sorry fates of Nicolae Ceausescu and Muammar Gadhafi have demonstrated to Kim Jong Un what might happen to him (and his loved ones) if he does not succeed in maintaining political stability. So, he is playing a deadly serious game where he has no safe exit options, and he knows it.

What are the major threats that the young authoritarian leader is facing now – or, to put things somewhat differently, which political forces, external and internal, can prevent him from staying in power for decades? At the first approximation, there are three such dangerous forces. These threats are: an elite conspiracy or coup; a foreign attack (perhaps intervening in some local crisis); or a popular revolt. Kim Jong Un's entire policy can be best interpreted as a series of highly rational (if sometimes brutal) measures aimed at neutralizing these three major potential threats.

Dealing with the threat of conspiracy

The first threat Kim Jong Un has to deal with is the ever-present menace of an elite conspiracy or military coup. Kim Jong Un's period of apprenticeship was too short, and he had few opportunities to establish his own power base, so he inherited his father's top bureaucracy: a bunch of generals, ministers, and party secretaries, who were at least twice his age. It would be a problem in any country, but it is much more of a problem in a Confucian society like North Korea where age matters a lot.

To complicate things further, the policy Kim Jong Un intended to follow contradicted in many important regards what his top officials believed to be right and proper. In order to survive and stay in power, as well to develop his country and improve his people's lives (a secondary, but still important goal for him), Kim Jong Un had to initiate reforms to stimulate economic growth that go against many convictions of the old guard. These people, overwhelmingly old, do not see the reasons to take risks; they believe that the system has enough strength to last for another decade or two. Such a period is good for an octogenarian dignitary, but clearly not good for a young leader.

Kim Jong Un dealt with the conspiracy/coup threat in a rather traditional way: with intense purges. Nothing shows better what happened in Kim Jong Un's North Korea than the fate of seven top officials who, together with Kim Jong Un himself, walked next to Kim Jong Il's hearse during the late dictator's funeral procession in December 2011. In two years' time, five of the seven people have disappeared, and two of them are known to have been executed on Kim Jong Un's orders.

Contrary to what is often believed, such harshness is unusual for North Korea. The early period of North Korean history, from the late 1940s to the early 1960s, was indeed marked by frequent and bloody purges, with communist leaders killing one another in large numbers. However, by the late 1960s things changed, so the North Korea of the first two Kims became a place where the top leader seldom ordered executions or even long-term imprisonment of people whom he happened to know personally. Commoners could be sent to prison camps in the thousands, but the top elite was remarkably secure. Usually, a disgraced dignitary would be sent for "re-education" to a remote area and then often recalled back and restored to his earlier power and glory.

Under Kim Jong Un, this old soft approach to the top officials was gone. A surprising number of people, especially top military officers, were executed or disappeared in prisons – including Chief of the General Staff Ri Yong-ho (purged and presumably executed in 2012) and Minister of Defense Hyon Yong-chol (executed in 2015).

It is also important that under Kim Jong Il top North Korean military and security officials kept their positions for a remarkably short period of time, playing a sort of involuntary musical chairs game. Within seven years of Kim Jong Un's rule, North Korea has had seven defense ministers, the longest serving of whom kept this position for less than three years. To put things in comparison, during the 1967-2011 period, lasting forty four years, there were merely five (!) defense ministers. So, the average length of their tenure under Kim Jong Un shortened nearly ten times. Other key figures in the top military leadership are also replaced with similar frequency.

The major goal of this policy is clear: the frequent rotation creates a situation when no ambitious general can establish a power base and create a network of connections which is vital for successfully staging a coup or making a conspiracy.

This policy of purges is often described in foreign media as a "reign of terror" but this description is misleading. When it comes to dealing with the common population, Kim Jong Un's policy, repressive as it is, is not much worse than policy of his father – and is arguably less repressive than policy of his grandfather. Kim Jong Un's purges are specifically directed against a narrow circle of people who occupy the very top of North Korea's power pyramid – and, more specifically, against "people with guns," the military and police commanders. Kim Jong Un is targeting, above all, generals, whom he sees as people in control of a potentially dangerous force.

This does not mean that common people are immune from persecution – on the contrary, North Korea's ratio of political prisoners to the general population seems to be by far the world's highest, with some 80-100,000 people in the political prison camps. However, this figure, high as it is, did not seem to increase considerably under Kim Jong Un. North Korea is a dangerous place to live for everybody, commoners or dignitary, but under Kim Jong Un the risks for dignitaries and generals increased while risks for the commoners have stayed on the old high level.

Among the purge victims, there were two members of Kim Jong Un's own family. This is also unusual because, in spite of frequent clashes within the ruling clan, since the 1960s family members have been largely safe from anything but comfortable exile in the countryside, or better, a diplomatic position in a remote country. Kim Jong Un broke with this tradition and showed his willingness to use force against potentially dangerous members of his own clan.

In December 2013, Kim Jong Un's uncle (to be more precise, his aunt's husband) Jang Song Thaek was arrested during a government meeting, in front of cameras. The unlucky dignitary was dragged away, stood a show trial and was executed in few days' time. In an unprecedented move, both his arrest and his execution were reported by the state media in some detail – with a large indictment being published in newspapers.

A few years later, in February 2017, North Korean operatives managed to kill Kim Jong Nam, the oldest son of the late Kim Jong Il and Kim Jong Un's half-brother. He was poisoned with a toxic agent while he was waiting for a plane in Kuala Lumpur Airport in Malaysia.

This murder of family members is often presented as a sign of Kim Jong Un's irrationality. However, the opposite is true: he removed two members of the Kim clan who were independent of him and had independent political aspirations. Jang Song Thaek, in the early days of Kim Jong Un's rule, began to fancy himself as a regent to the young ruler; perhaps this was indeed the initial hope of Kim Jong Il who promoted Jang when he chose Kim Jong Un as a successor. In the first years of the new rule, Jang Song Thaek was clearly second in command. He concentrated too much power and was occasionally even trying to tell Kim Jong Un what to do. Predictably, Kim Jong Un sensed danger coming from him.

The same is applicable to Kim Jong Nam, who lived overseas, in Macao and China, since the early 2000s. Kim Jong Nam occasionally contacted foreign media and conducted remarkably frank interviews where he even made some mildly critical remarks about North Korea. To make things even worse, there were signs that Kim Jong Nam was actually protected by the Chinese authorities who perhaps saw him as a potential head of a pro-Chinese regime in North Korea, should the need to establish such a regime arise in future.

Thus both Jang Song Thaek and Kim Jong Nam were actually quite dangerous. It's not clear whether they were really involved in some conspiracies, but, by being two only members of the ruling family who were also remarkably independent from Kim Jong Un himself, they could easily become a nucleus of such resistance. This sealed their fate.

Dealing with the threat of a foreign attack

The second threat Kim Jong Un deals with is the threat of a foreign attack. It can possibly take two shapes. On one hand, he's afraid of something that can be called the Iraq scenario, that is, a direct attack by the United States or, perhaps, some other great power (there is some fear of Chinese action).

On the other hand, Kim Jong Un and the entire North Korean elite fear what can be described as the Libya scenario, that is, a domestic rebellion supported by a foreign invasion.

The North Korean leaders are certain that without the nuclear program they are vulnerable – and, given the events of recent years, it's difficult to accuse them of being paranoid. They have seen how Iraq, which tried but failed to develop its nuclear program, was defeated and occupied by a U.S.-led coalition under what was by then the false assumption that it was developing nuclear weapons, and how its leader died on the gallows (most of Saddam's elite did not fare well, either).

Even more important for North Korea is the fate of Libya. Kaddafi did exactly what the U.S. and world demands that North Korea do: he surrendered his nuclear program in exchange for sanctions relaxation and preferential economic treatment. When a rebellion broke out in Libya, however, the Western powers intervened, banning Kaddafi and his supporters from what was their major military advantage – air power. Soon Kaddafi was intercepted and tortured to death, and his regime collapsed. For North Koreans there is no doubt that the existence of Libyan nuclear weapons, no matter how rudimentary, would have stopped the Western powers from forcing on Libya the "no fly zones" and downing the regime's air forces at the decisive moment of the civil war.

North Korean leaders have good reasons to believe that only some powerful deterrent can save them from a foreign attack. Their country is too poor and backward, in spite of recent economic improvement, to afford sufficiently powerful conventional forces, so WMD – especially, nuclear weapons – come as their natural choice. Indeed, the Kim family began to entertain nuclear ambitions as early as the 1960s, and worked on the nuclear weapons program for decades. In 2006 they succeeded in exploding their first nuclear device and in 2017 they tested what is claimed to be a thermonuclear device. They also worked hard to acquire delivery capability, and in 2017 they successfully tested two types of ICBM seemingly capable of delivering a nuclear warhead to the continental U.S.

It has been often argued that a combination of pressure and promises of economic incentives will persuade the North Korean leaders to change their position and consider denuclearization. The U.S. policy on the North Korean nuclear issue has been based on this assumption for decades. However, this assumption is wrong, and there is little surprise that the U.S. policy failed miserably.

Kim Jong Un and the entire North Korean elite – say, between one and two million people, including the family members – would definitely like to improve the lot of the commoners and would prefer to preside over a country with a healthy and growing economy. However, unlike most elite groups in the modern world, they face an existential threat, or at least, they sincerely believe that they face such a threat.

Being rational human beings and intelligent political actors, the North Korean decision makers understand that survival is more important than prosperity: after all, dead people don't need riches. Even if they were to survive a possible violent collapse of the regime, they are unlikely to stay in control since such a collapse would likely result in a German-style "unification by absorption" with a bankrupt and defeated North being swallowed by the triumphant and powerful South. It means that the North Korean elite, everybody who is anybody in present-day North Korea, would lose power and perhaps freedom, and some cases, even life.

To put things differently, not only Kim Jong Un, but all North Korean mid- and high-ranking officials, would like to witness a North Korean economic miracle, preside over it and profit from it. However, they are definitely not interested in this option if they are going to enjoy the view of newly erected high-rise buildings in Pyongyang downtown through the bars of their prison cells. Therefore, no matter what, they are not going to surrender their nuclear weapons, even though it is quite possible that they will eventually accept some partial compromise – like, say, a freeze or even partial reduction of their nuclear program, if the risk/benefits calculation suggests that this was going to be a rational action.

The sad fate of the Iran nuclear deal, so carefully negotiated by the Barack Obama administration, is another bitter lesson for North Korea to learn. Once Donald Trump took power, he immediately denounced this agreement. What can guarantee that the next U.S. president whose policy is likely to be ABT (that is, "Anything But Trump") will not treat any potential agreement with North Korea in the same way? If it happens, the North Korean leadership will find themselves without their much cherished nuclear deterrent, and with a few pieces of useless papers.

Therefore, the North Korean nuclear policy is clear. When outside pressure (largely from the U.S. but also from China) gets dangerously high, as happened in 2017, North Koreans can engage in negotiations, making (rather empty) promises in order to win time. There is even some probability of North Korean leaders accepting a reduction of their nuclear weapons stock – if threats are sufficiently plausible and promises of rewards are sufficiently believable. However, there is a bottom line that is never going to be crossed, and this bottom line is quite simple: no matter what, North Korea should have a certain number of nuclear devices, and ideally, delivery systems, to ensure that no reasonable outside power would ever either attack it, or intervene in a domestic political crisis.

Dealing with the economy: the threats of reforming, the threats of non-reforming

The third threat Kim Jong Un deals with is the threat of popular discontent, the ever-looming risk of some kind of popular rebellion. Such a rebellion could get some overseas support and/or get intertwined with some kind of the elite conspiracy – pretty much as happened in 1989 Romania, where a combination of an elite conspiracy and popular rebellion resulted in the violent collapse of the Ceausescu regime. In order to reach his main goal and die as the nation's almighty leader at a ripe old age, Kim Jong Un should stay in power for many decades, ideally for half a century. That outcome is virtually impossible if the economic situation of North Korea does not improve, and Kim Jong Un understands this very well.

Back in the 1940s when Korea was divided into North and South, the territory of the present-day North Korea, with its massive steel mills, chemical plants and power stations, was the most industrially advanced region in East Asia outside Japan. Nowadays, it is a basket case. In 2018, the North Korean government published its own estimate of the country's GDP which, remarkably, does not differ that much from the estimates made by foreign observers. The nominal per capita GDP in North Korea is, according to the government's own official data, merely $1,214. To put things in comparison, the same indicator for China is seven times higher – $8,826 in 2017.

Of a greater political significance is the gap with neighboring South Korea which, before the 1945-50 division, was an agrarian backwater, but has now become a powerhouse of the world economy. Currently the nominal per capita GDP in North Korea is just below $30,000, that is, some 25 times higher than in the North. Worldwide, this is the largest gap between two countries that share a land border.

The existence of a rich and prosperous South Korea whose population speaks the same language is a massive destabilizing factor which makes the situation in North Korea dramatically different from, say, the situation in China.

When, in the late 1970s Deng Xiaoping launched China's 'reform and opening policy,' he did not need to care about a mighty and attractive "another China" nearby. The Republic of China on the island of Taiwan might have been very prosperous by the then-standards of the continental China, but, after all, it was merely a tiny island state. When the common Chinese in the 1980s learned about the prosperity of, say, Japan, or the United Sates, they did not see it as a political problem, because it was prosperity enjoyed by foreign nations whose history, culture, and geography were completely different from those of China. The economic success and prosperity of, say, Japan could not be construed as irrefutable proof of the failure of the Chinese Communist Party policies.

On top of that, in the reforming China, nobody would even think about unification with, say, the United States, or Japan, or other prosperous nation of the world. China could not possibly become the 51st state of the United States of America or a Japanese prefecture. However, in North Korea the situation is very different.

First, the previously unimaginable economic success of the South is likely to be seen as proof that the North Korean political and social system did not deliver. Therefore the spread of knowledge about this success, especially if it were combined with a measure of domestic political relaxation, is likely to constitute a grave threat for the domestic stability of the nation. On top of that, unlike the Chinese, many North Korean commoners are likely to entertain a (rather illusionary) belief that German-style unification with the rich South would immediately deliver to them the living standards the average South Korean enjoys now.

It also does not help that North Korea is run by a hereditary elite, some 100-150 families, so the current leaders cannot even fully blame their predecessors for the sorry state of economy. Deng Xiaoping, a former victim of Mao Zedong's purges himself, could say that Mao was "30 percent wrong" and denounce the Cultural Revolution. Kim Jong Un cannot possibly admit that his father or grandfather was even "1 percent wrong."

In other words, in a divided country, a China-style policy of openness and reforms is highly risky. There are prohibitively high chances that in the peculiar case of North Korea such a policy, instead of delivering a China-style economic miracle, would deliver an East German-style political crisis, followed by a regime collapse and absorption of the North. Needless to say, in a divided nation, the North Korean elite has good reasons to suspect that in case of such a collapse, it will have little chance to stay in power. In the unified country, all key positions would very likely be taken by the South Korean elite and those few North Koreans who somehow achieved close connections with Seoul, while the current elite would be, at best, marginalized, and, at worst, incriminated, for the massive human rights abuses of the Kim family regime

'Reforms without openness' as a possible solution

There are good reasons to believe that the fear of unintended consequences which might result from Chinese-style political and economic reforms was the major reason which, for nearly two decades, prevented the Kim Jong Il government from emulating China, of whose success Kim Jong Il himself as well as all his advisors were perfectly aware.

However, the deliberate decision not to emulate China does not mean that the Kim Jong Il government in the 1990s and early 2000s succeeded in freezing the country's economic and social structure – even though such a freeze was the authorities' obvious goal. On the contrary, North Korea in the early 1990s underwent massive social and economic transformation which can best be described as 'de-Stalinization from below'.

In the early 1990s, the Soviet subsidies, which for long had been vital for keeping the North Korean economy afloat, were suddenly discontinued. This predictably led to a massive economic crisis. Industrial output nearly halved, agricultural production collapsed, food rations were not delivered and the resultant famine led to 500-900,000 excessive deaths.

Facing this situation and being suddenly deprived of the official salaries and state-delivered rations, the North Koreans essentially rediscovered the market economy. Initially they began small-scale market trade and household production. The farmers began to work on the steep mountain slopes, growing food for themselves and for resale. Workers used their time and equipment of their factories to produce consumption items for resale at the markets. Cross-border smuggling flourished, and up to 200,000 North Koreans moved to China – partially escaping famine and partially looking for work.

In due time all kinds of private economic activities reemerged. In some cases, the more successful entrepreneurs eventually amassed enough money to operate rather large enterprises which, however, had to be disguised, through official registration, as state property. For example, pretty much all restaurants currently operating in North Korea are, on paper, considered to be state property but in practice are run by private operators. The same is applicable to a large part of North Korea's fishing industry: small wooden boats, which can be seen in large numbers along the Korean costs, are formally registered as state property but are actually owned privately. There are privately operated factories and mines – also, of course, with some paper registration as state property. Around 2010, it was estimated that the private sector produced between 25 percent and 50 percent of North Korea's actual GDP.

Kim Jong Il and his close advisers were uncertain what should be done about this spontaneous privatization. There were periods (like, say, 2002-2005) when Kim Jong Il listened to his pro-market advisers, and was inclined to cautiously support such changes. However, for most of his 17-year rule, Kim Jong Il was either ambivalent or hostile towards the slow-motion collapse of Soviet-style state socialism. He could not stop this collapse, let alone reverse it, but in most cases he did what he could to slow the transformation down.

This approach was actually quite rational. Kim Jong Il understood that all reforms were inherently risky and might speed up political disintegration, his worst fear. Kim Jong Il, then in his late 50s and early 60s, obviously hoped that the system, in spite of its slow-motion decline, would still survive until his physical death, while hasty attempts to reform the system would have roughly equal chances of either saving it or speeding up its collapse. So, he preferred to remain passive.

However, his son, being much younger, cannot afford to take the same stance. If nothing is done, sooner or later the spontaneous disintegration of the system from below, combined with the steadily growing gap between North Korea and its neighbors, especially South Korea, will make the political structure unsustainable and provoke its disastrous and violent disintegration. So Kim Jong Un had no choice but to make the first move: unlike his aged father, he cannot afford to ignore the ongoing changes if he wants to survive as the country's leader for a really long time.

Kim Jong Un's personal background also helps. The worldview of his grandfather, Kim Il Sung, largely comprised ideas about the economy formed during the indoctrination sessions in the Chinese communist forces and then the Soviet army. His father, Kim Jong Il, once majored in Stalinist economic theory at Kim Il Sung university, and hardly changed his attitude much. Unlike them, Kim Jong Un spent his early teens in hyper-capitalist Switzerland, attending an elite school there. He knows well enough how the modern world operates, and he hardly has any sentimental attachment to the outdated ideas of state socialism. Therefore, his economic policy was aimed at emphasizing the introduction of market mechanisms – a topic that will be discussed at length in a later chapter.

However, Kim Jong Un and his elite cannot afford the Chinese-style 'reform and openness policy'. His regime, due to the existence of very prosperous, and very attractive 'other Korea', is unlikely to survive the Chinese level of openness towards the outside world or the Chinese level of relative political permissiveness, and Kim Jong Un understands this. So, his policy can be best described as 'reforms without openness.' His aim is to build a North Korean variety of the 'developmental dictatorship', somewhat similar to the Chinese model, but without post-Maoist political relaxation. (Yes, even under Xi Jinping China is far more politically relaxed than Mao's China or the Kims' North Korea.) Like any tradeoff, such compromise will be damaging for economic performance: presumably, a less open system, overloaded with political constraints, will not work that well. However, survival is more important than prosperity, so Kim Jong Un will have to accept the lower economic performance as a necessary, if regrettable, price for improved security.

So, unlike Chinese leaders of the 1980s, Kim Jong Un and his advisors, while promoting the growth of the market economy, did not relax political surveillance and control over the population. They did not encourage openness to the outside world. They made little if any change in the official ideology. If anything, North Korea under Kim Jong Un has become a more closed society than it used to be in the final years of Kim Jong Il's rule. Having taken power, Kim Jong Un not merely launched market-oriented economic reforms, but also began to repair the mechanism of state surveillance and control, which had gotten rusty under the watch of his aging father.

North Korean authorities stepped up the efforts to counter the penetration of foreign media. Starting from the early 2000s, many young urban North Koreans were secretly watching South Korean movies and TV shows which were in large quantities smuggled from China. While technically illegal, such activities seldom provoked serious persecution under Kim Jong Il. But this permissiveness disappeared under Kim Jong Un who began a massive crackdown on all people involved in the smuggling, reproducing, and selling of the banned South Korean videos.

Kim Jong Un also dramatically increased control of the border with China, aiming at reducing the number of defectors who were going to South Korea from the North. This policy was remarkably successful: the number of defectors went from roughly 2,500 around

2010 to about 1,000 in 2018. This was achieved through increase in the number of border guards and rotation of units, but also through massive and sophisticated propaganda campaigns that presented defectors as naive and helpless victims of hostile propaganda.

Kim Jong Un's major long-term strategic goal is clear. He wants to develop the economy through the encouragement of market mechanisms. But he also wants to make sure that his people remain as ignorant as possible about the outside world, and as fearful as possible of the authorities, especially the secret police.

Only time will tell whether Kim Jong Un's policy of "reforms without openness" will succeed, but for time being, it appears that nowadays, if one looks at the situation from the North Korean elite's angle, no realistic alternative to such a policy exists. In order to stay alive, the young North Korean autocrat and his support base have to do pretty much what he is doing now.

5

What Makes Kim Jong Un Different?

John Delury

Jalan-jalan

It is the evening before one of the biggest surprises in 21st century diplomacy – a summit between the President of the United States of America and Supreme Leader of the Democratic People's Republic of Korea. President Donald J. Trump is ensconced somewhere safely behind the security cordon walling off the Sentosa Island resort where the two leaders will meet the next day – perhaps he is recovering from the flight, or preparing for the meeting, or catching up on TV news. Chairman Kim Jong Un is not in his room. He is standing against a wall of begonias, looking straight into the cellphone camera lens, a broad smile across his face. He is flanked by Singapore's education minister and Foreign Minister Vivian Balakrishnan, who, arm extended, snaps a photo. It may be Kim Jong Un's first selfie, or if not that, then the first selfie to be "shared" with the world – the foreign minister posts it to his Twitter account with the hashtags #jalanjalan ("to go for a stroll") and #guesswhere?

I was in Singapore to comment on the summit at the invitation of Channel News Asia, and the following day – as Kim and Trump held their historic talks – I went in search of the answer to the foreign minister's tweeted question by retracing Kim's step on his *jalanjalan*. Unfamiliar with Singapore's landmarks, I had to ask locals for help – "Was the North Korean guy here last night?" I would ask, and friendly shop-owners, security guards, and hotel staff would show me the way. I took the elevator to the top of The Marina Bay Sands hotel, built by a South Korean construction company, and imagined the half-dressed patrons in its famed infinity pools waving to Kim. Then I wandered into The Gardens by the Bay, a spate of reclaimed land that juts out into the Singapore Straits. Crossing the elevated path from the hotel's 6th floor into The Gardens reminded me of a moment on a trip to North Korea, overlooking the West Sea Barrage built around the port at Nampo. It was a beautiful spot, mountains rolling into sea, but it was eerily still – the few ships in sight sat high in the water, cargo-less. Could Nampo one day become a bustling trading hub, a mini-Singapore? Did this thought occur to Kim?

Finally I came to the spot where Kim stood for his first known selfie, and took one myself. At that moment, the US-DPRK summit was winding down, but I couldn't help thinking that Kim's selfie in front of this wall of begonias was of greater significance than the photo-op in front of the line of flags. Kim's willingness to fly to Singapore – on a borrowed Air China plane no less – revealed him to be a different kind of North Korean leader, quite unlike his father Kim Jong Il, who traveled by rail under a veil of secrecy, and only to visit the two countries he thought he could (somewhat) trust – China and Russia. Once on the ground in Singapore, Kim did not hole up in his hotel room. Instead, he bounded off for a *jalanjalan* in the Singapore night, smiling at random crowds with their cellphones filming, taking a selfie with his new pals from the Singaporean government.

For leaders of "normal" countries, there would be little significance in something as mundane as a downtown stroll the night before a summit in a foreign capital. But for the Supreme Leader of the North Korea to take such steps has profound implications. Kim Jong Un shows a readiness to stray far outside of the typical North Korean comfort zone, where everything is choreographed and scripted, where society, economics and politics are designed to operate on the principle of total control, where there is nothing to learn from a hostile, forbidden world and North Koreans have "nothing to envy." Step by step, Kim is walking away from that logic. His inclination to "normalize" North Korea is the key driver to the transformative process we are seeing begin to unfold in terms of diplomacy.

The king's speech

The dramatic summitry of 2018 gave world leaders their first look at another side of Kim Jong Un and the direction he wants to take his country in. But to the discerning eye, there have been important signposts for years that Kim was a young leader with rather un-North Korean instincts – in fact, from as soon as he inherited rule after his father's death in December 2011. After fulfilling the filial duty of prime mourner at the memorial services, Kim wasted little time in getting to work on affairs of state. North Koreans were gearing up for a historic anniversary – the centennial of his grandfather Kim Il Sung's birth on April 15, 2012 – and rather than call off the party, Kim used the celebration to make his grand entrance onto the public stage. North Korea watchers got one of their first surprises of the new era on April 12, when Kim give a nationally-televised speech in Kim Il Sung Square. It was a striking contrast to his father, whose image was omnipresent in propaganda, but who never gave recorded, let alone live broadcast, speech in public.

Kim's continued to reinvent political traditions when, on January 1, 2013, he delivered a New Year's Address. In his grandfather's day, the New Year's speech was a kind of North Korean State of the Union, but his father stopped giving the speech, and replaced it with new year's statement published in all the newspapers and known as the Joint Editorial. Kim Jong Un's willingness – even eagerness – to be seen and heard, for maximum dissemination, defines and distinguishes his political style. It bespeaks a certain populism, a typical politician's desire to "connect" with constituents. Live broadcast speech-giving in particular requires a comfort with spontaneity, with little things going wrong or not quite as planned, even when the world is watching and the cameras are rolling.

Kim used his comfort in front of the camera to powerful diplomatic effect in September 2018, when North Korean state media released an unusual video of Kim sitting at his desk, delivering stern remarks in response to Donald Trump's warning at the United Nations General Assembly that the U.S. might have no choice but to "totally destroy"

North Korea. Kim's Victorian-era insult that Trump was a "dotard" whom he would "tame with fire" lit up Twitter – probably impressing Trump as much as insulting him. Weeks later when a North Korean foreign ministry commentary called Trump an "old lunatic," the President tweeted, "Why would Kim Jong Un insult me by calling me 'old,' when I would NEVER call him 'short and fat?' Oh well, I try so hard to be his friend – and maybe someday that will happen!" In those days of talk of "fire and fury," the tweet seemed like yet another round of acrimony inching the Peninsula closer to real conflict. But in hindsight, Trump's coy reference to wanting to become Kim's friend reads like diplomatic flirtation. Kim for his part eagerly engaged in the rhetorical dueling.

The victory of Byungjin

Skeptics might naturally object that examples such as these drawn from Kim's public speeches are merely cosmetic and stylistic – superficial changes like the shorter length of performers' skirts in Kim's favorite girl band, Moranbong. But in terms of hard policy choices, there are equally strong indications that Kim wants to lead his country in a new direction. He took power facing the same dilemma that has bedeviled North Korean leadership for decades – how to promote economic prosperity and international standing while protecting national security and regime stability? To see how Kim is trying to answer this question in a new way, we cannot judge him in a vacuum; rather, we need to interpret his words and deeds in light of the legacy he received upon inheriting power.

His father Kim Jong Il tried but ultimately failed to solve the riddle of "wealth and power" for North Korea after the Cold War. Taking full control in 1994, Kim Jong Il initially sacrificed butter for guns, relying on the military and security services to keep the system intact, and announcing an official line of "military-first politics." North Koreans suffered horrifically for it, enduring a nationwide famine known euphemistically as the "Arduous March." They were told they would have to "tighten their belts" for the sake of the independence of the nation and people.

By the early 2000s, Kim felt confident enough to allow modest experiments with market-oriented economic reforms and increased foreign trade, including with South Korea. But the reforms had mixed results in the short term, and Kim's instincts toward caution and control won out over the spirit of trial and error. Market crackdowns were a recurring feature of the Kim Jong Il era, and a currency redenomination in late 2009 wreaked havoc on people's hard-earned savings and expectations of their economic future. By the time of his death in 2011, "neo-orthodox" socialist economics, as the University of Vienna's Ruediger Frank termed it, had come back with a vengeance. The arc of the Kim Jong Il era bent toward security, control, poverty and isolation. The lesson of the interlude of economic experimentation in the early 2000s was: better not to try at all than to try and not completely succeed right away.

We have no way to know how long the arc of the Kim Jong Un era will run and where it will land in the end. But so far, he is bending the country toward development and opening, even if that involves compromises in terms of security and ideology purity. Kim's focus on economic development was apparent from the get-go. His first public speeches in April 2012 articulated an unmistakable stress on the economy. In an implicit rebuttal of his father's "military-first" approach, Kim promised that he would not make the people tighten their belts again, and senior officials talked about the need to build a "knowledge-based economy." On my fourth visit to Pyongyang in January 2013, as part of a delegation including Google's Eric Schmidt, I saw the new zeal of North Korean cadres as they tried to get in line with their young leader's message. In March of that year, Kim gave his strategy an official name: "simultaneous progress" (*byungjin*) on economic development and nuclear deterrence. Washington focused on the nuclear "threat" implicit in Kim's strategy, and watched first in condescension and then in consternation as Kim delivered on his promise to improve the nuclear capability "qualitatively and quantitatively."

Very little attention was paid to Kim's consistent emphasis on the other half of *byungjin*, the economy. The results were not as dramatic or impressive as the nuclear and missile technology breakthroughs. Careful observers however noticed that Kim introduced pragmatic reforms in 2012-13 that empowered farmers in the countryside and managers in cities and towns to make their own decisions about how to run their farms, factories and stores. He left the informal markets alone and encouraged expansion of the official market network, moving the North Korean economy in a Sino-Vietnamese direction. *Byungjin* also implied a subtle reallocation of resources away from military defense on the whole by targeting investment in the narrower goal of a "strategic deterrent." Like the "new look" policy of the Eisenhower era, Kim hoped to reduce defense expenditures by concentrating on the ultimate weapon, or as he came to call it, the "treasured sword" of the Bomb. Freeing up a bloated armed services to engage in productive labor is a low-hanging fruit of North Korean economic reform – Kim's nuclear focus may help explain the paradox of how economic conditions appeared to improve despite increasing sanctions and diminishing trade.

The "laissez aller" tendencies of economic policy under Kim speak to the same defining characteristic of his leadership – a willingness to tip the balance away from militancy and control, toward spontaneity and openness. Similarly, the remarkable success of the nuclear and missile program, maddening and threatening as it appears from the outside, stems from a positive quality in Kim's leadership style – his embrace of trial and error. When the first big test of his era, a satellite launched to commemorate his grandfather's centennial in April 2012, was a dud, Kim did not hide the failure (as his father had done in the past). Instead, state media released a terse acknowledgment the rocket "failed to enter its present orbit." Kim ordered his scientists and technicians back to the drawing board. In December, he oversaw another satellite launch – the most successful to date – and ushered in a stretch of intensive rocket and missile testing that culminated in late 2017 with the testing of the Hwasong-15 ICBM, capable of hitting the continental United States.

Trial and error, acknowledging failure and redoubling efforts, loosening and opening up – these are the hallmarks of the Kim Jong Un era. Their sounds are muted by the fact that North Korea as a system and culture remains one of the most isolated, militant and orderly in the world. Yet the trajectory is there, for those who know the historical baselines and are willing to see the signposts. And if *byungjin* was too subtle for people, Kim made his strategic intentions even clearer in April 2018 at a high-level party meeting (the 3rd Plenum of the 7th Central Committee). The timing was ripe with diplomatic significance – Kim had met with China's Xi Jinping for the first time the previous month, was about to have his first summit with South Korean president Moon Jae-in, and an unprecedented meeting with U.S. President Trump was in the works. As these diplomatic horizons opened up, Kim made a dramatic internal announcement: *byungjin* was over. No longer would party cadres and government officials be expected to put half their energy into the economy and half into the "treasured sword" of nuclear deterrence. Instead, going forward, the new strategic line called for putting "all efforts" into economic construction.

Byungjin became a victim of its own success; its "victory," as Kim put it, meant its dissolution. And here was another break from the past. U.S. analysts had downplayed Kim's initial invocation of *byungjin* by pointing to the fact that he was merely borrowing one of his grandfather's slogans. Indeed, back in 1962, Kim Il Sung declared a *byungjin* line of equal emphasis on economic development and military strength. But in 1970, at the 5th Party Congress, Kim was forced to admit the failure, not the victory, of his *byungjin* policy. Not only that, he dealt with the failure by doubling down on defense spending, pushing North Korea deeper into the rabbit hole of militarism, and missing out on another wave of East Asian economic growth. Kim Jong Un once again was departing from the "playbook." Already, his *byungjin* was a rejection of his father's "military-first politics" and, by substituting "nuclear deterrent" for "defense," a revision of his grandfather's *byungjin*. More importantly, by declaring the victory of byungjin, Kim announced a fundamental redirecting of North Korea's trajectory onto the path followed by almost all its neighbors in the region – putting the economy first.

Inter-Korean chemistry

Experts in Washington are chary of seeing anything novel or promising in the leadership of Kim Jong Un. But the government in Seoul, and a majority of the population in South Korea, appear to be much more open to the possibilities of a new kind of North Korea, and the opening of a new era in inter-Korean relations. Inter-Korean chemistry is altering quickly, and their rapprochement is entirely bound up in the person of Kim Jong Un, the personal rapport he has developed with ROK President Moon Jae-in, and the public's sense that, through them, a fundamental change is at work on the Peninsula. Moon's approach is taking maximum advantage of the opportunities that Kim presents. Is the United States?

Even before the breakthroughs of early 2018, the Kim Jong Un era had actually been comparatively peaceful in terms of inter-Korean conflict. The disputed maritime border in the West Sea, site of numerous violent clashes, was quiet. Tensions spiked in the spring of 2013, but aside from a lot of posturing on both sides, no one was injured. The only injuries of the Kim era, in fact, were caused by a land-mine incident in August, 2015, when ROK soldiers on patrol in the DMZ were wounded by stepping on a mine – it remains unclear if the casualties were deliberate or inadvertent. Not a single South Korean soldier or civilian has died at the hands of the North Korean military since Kim Jong Un took power – yet another contrast to the record of his father's reign, let alone that of his grandfather.

Although no one was killed along the border, relations remained tense between Kim and his first two counterparts in Seoul, conservative leaders Lee Myung-bak and Park Geun-hye, as well as during the first year of the liberal Moon administration. The April, 2018, summit in the DMZ between Kim and Moon, following on joint participation in the Winter Olympics, marked a dramatic shift from hostility to partnership. The first moment of encounter between the two leaders once again revealed Kim's penchant for spontaneity – as he and Moon made small-talk, cameras clicking, the world watching, Moon said he wished that he could visit the North soon, and Kim, impishly, invited him to take a step north then and there. Moon did not miss a beat; playfully, the two men clasped hands and stepped first north, paused for the cameras, then proceeded back to the southern side for the day's events. They were willfully transgressing the line of division and hostility, which, as Professor William Ury points out in the case of Anwar Sadat's visit to Jerusalem, can be a powerful demonstration of peaceful intent. Kim was also proving his readiness to step outside the North Korean theater state, and engage in the give and take of "normal" diplomacy and relationship building. Kim and Moon went off-script again later in the day when what was scheduled as a brief walk in the woods turned into a prolonged tête-à-tête over tea. President Moon and his advisors emerged from the daylong summit with a reinvigorated faith in Kim's ambition to lead his country in a very different direction, including fundamentally improved relations with the South.

In the months to follow, North and South opened up long-clogged arteries of dialogue and interaction – from sporting events and cultural performances to military talks and political dialogue. At the diplomatic level, this culminated in Moon's September visit to the DPRK for the third meeting with Kim (a second, spontaneous meeting took place in late May). Moon's visit stay featured typical North Korean choreography, from ecstatic, flag-waving crowds welcoming him at the airport to a performance of the "Mass Games" at May Day Stadium. But at those Games, Kim again departed from convention by inviting Moon to give a speech of his own to the crowd of 150,000 Pyongyangites. Calling attention to the novelty of the moment, Moon began his speech, "As President of the South, I cannot express in words how overwhelming it is to be given this opportunity by Chairman of the State Affairs Commission Kim Jong Un to greet you. Citizens of Pyongyang, we are now forging a new era together in this way."

On the final morning of Moon's three-day visit, the leaders flew to the border with China for a joint pilgrimage to the sacred Korean peak of Paektu Mountain. International media interest in the summit had waned by this point, but South Koreans were stunned and bemused as they watched raw video clips of Kim, Moon and their retinues on the mountaintop. They stood together clapping for a K-pop star's *a capella* rendition of the iconic folksong Arirang, and posed for group photos against the stunning backdrop of Heaven Lake. In one clip, Kim's body language suggested embarrassment at the fawning behavior of a senior advisor, while Kim looked comfortable in his interactions with Moon and the two "first couples" seemed genuinely to enjoy each other's company. The symbolism of rapprochement took concrete form in the Pyongyang Declaration, which reaffirmed the shared goal of "peace and co-prosperity," along with a "comprehensive military agreement" signed by defense officials that laid out specific steps in reducing risks and building confidence. Kim and Moon positioned themselves to transform the Cold War status quo on the Peninsula of an armistice regime into a new order of real peace.

The future of U.S. diplomacy

Kim as a political leader is cut from a different cloth than his father, and the implications for his country are profound. Understanding Kim's true nature is critical to the success of diplomatic efforts by the United States and South Korea to realize a better future for the Korean Peninsula. Kim is opening a historic window of opportunity to draw North Korea, at long last, into the fold of East Asian "normalcy." The driving force in this normalizing process is likely to be inter-Korean dynamics, as the North and South move from a hostile relationship to an amicable one.

In geopolitical terms, Kim's normalizing instinct is likely to lead him toward the East Asian "norm" of seeking the optimal point in between the United States and China, the two great powers determining the economic and security architecture of the region. It seems unreasonable to expect Kim to go all the way into the arms of the United States – indeed, who in East Asia does? Still, he can be expected to develop significant areas of partnership and cooperation with the U.S., and its ally South Korea, on a range of strategic concerns, in ways that help keep balance in the region. This is the significance of the most often used phrased in the Singapore Declaration signed by Kim and Trump: "to establish new relations." Normalizing relations with the United States, and using that linkage to keep balance as power tilts toward Beijing, conforms to Kim's overall strategic approach and tendencies as a leader.

To realize the full potential that Kim Jong Un represents, Americans therefore need to think hard about North Korea in different ways and see the country's leadership and people through a new lens. If the media only pays attention to Pyongyang only when it stages a "provocation," and otherwise assumes everything North Koreans say is a trick, then the U.S. public will have a hard time imagining what "new relations" with the DPRK could look like. For the analytical community, North Korea can no longer be assessed purely in terms of threat; opportunity analysis should occupy as many resources as threat assessment. In policy terms, the over-reliance on economic sanctions, international censure, and shows of force as means to "sharpen North Korea's choices" needs to give way to proactive and sustained engagement, positive inducements and flexible diplomacy. In place of bromides about how Pyongyang is only hurting and isolating itself, an enlightened policy will seek opportunities to draw North Korea politically and economically into the region, to widen and deepen the licit linkages between North Korean people and the rest of us. Kim looks ready to engage in a transformative process – now it is up to the United States to reciprocate.

North Korean finally has a leader who is ready to go beyond the staged, controlled and militant ways of the country's public life and political culture. From his first speech as leader in 2012 to his dramatic entry onto the diplomatic stage in 2018, Kim has proven again and again a willingness to put himself in situations that are unscripted and spontaneous. South Korean, American and Chinese who have interacted directly with Kim describe a young man who is sophisticated and "well mannered," as one senior official in Seoul once put it to me. For lack of a better word, Kim is a normal head of state. Kim's normalcy is the living blueprint for a new North Korea – for a nationwide transformation into a place that, in economic, social and political terms, moves into the band of "normal" by East Asian standards. Kim is signaling a will to change North Korea's place in the world. From tension, hostility, and paranoia, toward openness and partnership. The future can be seen in that selfie in front of a wall of begonias. To borrow Wittgenstein's injunction, "Don't think. Look!"

6

Development Strategies Available to North Korea and Their Political Risks

Dwight H. Perkins

It has been widely reported that Kim Jong Un, having "solved" the nuclear weapons problem, now wants to turn the attention of his country to the task of economic growth and a rising standard of living for the people of North Korea. As this essay is being written, there is no information available, to this writer at least, as to how he hopes to achieve those goals. The development strategies available for turning North Korea into a middle or high income country, however, are not infinite. Each of the small number of alternative strategies available has potential existential political costs for the current North Korean leadership. The remainder of this essay will attempt to outline the major choices facing that leadership.

To begin with, North Korea has only 25 million people and the average GDP per capita is low, probably above US$1,000 but not far above. (The Bank of Korea has estimated that it may be around US$1280 but, as astute observers such as Marcus Noland have indicated, this figure is based on little data and could be off by as much as $1,000 per capita or a bit more.) Whatever the precise number, total GDP and total household incomes are very low (comparable to countries like Bangladesh and Pakistan or perhaps a bit higher like South Korea in the early 1970s) and the total domestic market for goods and services is also very small. Sustained economic growth, therefore, is not likely to be obtainable through a closed economy development strategy that industrializes mainly through import substitution. North Korea, as in the case of South Korea in the 1960s, will have to promote the development of exports in order at a minimum to be able to import the requirements of a growing industrial sector.

Unlike South Korea, which had no agricultural or natural resource exports in the 1950s, North Korea has some minerals and its largest single export is coal sent mainly to China. Exports of these and other small items together with weapons and certain illicit sources of income have given the country sufficient foreign exchange to sustain the current level of activity with very modest growth. To achieve sustained high level growth, North Korea is essentially in the same position as South Korea was in the 1960s except that South Korea met its minimal needs for foreign exchange through foreign aid and UN force payments. In South Korea then and in North Korea today either exports of manufactures will grow at a rapid rate or sustained economic development will not be possible. If sanctions on North Korean trade remain in place, therefore, rapid manufactured export growth and hence substantial GDP growth will remain impossible. In the absence of manufactured exports growth, North Korea could improve the living conditions of its population including a higher level of food production and consumption by freeing up agriculture prices and by returning to household farming, but this will not sustain a steady and rapid increase in GDP or of household incomes nationwide. Much the same can be said about a policy that allows private markets to develop even though still technically illegal, a possible approach by the North discussed in another essay in this volume.

But assuming that the nuclear situation is solved and sanctions are removed, would North Korea be able to promote the rapid growth of manufactures and of the export of manufactures in particular? Certainly the labor force required for industrial growth is available. The large share of the younger parts of the labor force that is diverted to military service could be a problem, but the military also provides training and discipline that should make those discharged from the military suitable for factory work and other modern sector employment. The education level of these potential factory workers is high when compared to many likely competitor countries. Furthermore, half of the younger labor force is women, most of whom are not in the military and typically make up a large share of the industrial workforce in the early stages of industrial development. The country also apparently has large numbers trained in engineering and other technical fields essential to industry even if today many are occupied developing and manufacturing weapons.

One missing element is that almost no one in North Korea has any experience with marketing or with how to manage an enterprise in a competitive market environment. North Korean enterprises are state-owned and are managed in accordance with the central plan, not with reference to markets of any kind. If the experience of other Soviet-type economies from Vietnam to Russia is any guide, the quality of industrial products today is low and few could be sold in markets where goods from China or other market economies were available.

Another missing element is that North Korea acting alone, if it maintains its current level of military related expenditure, has limited investment that could be directed toward market oriented consumer manufactures. Most estimates of North Korea's military expenditures indicate that the total is more than 20 percent of GDP although neither the actual size of military expenditures nor the size of GDP is known with any precision. However, keeping 16 percent of the country's male labor force in the military must have an opportunity cost of lost non-military production of nearly US$3 billion and that would not include the cost of military equipment (or any of the costs of the nuclear and missile program). The opportunity cost of this labor (the amount of civilian production lost by having a significant part of the labor force in the military), assumed to be around US$2,000 per person or higher, is likely to be higher than the actual wages paid to them plus whatever subsistence is provided in kind and there are nearly 1.5 million in the North Korean armed forces. These are among the most able bodied workers in the country.

The funds that are available for investment, whatever they are, are completely controlled by the government. There are no private entrepreneurs with significant capital and it is unlikely that any senior officials, other than a handful at the top, have any significant personal net worth. If the solution to the nuclear problem included a substantial reduction in conventional forces, that would free up considerable capital for other purposes. It would also make it easier for North Korea to gain access to international funding from the World Bank and from bilateral aid.

The simplest solution to the shortage of investment capital would be to turn to one of the country's two principal neighbors, China and South Korea. South Korea would at first at least seem to be the easiest choice. Their business and government people speak the same language and they have a powerful incentive to help the North overcome its poverty provided that the issue of war on the peninsula has been resolved. Only 3 percent of South Korea's GDP (in 2017) is more than the highest estimate of North Korea's current GDP. Two or three percent of South Korea's 2017 level of capital formation (US$9.5 to 14.3 billion) would more than double or triple North Korea's current level of capital formation if invested in the North. If the real constraint on expanding the North's investment level is the lack of foreign exchange, an investment from the South of US$ 9.5 to 14.3 billion using foreign exchange exclusively would be only 10 to 15 percent of South's average current account surplus (2015-2017).

South Korean money in anything like the required amount, however, is not likely to be available if the North's development model is similar to the earlier experiment with the Kaesong Industrial Park. That model involved South Korean businesses setting up factories in a nearby region in North Korea with a limited North Korean labor force that would produce goods for export. There was essentially no interaction of that limited labor force with South Koreans except for a handful of plant business managers. Even if this model was to involve the creation of several industrial parks, each with two or three times the amount of investment in Kaesong, it would not be remotely sufficient to unlock a sustained high rate of growth of GDP in the North. It was a model designed to provide the North with enough foreign exchange to keep the economy (and the military) functioning without the need for political system changes of any kind by the North.

For South Korean investors to put tens of billions of dollars of investment into the North, they would presumably expect to achieve a substantial rate of return on that investment. But could they find high return investments if they were given only limited, controlled access to the country? Would they be prohibited from bringing large numbers of personnel from the North to their factories in the South for training? Would they be able even to recruit the ablest people as employees or would the North's central planners select who was allowed to work for them? Would they be allowed to invest in infrastructure that served more than just the needs of their own factory or office? Could they sell the products produced in their enterprises in the North to the broader population there or could they only produce for export?

The freeing up of labor in the North would in many ways be the most dangerous politically for the North Korean government and political leadership. Political control in the North is achieved first and foremost by a tight control on information available to the population. That control would be lost by a flood of information being brought back by the large numbers of workers going to the South for training. There would also be the problem that many would probably not want to return to the North. Would the South force them to return? It doesn't seem likely. And if businessmen from the South were allowed to roam freely in the North looking for investment opportunities and discussing these opportunities with local people, would that be acceptable politically in the North? One could go on in this vein, but the bottom line is that it is difficult to see how there could be sufficient involvement by the South in the North Korean economy without a major change in the way that the North is governed. The South Korean Government might well agree to a policy of continued control by the current leadership of the North Korean Government, but would that leadership be confident that they could hold onto their positions in these much more liberal circumstances? They certainly have not been willing to take such risks in the past.

If a South Korean large scale involvement in the development of the North is too great a political risk, would a similar level of involvement by China be less risky? Certainly China has the capacity to build modern infrastructure for North Korea. North Korea is comparable in size to one of China's smaller provinces and Chinese government investment has transformed the transport infrastructure of all of its provinces over the past two decades. China's Belt and Road Initiative is geared to doing much the same thing for large numbers of other countries in Southeast, South, and Central Asia and elsewhere. China's total gross capital formation is over US$4 trillion each year and one percent of that would transform the North Korean economy in well under a decade even if North Korea invested little on its own.

China also has the managers and entrepreneurs who know how to produce and market manufactured exports. If large numbers of North Korean workers were to spend time in training in factories and businesses in China, there would not be much danger of China allowing them to stay permanently. Nor would those workers and managers in training be exposed to as much information about the outside world as they would in South Korea although China today is far more liberal in that regard than North Korea.

Chinese businesses, however, also have little interest in large scale investments unless they can receive a significant return on those investments. North Korea would have to loosen up its tight controls over its domestic society and economy just as it would for South Korean businesses. Would the Chinese Government be willing to simply subsidize the required expenditure without expecting an economic return? The probable answer to this question is yes, but what non-economic return would China expect? Certainly China would want North Korea to give up its nuclear weapons, but in this short essay we assume that North Korea would already have done this. Would the Chinese accept the leadership of North Korea as it is today or over time would they want to use their influence to shape a leadership more to their liking – one that would follow the leadership of China? I certainly do not know these questions but think the latter alternative is more likely. Turning to the Chinese to solve the dilemma of how to achieve sustained development would not involve North Korea in a risk of losing as much control over its population, therefore, but it might involve greater risk to the way the North currently chooses its leadership.

When one moves beyond South Korea and China as possible supporters of North Korean development, there is no other country that is likely to contribute anywhere near as much money or skilled training and manpower and the political risks would often be as great or greater. The United States and Japan could provide some financial aid as well as education and training, for example, and together or separately they could encourage the World Bank and Asian Development Bank to do the same. It is likely, however, that one or both countries would attach substantial conditions to such aid, conditions that would involve significant political liberalization by the North and a substantial reduction in its military expenditures beyond simply eliminating its nuclear and missile programs.

To conclude, given North Korea's small size and its limited natural resources, the development strategies that could achieve sustained substantial economic growth are largely limited to moving toward a market economy oriented toward the export of manufactures. That is the case even though the international trade environment is less favorable for exporters of manufactures than it was when South Korea began its rapid development. A closed economy that relies mainly on producing goods for the North Korean market will perform poorly. If all or most of the enterprises are state-owned and managed and run through central planning and administrative commands, it will perform even more poorly. A policy of liberalizing agriculture by going back to household agriculture and freeing up rural markets would help raise living standards for the general population, but North Korean agriculture and its natural resources more generally are not sufficient to sustain rapid economic growth. A large reduction in military expenditures would free up funds for development but would certainly be seen as creating risks for the survival of the North Korean leadership.

North Korea, therefore, is likely to muddle along at a modest growth rate of perhaps 2 or 3 percent per capita unevenly distributed and regime survival will depend on current methods unless it pursues an appropriate development strategy and turns outward for economic support for that strategy. As this essay has suggested, any turn outward involves substantial political risks, risks that the North Korean leadership has to date been unwilling to take. The current strategy of achieving security through nuclear weapons and missiles, however, also entails risks. The risk involved in opening up and liberalizing the economy to this writer at least appears to be less than that of the current strategy, but is it likely that the North Korean leadership will see it that way?

7

The New Leader, the New Economic Model

Andrei Lankov

When Kim Jong Un took power in North Korea in December 2011, he did not waste time, and almost immediately launched what was soon to become an ambitious program of economic reforms. Unlike his father and grandfather, Kim Jong Un had very few illusions about the potential efficiency of the Soviet-style economic system which had been championed by the Kim dynasty since the late 1940s. He understood that in order to achieve economic growth, the country had to implement market mechanisms. It will be just a minor exaggeration to say that Kim Jong Un is the most pro-market leader North Korea has seen since the late 1930s (after all, the last Japanese governor generals were not known for their enthusiasm for the free market economy).

When it comes to the economic policy, in the first years of Kim Jong Un's rule significant probability that in North Korea we could see the emergence of a peculiar version of what is known as a "developmental dictatorship" – a model of economic growth pioneered by South Korea and Taiwan and then followed by China and Vietnam. This model combines authoritarian control in politics with the acceptance of market economy, and usually pursues the export-driven economic strategy which allows the country to take full advantage of the abundant, cheap, docile and relatively skilled labour force of those countries.

North Korea's economic policy under Kim Jong Un has been greatly influenced by the brilliant success of Chinese reforms. China's example is really attractive, and it also helps that majority of the North Korean political elite have a pretty good understanding of what is going on in China: after all, they travel there frequently.

It is not incidental that from the beginning of Kim Jong Un's rule, North Korean government agencies began to collect systematic information about the Chinese economic reforms. These studies, which were often conducted by teams of North Korean experts specially dispatched to Chinese universities for this purpose, much influenced economic policy of Kim Jong Un's era. While there are some serious differences between North Korean and Chinese reforms, the Chinese impact on Kim Jong Un's thinking is quite apparent, even though the North Korean authorities are not going to admit this obvious fact. This silence is important because in order to maintain political stability, the North Korean propaganda emphasizes the nationalist myths and cannot possibly admit that North Korea, being unique by its nature, is emulating any other nation, especially China, which is perceived as a source of potential threat.

Reforms in agriculture

Like China, the North Koreans began their reforms with agriculture, as was only logical given the late 1990s famine and its impact. In 2012, Kim Jong Un issued what was then known as "the June 28 Instructions," a set of regulations dealing with the ways in which agriculture should be organized under the new rule.

The major feature of these regulations was the introduction of the field responsibility system.

Under the new structure, farmers are allowed to establish small work teams (punjo), each team consisting of some 5-8 members. This is roughly equal to the number of members in a large farming household, or perhaps, in two small neighboring households. So in practice, work teams are actually households or, sometimes, alliances of neighboring households in disguise – and this is what is expected by the managers, according to plentiful anecdotal evidence.

Each work team is allocated some plot of land for cultivation; this is why the new management model is often known as "field responsibility system." It is assumed that the same team would work this field for years to come, even though, unlike China of the 1980s, the North Korean authorities are not specific on the length of period when the team will retain usage rights in regard to a particular field.

Once the harvest is collected, the team is supposed to give a part of it to the state. Since most of the regulations on this issue remain secret, it is not clear how much a team should give to the state, but it appears that in most cases, we are talking about 30-40 percent of the total harvest. The remaining part can be disposed of by the team at its own discretion. So, in essence, we are talking about the introduction of a in-kind tax.

For decades, the North Korean farmers worked for fixed rations, which depended little on the actual efficiency of their work. Under the "field responsibility system," there is a clear incentive for farmers to work harder and take better care of the harvest: after all, the more they harvest, the more they will retain. The predictable result of the switch to this field responsibility system is an increase in food production, in spite of adverse climate conditions, in the years of Kim Jong Un's rule. While the nutrition problems remain widespread, especially in the remote parts of the country, the threat of famine does not loom large anymore.

Reforms in industry

Around 2014-15, reforms in industrial management began as well. In 2014, the KWP Central Committee and the DPRK Cabinet of Ministers adopted a set of government regulations known as the "Measures of May 30" or "5.30 measures" which implied a switch to the new model. After some local experiments and delays, the switch began in 2015. The state-owned enterprise began to use what was known as the 'socialist enterprise independent management system' (hence SEIMS).

The SEIMS is remarkably similar to the so-called dual price system which existed in China in the early stages of the Chinese reforms, in the 1980s. Under the new system, a North Korean state-owned enterprise is issued some plan indicators which it is expected to meet. However, unlike the old system, the plan indicators under SEIMS are well below the enterprise production capacity. In practice it means that only part of what is produced is supposed to be shipped to the state, or rather, another state-owned enterprise assigned by the state. For this part of what is produced, the enterprise paid the official state prices, which are usually well below the market prices for the similar types of goods and services.

However, the state-owned enterprise is allowed to sell what it produces in excess of the government-issued planned quotas at the free market, and for market prices. The money which is earned in such a way can be used for purchasing the necessary spare parts and raw materials, for paying workers, and also for investing into the further increase of the industrial production.

Under the SEIMS, the autonomy of the industrial managers increased greatly. They received rights to hire and fire workers, and also to pay them wages which reflect the workers' skills and productivity – unlike the old system where labor was assigned to the enterprises by the government agencies and payments were determined by the central bureaucracy. Actually, the additional wage is officially described as merely a 'bonus,' but this 'bonus' greatly exceeds the basic wages it is supposed to augment.

In practice, the switch to SEIMS means a significant increase in wages at those state-owned enterprises which are successful enough and sell a significant part of their production at the free market. While the official basic wages, if calculated by the black market exchange rate, still seldom exceed a 1-2 dollars a month, and are well below subsistence level, in 2018 the average salary at Pyongyang state-owned enterprises was between $30 and $70 a month, while skilled workers at more successful factories could earn more than $100 a month. It does not sound like prosperity, but this is clearly a significant improvement.

On paper, however, all industrial enterprises remain state property. It is not clear how the top management of these enterprises extract additional income from the new opportunities they have been awarded by the SEIMS. Indeed, it is possible that these people are supposed to work for the modest state-determined salaries, so everything they get above some basic level is acquired through assorted corruption schemes. At any rate, the increasingly luxurious lifestyle of North Korea's factory managers and the visibly growing income gap between managers and workers clearly indicate that managers are somehow rewarded for their performance – or perhaps find numerous ways to reward themselves quietly, with the tacit approval of the authorities.

The major goal of the SEIMS is to create a situation when the state-owned enterprises, without undergoing privatization in a strict sense, will have to operate according to the rules of the market economy, compete between themselves and do what they can to increase the volume and quality of their output. At the same time, the model implies that the enterprises will remain in the state property, even though the government is willing to turn a blind eye at the legal and illegal self-enrichment by the managers. It remains unclear to which extent such system will help to overcome major structural problems of the state sector, but there is little doubt that in the short run it is likely to deliver good results.

The new attitude to the "new rich" and private business

The last 25 years of North Korean history have been marked by the dramatic increase in the scale and significance of private business. While North Korea is still often seen and described as a "Stalinist state," such perception is outdated. When the Leninist central-planned economy was deprived of outside aid after the collapse of the Communist bloc in the early 1990s, it greatly shrank, and a new private economy emerged.

The best indicator of the growth of market activities is the steady increase in number and scale of markets. According to satellite imagery, there were some 490 officially licensed permanent marketplaces in North Korea – more than a twofold increase throughout Kim Jong Un's rule, since in 2010 there were only 200 markets in the country.

In most cases the scale of markets – number of merchants, total area etc. – increased as well.

While the market activities largely began from small trade and household production, over the course of time much larger enterprises appeared. Since the North Korean legislation remains hostile to the very idea of a private enterprise, a peculiar form known as a "pseudo-state enterprise" has appeared. Under this model an aspiring entrepreneur-investor makes a deal with some state agency or industrial enterprise. The deal allows him or her (women are remarkably numerous among the North Korean new entrepreneurial class) to register the enterprise as a state property, even though in practice it is established solely on investor's money and run by an investor who makes all managerial decisions, hires and fires personnel, and pockets most of the profits. His or her relations with the state agency that provides the official cover are usually limited to paying a regular fixed contribution to the agency budget.

Such deals are especially common among the numerous foreign trade companies. Such a company, usually established by some large government enterprise or government agency, usually is supposed to generate hard currency income (normally, through trade with China), but in practice its top management, in spite of good connections, has neither money nor experience nor skills to engage in the international trade successfully. To overcome these difficulties, the managers of the foreign trade company tend to make deals with rich individuals who are willing to invest and establish pseudo-state enterprises. The great autonomy granted to foreign trade companies by the current regulations usually facilitates such a deal. This approach makes possible the emergence of very large private enterprises, including mines, oil refineries, etc.

Private capital is prominent in such fields as retail trade, restaurant and catering industry, intercity transportation (with the exception of railways).

A peculiar feature of post-famine North Korea was the emergence of successful and rich private entrepreneurs, who are known as "donju" or, literally, "masters of money." This term is applied not to any market operator but only to people who have amassed significant wealth and are capable of making significant investments. The first donju appeared in the mid-1990s. Most of these people initially made their fortunes in semi-legal activities, often related to foreign trade and/or smuggling, and continued to build up their fortunes investing into the pseudo-state enterprises. As of the early 2010s, their operational capital was counted in hundreds of thousands of U.S. dollars, and some of them were millionaires. Remarkably, the 'masters of money' are seldom officials; direct involvement of nomenklatura in market operations has been explicitly banned, and this ban has been largely followed.

Under Kim Jong Il, the North Korean government was quite uncertain about how the emerging bourgeoisie should be treated. Periods of passive acceptance and benevolent neglect were interrupted by periods of persecution and intense campaigns against the "anti-socialist elements." In the 1990s and early 2000s, many of the new rich North Korean individuals perished in prisons or were even executed since pretty much all their activities were, strictly speaking, a blatant violation of the existing North Korean laws.

However, Kim Jong Un has a different attitude towards private money. Under his watch, the new rich North Koreans were basically left alone. Since his rise to power in 2011, North Korea experienced few, if any, campaigns targeting individual businesses. Furthermore, Kim Jong Un made explicit remarks to managers of the state-owned enterprises indicating that they should try to attract private investment in order to increase their production. In 2014, the new law of industrial enterprise explicitly stated that state-owned enterprises are allowed to attract individual capital, or, as the law puts it, "excessive funds of the individuals." One market trader, echoing sentiments widely shared throughout the North Korean business sector, once told the author, "Our life has never been as good as in the days of Kim Jong Un."

The new attempts to attract foreign investments

Since the beginning of his rule, Kim Jong Un has undertaken systematic efforts aimed at attracting foreign investment, pretty much in line with what was done in China and Vietnam. Foreign investment played a massive role in producing the East Asian 'economic miracles' of the second half of the 20th century, so the North Korean leaders hoped to get foreign investment as well.

Actually, this policy is not new. The first attempts to attract foreign investment took place as early as the 1980s, when the 1984 Joint Venture Law was passed. The early 1990s, the last years of Kim Il Sung's rule, were marked by a much publicized, but ultimately rather unsuccessful, attempt to launch the Rajin-Snbong Special Economic Zone (SEZ) – obviously, yet another attempt to emulate China. These attempts did not stop under the second ruler of the Kim family: in 2002 Kim Jong Il approved a hyper-ambitious plan of a SEZ in the border town of Sinuiju, just across the fast growing Chinese city of Dandong. Had this radical plan been realized, the Sinuiju SEZ would enjoy a truly unique level of autonomy – using Chinese analogues, it was meant to be closer to those of Macao and Hong Kong than to a regular Chinese SEZ. However, the plan was abruptly stopped – unlike another SEZ, Kaesong Industrial Zone which was launched in 2005. The Kaesong Industrial Zone catered to the South Korean investors and relied on direct and indirect subsidies from Seoul. Probably, this is what made it viable, so it grew up to house more than a hundred South Korean companies that hired some 55 thousand North Korean workers. However, the Kaesong SEZ did not survive the period of the conservative administrations in power in Seoul and was closed in 2016.

So, the SEZ experiments have a long history in North Korea, but, generally speaking, the success was at best moderate. However, the rise of Kim Jong Un to power was marked by the establishment of a large number of Special Economic Zones.

First of all, Kim Jong Un dramatically increased the number of SEZs. Now North Korea technically has 25 SEZs, even though only one of them (Rason, former Rajin-Sonbong SEZ) actually operates. Obviously, like his father and grandfather, Kim Jong Un was much inspired by the example of the Chinese SEZs, and also sees SEZs as an ideal model since in theory the heavily controlled environment of the SEZ allows to attract foreign capital while minimizing the ideologically dangerous interaction between North Koreans and foreigners.

Apart from the SEZ, there were other attempts to attract foreign investment, as well as attempts to develop foreign tourism. Of somewhat peculiar, not to say bizarre, nature, was the decision to build a world-class sky resort on Masik pass, near the eastern coast of Korea. Obviously, this project owed much Kim Jong Un's sweet memories of his teenage years spent in Switzerland – the leader seemingly believed that it would be an easy way to earn money. The resort was built, but predictably failed to attract foreign visitors and turned into a subsidized playground of Pyongyang's new rich.

On balance, attempts to attract foreign investment have ended in failure. There were manifold reasons why very few foreigners were interested in investing their money in North Korea.

The first reason, of course, is the North Korean nuclear and missile program. As a result, North Korea is seen as a dangerously unpredictable place. Also it is widely believed that any commercial interaction with North Korea is likely to make the companies and individuals involved into targets of the international sanctions.

Second, the North Korean managers grossly overestimate the attractiveness of their country to foreign investors and entertain inflated expectations. Most of the newly established Special Economic Zones are inconveniently located and do not have even basic infrastructure – like paved roads, railways, electricity, and water supply. The North Korean managers usually assume that the foreign investors will also subsidize the construction of the necessary infrastructure – but this is definitely not the case.

Third, the North Korean authorities have shown themselves to be remarkably unreliable partners. In those rare cases when foreigners not merely make investments in North Korea, but start making a considerable amount of money there, these lucky investors immediately find themselves targets of official extortion of different kinds. The North Korean side unilaterally rewrites agreements, introduces new rules, and in some exceptional cases, even confiscates foreign enterprises which they deem 'excessively' and 'unfairly' successful.

Two most prominent cases of this kind are the story of Orascom, the Egyptian construction and telecommunication firm, and the story of the Chinese Xiyang Group, a large privately owned mining company from Liaoning. Orascom played a decisive role in rolling out the mobile networks in North Korea. However, once the fast growing networks began to generate profit, Orascom was prevented from repatriating its earnings. Xiyang built a large iron ore mine, but once the work was completed, the North Korean authorities confiscated the mine and expelled the Chinese personnel from North Korea. These two cases are the best known, but in many regards, they are quite typical – somewhat similar stories have been told by a number of foreign businessmen who dealt with North Korea.

Finally, the North Korean authorities are remarkably cautious in dealing with the investors. In most cases the foreign visitors are strictly controlled, all their meetings with the locals have to approved and carefully monitored, and even minor issues take long time to sort out. Even when a foreigner runs a business in North Korea, his operational control and managerial rights remain severely curtailed. This approach is understandable: the North Korean authorities see foreigners as vectors of dangerous ideological deceases, carriers of potentially subversive knowledge. This means that the North Korean decision-makers are willing to sacrifice economic efficiency for the sake of political security, and restrict the foreigners' freedom of action.

So, the unique combination of poor infrastructure, unrealistic expectations, habitual cheating, extreme isolationism and international sanctions, has made North Korea an unattractive place for foreign investment. However, on balance, one can say that the North Korean economic policy has been remarkably successful.

The reform works

Since North Korea ceased publishing their relevant economic statistics in the early 1960s (with very few exceptions) it is impossible to make precise estimates about the level of economic growth which was generated by Kim Jong Un's economic reforms. Nonetheless, there is little doubt that, at least, it was growing until 2017, when the UN Security Council began to introduce 'sectoral sanctions' – that is, sanctions targeting specific industries in North Korea.

The oft-cited estimates by the South Korea's Bank of Korea are almost universally seen as excessively conservative. Most of the foreign observers believe that economic growth in 2012-2016 was between 3-5 percent, while some others support even higher estimates of growth. Presumably, the introduction of very tough sectoral sanctions had some negative impact on the economic growth, even though the exact scale of this impact is not clearly known.

Nonetheless, there is little doubt that the living standards in Pyongyang and, to a lesser extent, other major cities are improving quite fast.

The 2010s were marked by large construction programs in Pyongyang. To a significant extent, these programs were financed by private money. The new rich, the donju, have few opportunities for profitable investment, and therefore, are much interested in investing their money in the emerging real estate market – and Kim Jong Un's policy essentially encourages the officials to accept the private investors. The houses are built together, with the government agencies doing necessary paperwork and private individuals investing money that is used to hire workers, rent equipment and purchase construction material. The flats are then sold at the market. Trade in real estate and even private ownership of the real estate is still technically illegal, so officially it is the residence/usage rights which are sold at the black market. However, the majority of the North Koreans do not see it as a problem.

The real estate market, in spite of its unofficial or semi-official nature, is flourishing, with prices going through the roof. Between 2005-2017, the price of houses in downtown Pyongyang increased ten to twenty times. Nowadays, a new good flat in downtown would sell for $70-100,000, while premium quality real estate is even more expensive, with price tags exceeding the $150,000 mark.

Big shopping centers and department stores have appeared in Pyongyang. Remarkably, the revival of local industries – especially light industry and food processing – means that a fast-growing part of the goods which can be found in these supermarkets is locally produced. People are much better dressed and fed than ever before and traffic is getting thicker. As sign of growing prosperity, one should mention the emergence of service industries: catering, home renovation, extracurricular studies are booming.

The growth of the market economy has produced significant inequality – as one should expect. There is a significant number of the new rich North Koreans who can afford to spend an equivalent of a worker's salary during just one night in an expensive restaurant. There is also a growing gap between Pyongyang and the rest of the country. However, it would be a mistake to think the improvement of the economic situation is limited to Pyongyang only. The rural areas are doing much worse than Pyongyang and cities located on the border with China, which are profiting much from legal and illegal exchanges with China. However, on balance the fruits of the economic growth are noticeable pretty much everywhere.

The deafening silence of media

However, it is remarkable that in spite of the ongoing changes, the North Korean official media is very reluctant to attract much attention to the ongoing reforms – or even admit that the reforms are taking place.

The general access media (like the official party newspaper, *Rodong Sinmun*) seldom writes about the new economic policies, and if it does so, it provides very imprecise description of the new system. Most of what is known about "field responsibility system" and "socialist enterprise independent management system" is based on refugees' testimony and some classified documents that have been smuggled outside the country. While references to some new systems can be occasionally encountered in the open access mass media, these references are remarkably, and deliberately, short and imprecise.

The specialized publications, including journals specifically deal-ing with economic issues, tend to be significantly more frank and detailed. Very often careful study of such specialized texts can provide a reader with a reasonable picture of what's going on, but even in such specialized publications many important things are not mentioned.

Such approach is not uncommon in North Korea: it is the country where important government policies have been routinely announced via closed channels even when those policies were known almost universally. A good example of such seemingly irrational secretive-ness is the 2009 currency reform. The reform touched virtually every-body, since it required all citizens to change all old bank notes for new ones within a very short period of time and very small exchange limits, but was never even mentioned in any open access publication.

There is little doubt that some of the new economic policies, in spite of being widely implemented and hence widely known, are not supposed to be much mentioned in the media. Obviously, this silence reflects the ideological uncertainties of the North Korean elite. The discussion of the new policies would require some justification for them, and this justification is not very easy to design.

For decades, it has been difficult to find in the official North Korean political vocabulary a word that has more negative connotations than "reform." It is implied that North Korea, being endowed with the world's most perfect social and political system, conceived by the greatest genius of all times and countries, does not need any "reform." North Korean propagandists are never tired of repeating that reforms in their country would be not only unnecessary, but deeply harmful and reactionary. In an editorial (published August 25th, 2016), the Rodong Sinmun characteristically fumed: "Under the army-first revo-lutionary leadership of the great general, we have completely annihi-lated the schemes of the imperialists who try to lure us into 'reforms' and 'openness' in order to infect us with the reactionary bourgeoi-sie liberal ideas." Similar statements, albeit with varying degrees of hysterical pitch, have been common in North Korean media for nearly three decades, and this sustained propaganda campaign makes difficult for the North Korean ideologues to find right justification for the ongoing change of the political line. Thus, they prefer to remain silent.

Even though Kim Jong Un himself probably has few problems with the market economy as such, he and his advisors might be quite reluctant to openly admit the ongoing transformation of the country, since such an open admission is likely to provoke discontent and ideological disorientation among the general public. This is not what the North Korean elite wants; their major goal is, of course, to keep domestic political stability, no matter what.

There are also good reasons to believe that Kim Jong Un's current vision of the ongoing reforms implies that the state property system would be preserved whenever possible, including cases when such an approach does not make much economic sense. While private capital is tolerated and encouraged nowadays, there is an explicit belief that state property should remain dominant even though the relations between state enterprises from now on should be increasingly driven by the logic of the market.

•

The jury is still out on the issue whether Kim Jong Un's new economic policy will be able to deliver economic growth without excessively jeopardizing political stability. Given that regime collapse could well be bloody, dramatic and wrought with all kinds of dangers (nuclear proliferation, incidental use of WMD, clash of great powers, etc.) the peaceful evolution of the regime seems to be a more preferable outcome, but is it possible?

To start with, there are possibilities that Kim Jong Un himself will reverse his course; after all, his father did this in 2005, after few years of supporting similar, if less radical, reforms. If Kim Jong Un receives significant subsidies from the outside world, he will face a great temptation to stop the inherently risky line he is pursuing now. If some political crisis strikes, he might react in the same way. Kim Jong Un might be removed from power by some conspiracy whose members can have a much more conservative view of the economy. Finally, with age and, perhaps, looming health problems (his lifestyle is self-destructive to an extent), he might lose the energy that is also vital for a radical reformer.

However, even if Kim Jong Un shows a great determination, he will face serious problems. To start with, it seems that North Korea will be unable to attract much foreign investment, and this might be decisive: all earlier "economic miracles" in the region were driven, to an extent, by the influx of foreign capital. Due to the compelling strategic reasons, North Korea will never surrender nuclear weapons, and this means that it will be subjected some international sanctions – again, a serious obstacle on the way to the economic breakthrough. The government's seeming unwillingness to openly admit that it is moving the country towards market economy, means that there will be problems with creating the necessary legal and institutional framework for the economic activities.

So, Kim Jong Un and a narrow circle of his trusted advisors, are engaged in risky experiment whose chances of success are not clear. Nonetheless, one can only hope that the North Korean leaders find the right path. If they make a mistake, they will pay a high price, but all other parties involved will suffer as well.

8

Can Moon Jae In Hold It Together Domestically?

Carter J. Eckert

South Korean leader Moon Jae In has defined his presidency in terms of a sweeping rapprochement with North Korea and staked his historical legacy on its success. He follows here in the footsteps of his liberal predecessors and mentors, Kim Dae Jung, and, especially, Roh Moo Hyun, and carries the mantle of a generation of Koreans, the so-called 3-8-6 generation,[1] who fought triumphantly for democracy in the 1980s against decades of military dictatorship. His ardor for a new peace regime with North Korea is also fueled by his own personal background as the son of North Korean refugees, part of a mass evacuation of tens of thousands of Koreans from the northern port of Hungnam during the Korean War after a disastrous defeat of United Nations forces by Chinese troops in December 1950.

If or when such a peace regime eventually emerges remains to be seen, but there is no doubt that Moon and South Korea have been key to whatever progress has been achieved to date. Moon's intelligence, boldness, and determination, as well as his deft personal cultivation of both American president Donald Trump and North Korean leader Kim Jong Un, have been at the core of a South Korean diplomacy that has adroitly negotiated and sustained a peace momentum despite complex and often sharply differing interests and understandings between the United States and North Korea. Considering that little more than a year ago the world was holding its breath over a possible war that would unleash what Trump at the time called "fire and fury

---

1 This is a South Korean term coined in the 1990s to refer to Koreans who were then in their 30s (hence 3); attended college in the 1980s (hence 8); and were born in the 1960s (hence 6).

like the world has never seen," the importance of this momentum should not be underestimated.

The political challenge

If Moon and his government have been dramatically effective on the international stage in fostering a new relationship with North Korea, they have been somewhat less so domestically. Indeed, some of the greatest challenges to Moon's policy – political, economic, and generational – may well come from within South Korea itself. Politically, Moon remains in a relatively strong position nearly two years after his rise to power in a special election in May 2017 following the impeachment of former president Park Geun Hye. He won the presidency by an unprecedented almost 20 percent margin over his closest conservative rival, and his popularity until only recently has hovered around 60-70 percent, buoyed by three well-choreographed summit meetings with Kim Jong Un. The most recent meeting in Pyongyang also included a spectacular visit by the two leaders to Mt. Paektu on the North Korea-China border, a site saturated with symbolic meanings of ethnic oneness for both Koreas as the birthplace of Tan'gun, the mythical progenitor of the Korean people and founder of the first Korean kingdom in 2333 BCE. South Korea's once powerful main conservative party, now known as the Liberty Korea Party (LPK), was rent apart by Park's fall from grace and removal from office and has yet to fully recover internally or in terms of popular support. So far Moon has been able to pursue his peace regime with North Korea without significant conservative interference.

But Moon is by no means invulnerable. Like Trump, who will require bipartisan congressional support for any kind of formal treaty he signs with Kim Jong Un, Moon will need support of the conservative opposition to realize his goal of an historic and irreversible new understanding with the North. While he won handily over his main conservative opponent in 2017, he received less than a majority of the full popular vote, and in the National Assembly his Democratic

Party also lacks a majority with only 44 percent of the seats, while the LPK still holds about 38 percent. And the broader forces of conservatism in the society, closely aligned with the LKP and always skeptical of any kind of accommodation with North Korea, are still powerful in South Korea, not least of all in the media, including the country's most influential newspaper, the *Chosŏn ilbo*. During the 2017 presidential election campaign Moon in fact acknowledged the residual power of the conservatives and his dependence on them by paying a respectful visit to the gravesite of former president Park Chung Hee, who, despite his daughter's disgrace, has remained an icon of conservative adulation.

Moon's timeframe for success is also politically constrained and growing shorter with each month that passes. As president he is limited by South Korean constitutional law to a single five-year term, and he is already nearing the end of his second year. Having made his new North Korean policy the centerpiece of his administration and channeled so many presidential and government resources into it, he needs as soon as possible to demonstrate substantive progress in relations with the North that go beyond mere summitry, as important as that has been. The problem, however, is that better relations between North and South are also dependent to no small extent on improvement in relations between the United States and North Korea, which is why the South Korean government has been expending so much time and effort in Washington and Pyongyang in trying to keep alive what they regard as the positive spirit of the June 2018 Singapore summit between Trump and Kim Jong Un. For the moment Trump and Kim continue to engage amicably, and as I write are even planning a second summit, but if there is a serious falling out on denuclearization or any other major issue, Moon could also face a very difficult situation domestically. If he is seen as siding with North Korea over the United States and thereby jeopardizing the US-ROK alliance, another conservative icon, or granting significant concessions to North Korea without reciprocal returns, the full force of the conservative political, economic, and social establishment is likely to rise up against him and his government. In effect this is what

happened in 2008 when conservative Lee Myung Bak was elected
president, in part because of differences between the United States
and South Korea over North Korean policy under Kim Dae Jung
and Roh Moo Hyun, and because the previous ten years of a liberal
"Sunshine Policy" toward North Korea, in which Moon himself was
deeply involved, came to be seen by many in South Korea as too
one-sided in favor of North Korea.

The economic challenge

While Moon's political challenges to a successful realization of his
North Korean policy are not to be discounted, even more daunting
are the economic challenges that he, and indeed the country, are
currently facing. The problems here are compounded by the fact that
they are largely cumulative and structural, having developed and
grown more acute over the past several decades, and are therefore not
easily or quickly resolved in a single presidency, whoever the president
might be. Director Lee Chang Dong's poignant new film, "Burning,"
which was submitted by the South Korean government for 2019 Oscar
consideration in the Best Foreign Language Film Category (though
failed to receive a nomination), touches on one of the most serious
and intractable of these economic problems, the issue of income
inequality. Before the late-1990s and the 1997-1998 financial crisis,
scholars of the South Korean economy were beginning to question
Nobel laureate Simon Kuznets' well-established theory that income
inequality would inevitably increase with economic development and
rising incomes, but not any longer. More recent studies all suggest
that South Korean inequality has grown significantly in the past two
decades. The population hit worst has been the country's workers,
especially those in the most menial jobs, but even South Korea's once
much vaunted middle class has seen considerable contraction. And
public awareness of the problem has also intensified. Lee's new film,
among other things, is testimony to a mounting popular perception
and anger toward this widening income gap and its cascading nega-

tive effects on society and social relations.

Moon has sought to alleviate the situation by increasing the minimum wage and reducing working hours, but these measures have created other problems, and in any case the question of income inequality is closely related to a host of other deeply-rooted issues, both as cause and effect. It is well known, for example, that South Korea is facing a serious demographic crisis. The country has the lowest fertility rate in the world and a longer-living, rapidly-growing elderly population, which is already beginning to put an enormous burden of medical expenses on lower income families, as well as on the government itself. About half the country's elderly are living in poverty, and elderly suicide rates, already twice that of other age groups, are growing at an alarming pace.

Common economic sense would suggest that the low birth rate, which also means a shrinking labor force, would help push wages upward in the logic of supply and demand, but again the problem is more complicated. While wages in the upper echelons of the work force have risen to some extent, the wages at the bottom have remained stagnant for years. More to the point, wages have stagnated because job growth has been slow, and job growth has been slow because production and economic growth have also been sluggish for some time. Unemployment is currently at a 17-year high; China, a key driver of international trade and South Korea's largest trading partner, appears to be experiencing an economic slowdown; and the latest projections for South Korea are not sanguine, forecasting even dimmer growth for 2019 than in the previous year.

The truth is that South Korea is at an historic juncture in its economic development trajectory. The original breakthrough in the 1970s under Park Chung Hee was structured on a manufacturing regime geared to cheap exports produced by low-cost labor at a time when South Korea faced few competitors. Today and for some time now the situation has been very different. If South Korea is to remain competitive in the world market relative to economic powerhouses like China and other developing countries, as well as relative to the most advanced economies, the country needs to implement a paradigm shift in its national economic strategy, from manufacturing to services and information technology. This is the "great challenge" that South Korea is confronting, according to a former head of the Korea Development Institute, the country's most prestigious government research and policy center, but South Korea still has a considerable way to go in this regard compared to other OECD countries like the United States and Japan. There the shares of manufacturing and services in total GDP are, respectively, about 19 percent/80 percent and 28 percent/70 percent, while by contrast in South Korea the figures are 35 percent/54 percent.

In pursuing his vision of a new deal with North Korea, President Moon Jae In can ignore the economic realities of South Korea today only at his peril. If he comes to be perceived as more focused on or more concerned about North Korea than South Korea, especially in the absence of any tangible benefits in the reconciliation process, he is likely to incur severe criticism from large swaths of the Korean public on both sides of the political spectrum who are feeling the pressures and pains of the current socioeconomic situation. Already there is some sign that this is happening, as his poll numbers have been dropping, and one can find increasing numbers of negative comments in the South Korean online media about his government's privileging of long-term North Korea policy issues over urgent, everyday problems in South Korea itself.

The generational challenge

More difficult to assess or analyze but also important is the challenge Moon and his government face in capturing the hearts and minds of South Korea's younger generations, including the country's millennials, with Moon's North Korea initiatives. Although they have disagreed on the means for attaining it, for Moon and the 3-8-6 generation, as well as for the older generation they opposed politically, reunification has been and remains a sacred national goal. It is not at all clear that the majority of younger South Koreans share that passion or sense of mission. Even nearly two decades ago, in the early 2000s, when I was concluding a historical survey class on the "Two Koreas" and suggested that one of the things that connected all Koreans was a desire for reunification, I was challenged by a student, a young Korean woman from South Korea, who told me that this was no longer the case and that she and most of her friends had many other ambitions, both personally and for the nation, that they would place above reunification. She added also that she and her friends were concerned about the financial costs of reunification, which they feared would be many multiples of the cost of the German reunification and disrupt or even threaten the South Korean economy on which they all depended.

Such attitudes are not by any means exceptional among South Korea's younger generations. The Korea Institute for National Reunification in Seoul recently reported that more than 70 percent of South Koreans in their twenties oppose reunification. For the most part these younger Koreans have grown up in a very different post-Cold War, democratic world, where two Koreas have been the norm, and where North Korea seems indeed like another country, despite commonalities of language and culture. North Korean refugees are often looked down upon or even shunned by the general population of the South, so much so that some refugees have even sought to return to the North. Only about 14 percent of younger South Koreans in their twenties consider North Koreans as "one of us," according to a recent poll by the Asan Institute.

Even though it is surely correct to say that there is strong general support for a better relationship with North Korea, perhaps even for a peace regime that would reduce or eliminate the likelihood of war, for younger Koreans North Korea is not necessarily the primary focus of interest and attention it was for their parents and grandparents, and the cherished dream of reunification that inspired the older generations is for the younger far less compelling, perhaps not even a consummation devoutly to be wished. While they have thrilled, like most South Koreans, to the dramatic North-South summitry of the past year and a reprieve from the frightening prospect of another devasting war on the peninsula stoked by Trump and Kim in late 2017, twenty-first century generations in South Korea are likely to embrace Moon's reconciliation efforts with the North only so far as they are not seen seriously to detract from or to impinge negatively on their own personal economic and social aspirations and concerns.

Can Moon hold it together domestically?

Given these formidable challenges within South Korea, can Moon hold it all together and continue forward on his ambitious reconciliation path with sufficient domestic support? As already noted, as much depends on what happens *outside* South Korea as within: what Trump does; what Kim does; how, what, and when they do what they do together; and whether what they do together is ultimately approved by the U.S. Congress.

But Moon also must act and act quickly to marshal as much support as he can from all segments of South Korean society. To no small degree the economy is key. It is the weakest link in his domestic support chain, and a significant turnaround, or even only a public sense that things are changing economically for the better, will greatly strengthen his position and help disarm his critics. Moon is clearly aware of the stakes, and since the beginning of the new year he has been actively promoting new economic initiatives, including an energy shift away from coal and oil to a "hydrogen economy" as a new growth engine for South Korea.

In a move that harkens back to the "Sunshine Policy" of Kim Dae Jung and Roh Moo Hyun, and was embodied in the now shuttered Kaesong Industrial Complex, Moon has also been at pains to promote the idea of North Korea as an economic opportunity, a place where South Korean capital and technology can merge with cheap, skilled, and disciplined North Korean labor to reprise in the North, as it were, South Korea's remarkable growth of the 1970s and bring significant new economic benefits to both parts of the peninsula. It was precisely this kind of thinking that led him to take the leaders of South Korea's biggest conglomerates with him to Pyongyang this past September, including Samsung's heir-apparent Lee Jae Young. It is not clear how enthusiastically South Korea's premier business-men share Moon's vision. Also, notwithstanding the advantages of language and culture, in any North Korean development scenario South Korea is likely to be facing considerable competition from China, which currently accounts for 90 percent of the North's trade, and has a decided political advantage given the longstanding relationship between the two countries since the 1950s and North Korea's fears of being swallowed up by South Korean capitalism. Still, the argument for economic cooperation is a powerful one, politically as well as economically, and the Kaesong Industrial Complex, while it lasted, was an encouraging sign of what might be accomplished on an even larger scale.

The road ahead will not be easy, but perhaps for the first time since the establishment of the two Korean states in 1948 the heads of all the most relevant major national players, North Korea, South Korea, China, and even the United States, are aligned in terms of seeking a fundamentally new arrangement on the peninsula, and Moon has shown himself to be a master diplomat on the international stage in helping to bring this alignment about. One cannot help but wish him well also on the domestic front in his quest for a permanent peace regime on the peninsula. It is hard to imagine that such a regime would not be beneficial for both Koreas, for the region, and for the world. And nearly thirty years since the collapse of the Soviet Union and formal end of the Cold War, it seems historically long overdue.

9

Thinking Realistically About Unification

Katharine H.S. Moon

Ever since the division of the two Koreas by the great powers in 1945, "unification" has been a mythical word, resonant with longing and loss and accompanied by hopes and fears. It may be natural to seek the rejoining of a divided land, people, and family members, but it is also natural to worry about how to achieve unification and what kind of sacrifices might be required for that goal. Very few on either side of the 38th parallel would favor war as a means to unification. But even with a peaceful process, economic insecurities and political dangers loom. This essay assesses three challenges regarding unification:

1. uncertain South Korean public opinion;
2. different premises of unification;
3. political challenges and pitfalls of unification.

For all South Korean presidents since Syngman Rhee (1948-1960), their *raison d'être* not only rested on national security and economic progress, but also on unifying the peninsula. No leader could have assumed or remained in power without enacting at a minimum lip service to "unification." Rhee went so far as to seek forced unification using ROK troops through a northward push. In more recent years, Kim Dae Jung developed the "sunshine policy" to induce North Korea toward peaceful engagement with the South and toward gradual unification. Park Geun-hye felt the need to highlight the potential gains rather than economic costs of unification through the notion of "unification bonanza" so that the younger generation of South Koreans with little memory of the Korean War and the pain of division might kindle a desire for keeping the unification dream alive.

Currently, Moon Jae-in has equated his presidential legacy (and political survival) with improving inter-Korean relations as "foundation for peaceful unification through mutually beneficial cooperation."[1] The complex quest for denuclearization of the DPRK, rapprochement between Pyongyang and Washington, constructive inter-Korean interactions all are intended for the ultimate realization of unification. The ROK Ministry of Unification clearly states: "We aim for unification that naturally occurs as part of the process of promoting the coexistence and co-prosperity of the two Koreas and recovering the Korean national community." However, there is nothing "natural" about unification.

First, the South Korean public's views of unification are divided by age, socioeconomic background, and political orientation. Young respondents (20s and 30s) in large N surveys tend to show most wariness about unification and prefer the status quo relative to their older counterparts. Even among twenty-somethings, more men than women view unification as a necessity (71.7 percent versus 49.4 percent in a 2017 survey) and strikingly only 19.8 percent of males versus 44.6 percent of females view unification as "not necessary" in the same survey.[2] Also, higher levels of education and income correlate with a higher preference for unification. And of course in the highly divided political society of South Korea, more than 80 percent of participants in a 2018 survey believed that left-right conflict among political parties and the citizenry at large would be a serious obstacle to unification.[3]

1   ROK Ministry of Unification, "Moon Jae-in's Policy on the Korean Peninsula: Four Strategies," https://www.unikorea.go.kr/eng_unikorea/policylssues/koreanpeninsula/strategies. Accessed January 10, 2019.

2   Seoul District Youth Hub Center, "Youth Generation Unification Perception Survey," November, 2017, https://youthhub.kr/wpcontent/uploads/2017/10/2017_ %EA %B8 %B0 %ED %9A %8D %EC %97 %B0 %EA %B5 %AC_ %EC %B2 %AD %EB %85 %84 %EC %84 %B8 %EB %8C %80 %ED %86 %B5 %EC %9D %BC %EC %9D %98 %EC %8B %9D.pdf. Access date January 18, 2019.

3   Korea Council for Reconciliation and Cooperation (민족화해협력범국민협의회), January 25, 2018https://www.kcrc.or.kr/files/FileDown.asp?idx=7942&gubun=file1. Access date January 18, 2019.

Do South Koreans believe unification is necessary?

Between 2008-2017, the percentage of positive responses remained around 50 percent. Events, however, can change public opinion. After Moon's third summit with Kim in September 2018 (and the first-ever visit of a South Korean president to the DPRK), 60 percent of 1200 South Koreans aged nineteen and older responded that unification was necessary. This was the highest since 2007 (64 percent), the year that ROK President Roh Mu-hyun and DPRK leader Kim Jong-il held the second inter-Korean summit. (These figures are from publications by the Institute for Peace and Unification Studies, or IPUS.) The generational gap also narrowed as 52 percent of respondents in their 20s and 30s supported unification as a necessity compared to 40 percent in 2017. Soon after the Pyeongchang Olympics in winter 2018, a survey of 1059 adults between March 13-14, 2018 showed that 56.7 percent "strongly agreed" and 25.8 percent "slightly agreed" that unification was a necessity.[4] According to a survey by the ROK Ministry of Tourism and Sports and Hankook Research Company between June 29 and July 6, 2018, soon after Donald Trump' s summit with Kim, 83.5 percent of 1521 adult respondents believed that unification is "possible." The vast majority, 79.9 percent, said in the long term, while 3.9 percent said in the near future.[5]

By contrast, the 2017 annual unification survey by Seoul National University IPUS showed that only 16.5 percent viewed unification as "extremely necessary" and nearly 38 percent regarded as "slightly necessary," in line with comparable figures from the 2016 annual survey. Among those stating that unification was "not necessary" were 22 percent of the respondents in 2017 and 24.7 percent in 2016.[6]

4   GonjungResearch,http://gongjung.org/generalboard/?board_name=generalboard&order_by=fn_pid&order_type=desc&vid=2&ckattempt=1. Access date January 16, 2011.
5   http://m.mcst.go.kr/m/s_notice/notice/noticeView.jsp?pTp=P&pTpCD=0302000000&pSeq=16807
6   ROK Ministry of Unification, Unification Perception Survey 2017file:///C:/Users/owner/Desktop/Publications/Unification/2017 %20 %ED %86 %B5 %EC %9D %BC %EC %9D %98 %EC %8B %9D %EC %A1 %B0 %EC %82 %AC_ %200326.pdf, p.18 of pdf. Access date January 18, 2019.

By comparison, only 13.9 percent believed unification was not necessary.[7]

What are the reasons for unification?

Consistently, "ethnic kin" or "same nation/people" leads by a significant margin (between 40 percent and 50 percent, 2007-2018) among several options, followed by "in order to reduce the threat of inter-Korean war" (between 14.5 percent and 32.5 percent, 2007-2017). Over the last decade as DPRK nuclear development, testing, and conventional aggressions such as the destruction of the ROK naval vessel Cheonan and the shelling of Yeonpyeong Island in 2010, as well as the 2015 land mine explosion at the DMZ heightened North-South tensions, there has been a slight rise in choosing the second reason. But for so many people, unification remains more about becoming whole again as a nation and reuniting families despite their fears and wariness of Pyongyang's military intentions. President Moon's vision statement on North-South cooperation on the Unification Ministry website makes things clear: "We will restore national homogeneity and build an inter-Korean community by expanding various inter-Korean exchanges."

Ethnic and cultural homogeneity is also a myth in South Korea. The reality is much more complex as over 2 million foreign nationals reside and work there and about a million South Koreans are part of what the government officially categorizes as "multi-cultural families." Currently nearly 4 percent of the population of 50 million is comprised of people from numerous countries speaking various languages and practicing an array of religions. By 2021, nearly 6 percent of the population is estimated to be foreign-born, even higher than the current OECD average of 5.7 percent.[8] This represents a spectacular demographic change from 1990, when fewer than 50,000

7   Gongjung Research.

8   Chosun Daily, http://english.chosun.com/site/data/html_dir/2016/07/28/20160728009 34.html. Access date January 19, 2019.

foreigners, comprising 0.1 percent of the nation's population lived in Korea.

Since the mid-2000s, the number of Korean nationals, overwhelmingly male, marrying "foreign brides" from other countries, such as China, Vietnam, the Philippines, Mongolia, Thailand and many others, have increased such that in some rural areas 40 percent of the population are not purely ethnic Korean. In recent years, over 150,000 foreigners, 70 to 80 percent of whom are female, have received naturalized citizenship in order to form a Korean "multicultural" family with their Korean spouses. Although former president Lee Myung-bak (2008-2013) was not noted for his progressive politics, he focused political rhetoric, funds, and bureaucratic attention on the welfare and integration of foreign nationals and multicultural families into Korean society. He also exhorted the mainstream society to live up to higher standards of global civility and fairness toward the foreigners and their families.

Although ethnonationalism dominates the individual and collective mindset, South Koreans, especially the young, are changing their views about national belonging and community. A 2015 Asan Institute survey found a significant drop from nearly 80 percent of respondents in 2005 and 2010 believing that "Korean bloodline" was essential to being Korean to nearly 66 percent in 2013. About one-third of the respondents believed that sharing the same bloodline was not important. It is interesting to note that only 14.4 percent of twenty-somethings in a 2017 survey believed that ethnic kinship was the main reason to pursue unification in contrast to about 60 percent who believed that national interests, including security and national status, are reasons for unification.

By contrast, we have no evidence that ethnonationalism is in contention in North Korea. Rather, as author B.B. Myers points out, "The celebration of racial purity and homogeneity is everywhere in North Korea." As Korea experts know, *Juche*, the guiding ideology, has had less to do with communism and internationalism and more to do with postcolonial nationalism based on "ethnic bloodline" and the notion of a family-state that encompasses the entire peninsula.

North Koreans do not acknowledge the changing faces and lifestyles in South Korea that result from intermingling with foreigners and have criticized the South for permitting the racial and ethnic mixing of Koreans through marriage migration. *Rodong Sinmun*, the Korea Workers Party newspaper, condemned the trend as an "unpardonable crime" and "poison" against the Korean nation and the prospect of independent unification.[9]

Many foreign nationals have resided in the ROK for long periods of time, for example ten to twenty or more years, and can speak excellent Korean and participate in various types of community life. And the birthrate among female marriage immigrants in South Korea is higher than that of native-born women. Yet the premise of "foreigners" comprising Korea would be anathema for most North Koreans, given the decades-long extreme ethnonationalism and xenophobia officially propagated by Pyongyang.

Any process of peninsular unification must be based on the fact that South Korea is increasingly becoming a multi-ethnic and multi-national society whose democracy must expand and protect equal citizenship and human rights for all Koreans. It is also a labor-importing country whose current and future economic survival depends on outsiders. The Korea Economic Research Institute issued a report in 2014 that the only viable way to sustain an adequate labor force and economic growth is through continued and increased immigration (4.3 million in 2030; 11.8 million in 2050; 15.3 million in 2060).[10]

Many South Koreans have assumed that once unified, North Koreans would serve as cheap labor and reduce, if not reverse, the labor shortage. But the DPRK birthrate has also been declining, and the economic costs of educating, retraining, and providing for various welfare needs of North Koreans will outstrip the economic contri-

9   Korea Central News Agency, "The Idea of a Multinational, Multiracial Society Means Destruction of the Korean Nation [다민족,다인종사회론은 민족말살론], April 27, 2006, http://kcna.co.jp/item/2006/200604/news04/28.htm#7, Access date September 24, 2015.

10   Kwanwoo Jun, "South Korea May Need Up to 15 Million Immigrants, Study Says," *Wall Street Journal*, December 15, 2014, http://blogs.wsj.com/korearealtime/2014/12/15/immigration-needed-to-bolster-workforce-study-says/. Access date March 22,2015.

bution North Koreans might be able to make in a unified country at least in the short, and possibly in the long run. Moreover, North Koreans undoubtedly will not endure second-class economic citizenship for any length of time, for they will have high expectations to earn money quickly and to improve their lifestyle. The robust diet of national pride that they have ingested for over half a century will also sensitize them to the kinds of discrimination and lack of access that would be inevitable at least in the initial period of unification. There is ample evidence of socioeconomic marginalization and psychological resentment among the 33,000 migrants/defectors from the DPRK who currently reside in the South.

Fighting over leadership and power

Even if peaceful, gradual unification were to take place, political fights among different types of North Korean populations as well as between Northerners and Southerners is highly likely. Many North Koreans in the South even now believe that they know and understand the "real" DPRK in contrast to South Korean experts in government and civil society. But even among the small numbers of what I call "defector elites," there is intergenerational, gender-based, and personal competition for political influence. Based on my interviews over the years, Northerners who are middle-aged and older are unaccustomed to democratic values and practice and demonstrate hierarchical and authoritarian forms of leadership (in some ways, not unlike their South Korean counterparts). But the younger generation, especially those who had been educated in the South since childhood or teenage years, who tend to be better suited to cooperation, compromise, and rational planning, see themselves as the critical future leaders because they are familiar with both societies. "Experts say that the South Korean-educated North Korean youth will be an important resource in linking the South and North Koreas together after unification."[11] But defector youths who are priming themselves for leadership positions tend to be male, like the older defector elites, in a refugee population that is between 70 to 80 percent female. Sexism against women dominates among North Koreans too. The question of representational legitimacy as well as competence will be up for grabs among North Koreans.

Without doubt, there will be severe regional contestation as well in any unified Korea. First, those who have stayed in the DPRK will fight for influence in any unification process and thereafter. They are unlikely to cede ground to Northerners in the South as well as South Koreans in determining their future. So a North-South rivalry is highly likely. Unified Germany today exhibits East-West tensions politically and in the economy nearly three decades after unification.

Any unification toward an integrated peninsular democracy will likely involve a proliferation of ideologically even more divided political parties. First, regional parties mostly representing Northerners and Southerners separately are possibilities, as are regional parties from within the North as well as the South. Democracy-building in the ROK was plagued by regionalism, with conservatives from Kyungsang Provinces dominating and so-called left-leaners and progressives in Jeolla Provinces shut out of power during decades of military dictatorship. It is also possible over time for the growing numbers of multicultural or hybrid Koreans in the South to form over time political parties that represent immigrant and anti-mono-ethnic goals. Most likely is a revitalization of labor parties as North Koreans seeking employment, training, and equal wages and welfare benefits on par with their southern kin, gravitate toward what they have been familiar with: a workers' party.

Although most of the academic and policy research on Korean unification focuses on economic needs and costs, the political aspects of unification, even if peaceful, require vigilant and clearheaded analysis. A rough road may be inevitable as part of a great transformation

11   http://www.durihana.net/board/view.aspx?b_id=214&tbname=bbs&pageIndex=0&-searchIndex=False

yet to be paved, but there is a real danger to democracy becoming destabilized and weakened as part of the political process. It may be rational for individuals to be self-interested about not paying lower taxes in the service of unification and vying for power. It may be efficient for entrepreneurs to seek out cheap labor with new entrants into the labor market. And the human desire to reconnect with family, landscapes of childhood, and wholeness as a people is so fundamental. But none of these should color or cloud the immense political challenges that will constitute unification.

10

China's Policy Toward North Korea

Jiyong Zheng and Xingxing Wang

Ever since the founding of their respective parties, militaries, and states, China and North Korea have been closely intertwined with each other because of their common historical and political origin. However, these two countries have been constantly alienated from each other and re-approaching each other as their respective political systems have evolved. Their political systems are "developing into different tracks from the same original path." More specifically, there already exists a large divergence between China and North Korea in terms of their world views, perceptions of situations, mentalities and logics, and operational modes to deal with real problems.

Although its path of development is disparate from the rest of the world, China continuously absorbs nutrients from the evolution of the whole world and integrates itself into this world, creating a far-reaching influence. It forms a set of logics of history and a system of discourses and perceptions for interpreting the real world, with Chinese characteristics. By contrast, the North Korean regime manages to survive by relating to the foreign world with the help of isolationism and mysticism. The distortions and misinterpretations of North Korea by the U.S., Europe, Republic of Korea (ROK) and Japan, which are based on their completely hostile political logics, makes it even more difficult for the external world to perceive and understand North Korea objectively and precisely.

Overall relations between China and North Korea

China-North Korea relations are highly complex because of the common – and still tightly intertwined – origin of their history, reality, and ideologies. This set of bilateral relations are reflected by a diversity of issues and problems that have been evolving from distant history. Generally speaking, China-North Korea relations can be broadly analyzed from the following perspectives:

Historical memory and regime security

There are no clear-cut boundaries between the histories of China and the Korean Peninsula. Particularly, the northern half of the Korean Peninsula had been an integral part of the historical process of ancient imperial dynasties of China. This peculiar phenomenon can be summarized as *"one history with two descriptions"* because a large section of the history of Korean Peninsula has always been included and recorded in the history of ancient China. A common history with two differentiated interpretations by historians in China and the Korean Peninsula led to the 2003 *"Goguryeo Event,"* a displeasure between China and South Korea.

China's involvement in the Korean Peninsula can be traced back to the Shang and Zhou Dynasties, the earliest dynasties of China's ancient history. Ancient historical records in China revealed that the first state ever established on the Korean Peninsula was the Jizi Joseon, a regime founded by Jizi, a close relative of the last monarch of China's Shang Dynasty (in around 11th century BC, during the Shang-Zhou dynastic transition). Upon its original establishment, Jizi Joseon submitted itself to the continental regime on mainland China. Since then its relations with Chinese dynasties shuffled back and forth between submission and being conquered. Generally speaking, China maintained an effective control over the territory north of the Taedong River for a very long time since the Han Dynasty established *"the Four Prefectures."* During that period, continental dynasties on mainland China always viewed as "internal disorder" any disobedience or strife within the area north of Taedong River of the Korean Peninsula, and was determined to send military force to put down this kind of "disorder." In China's ancient dynasties, the highest achievement in the governance of civil affairs was success in controlling the flooding of the Yellow River, while the most spectacular military accomplishment was completion of a mission such as pacifying disturbances on the Korean Peninsula.

However, the central dynasties of ancient China were unable to establish a clear position of the Korean Peninsula within their vast domains, because they did not know whether the Korean Peninsula should be dealt with through an "internal ruling" or an "external governance." In a broader sense, the Korean Peninsula was an enormous dilemma for China. At that time, the Koreans were almost identical to the Han Chinese in terms of ethnicity and culture, but they lived in a remote and barren area with difficult and costly access. For Chinese dynasties, any long-term occupation on this peninsula would prove to be unprofitable and unworthy, creating endless troubles and costs. On the other hand, it would be equally troublesome to leave it alone because external forces could invade and use it as a stepping stone to threaten the security of China. Also, it was fruitless or ineffective for Chinese monarchs to conquer, or forge political marriages, or send hostages. The kings of Korean dynasties always hedged doubly towards Chinese emperors: They appeared to be submissive to Chinese emperors when they were weak, but would struggle for equality with China or even harass the country when they were strong. Chinese dynasties tried a variety of means to control this peninsula, including establishing prefectures, abandoning direct administration, conquering, requesting tributes, or creating protectorate, but none of these means was effective over the longer term. Therefore, in the long history of Chinese dynasties, Chinese emperors regarded the Korean Peninsula as a problem and distanced themselves from this peninsula, while also preventing any external force or entity from meddling in the Peninsula for their own gains. This muddy and passive approach proved to be useful and was maintained by Chinese emperors for long time. Some Chinese dynasties even gave up some land to Korea so as to convert it into a stable buffer zone.

In history, the most subversive and dangerous threats towards Chinese dynasties always came from the north, particularly the steppes and grasslands near the Korean Peninsula. China's Han Dynasty was harassed and ravaged by the Nomadic Huns for many years and only managed to drive them away after constant wars lasting over a hundred years. The Sui and Tang Dynasties of China rose by successfully defending themselves against invaders from the steppes of Northeast China, and finally collapsed after being plundered by northern nomadic forces. China's Song Dynasty strenuously fought continuous wars against the Nuchens and Mongols and was finally destroyed and swallowed by the Yuan Dynasty of Mongols. China's Ming Dynasty was wiped out by the Qing Dynasty of Manchus, and then the Qing Dynasty perished because it lost the Korean Peninsula to Japan.

Therefore a historic challenge for China has been to avoid being attacked by any force from the North and to suppress any possible rise of a powerful and threatening force in the North, otherwise China itself would be destroyed or even engulfed by this sort of force. Just as Huang Zunxian argued: *"China would absolutely go to compete for Korea even at the price of exhausting its resources and fiscal incomes whenever some unrest appearrf in that area."* Maintaining a controllable and stable situation on the Korean Peninsula played a large role in determining the fate of a Chinese dynasty. Therefore, connections to this peninsula have a strategic and political heritage developed by China's ancient dynasties. Ever since the 2nd century BC, various Chinese dynasties that established a unified rule over the whole of China, including the Han, Sui, Tang, Song, Yuan, Ming, and Qing Dynasties, all launched large-scale military actions to the Korean Peninsula; some of them even collapsed due to unbearable costs associated with fighting wars in this area. Although they had to pay huge prices to send troops to Korean Peninsula, Chinese dynasties never hesitated to do so from ancient times until the late 19th century. In 1950, the newly-founded People's Republic of China still sent troops to this peninsula. The PRC fought its first war on the Peninsula against UN troops led by the United States, despite still recovering from a civil war that had concluded in 1945.

Ideologies

When the PRC was founded, the first generation of its leadership led by Mao Zedong not only retained the historical memory that "China's influence shall cover all of its peripheral areas," but also held an internationalized perspective regarding the whole world, which was very typical for communists in the early years of cold war. They had to consider how to strengthen ideological uniformity for the purpose of protecting their newly-born regime against powerful threats. Under such circumstances, the communist leaders of China adopted the policy of "*leaning one-sided to the Soviet bloc.*" Propelled by this policy and based on the common stand of fighting against the U.S. bloc, a shared emotional heritage left from history and a consideration on the Taiwan issue, China and North Korea approached each other quickly and formed one of the closest bilateral relationships in the world.

Both China and North Korea ideologically supported the communist Soviets, but they behaved differently towards the Soviet Union. Later, when disputes and confrontations erupted between China and the Soviet Union, North Korea made a double-hedge and managed to get benefits from both sides. Because of this experience, China does not regard North Korea as truly "Loyal and Honest." Moreover, China regards North Korea's "*Juche*" ideology as divergent from China's general stand of opposing personal cults and running counter to the original faith of socialism. Conversely, North Korea became very disappointed when China declared a détente with the United States and came to view China as stepping onto a "revisionist" path. North Korea began to regard itself as the world center of socialism. Today, a huge ideological gap exists between China and North Korea.

Since the collapse of Soviet Union and the dramatic turnovers in Central and Eastern Europe, tremendous changes took place in the external environments of China and North Korea, which further deepened the cleavages between them. China improved its relations with the United States and relieved its security dilemma. Taking full advantage of new opportunities appearing in the international community, China realized sustained economic growth and secured a more and more benign external environment. The Chinese leadership judged that the world's overall trend was toward peace and development, not revolution and war. Based on this insight, China further opened itself to the external world and relieved its previously tense relations with the U.S. after 1989. Meanwhile, the end of cold war terminated an international system in which North Korea was able to double-hedge between China and the Soviet Union for double gains. Pressed by the fundamental transformations of the China-U.S.-Russia trilateral relationship after the cold war, North Korea's trust of big powers reached its lowest point. It had to deal with unprecedentedly serious problems in domestic and foreign affairs.

Due to the collapse of the Soviet Union and the improvement of China-U.S. relations, North Korea was brought into an isolated position encircled by hostility regarding its style of socialism. It was aggravated by the U.S. claim that it might launch military attacks on North Korea in the first Korean nuclear crisis, the exacerbated deterioration of its national economy, and the noisy prediction of "*a fast collapse of North Korea regime.*" For the first time in history, the North Korean regime had to be concerned with the possibility of its collapse. Even more miserably, it seemed that China was indifferent toward it and was becoming more enthusiastic about developing China-U.S. relations. From North Korea's point of view, China undoubtedly betrayed North Korea and its socialist revolution. The divergent perceptions of these two countries on the international trends made the China-North Korea rift even wider and deeper. North Korea became increasingly restless and disturbed. In the end, the establishment of China-ROK diplomatic relations became the last straw that pushed China-North Korea relations into full-fledged frigidity. At the request of North Korea, China moved its representative out of Panmunjom and completely terminated its military presence on the Korean Peninsula.

Personal sentiment

Personal sentiment has always been an important factor in China-Korea relations. When the Chinese-Silla joint force unified the whole Korean Peninsula in the 8th century, the Tang Dynasty gave up to Silla its territory to the north of the Taedong River as a reward for Silla's loyalty and homage to the Tang Dynasty. China's Ming and Qing Dynasties sincerely assisted the Korean kings in driving out Japanese invaders or put down Korea's domestic rebellions. Personal sentiment could also be found in the decision of the leaders of Communist China to get involved into the Korea War in 1950. The communist leaders of China and North Korea cooperated with each other in their respective military struggles against Japanese occupations. As a matter of fact, North Korea's Workers' Party was originally founded within the Chinese Communist Party. Therefore, it was natural and inevitable that China and North Korea built very close relations after 1949.

Yet this commonality did not prevent the leaderships of these two countries from quarreling with each other during the Korea War. During wartime, China regarded North Korean issues as an integral part of Chinese affairs. However, North Korea agreed to view its issues as part of Chinese affairs only when it needed China's support, and denied China's involvement when it did not need China's support. This dynamic has continued to characterize China-North Korea bilateral relations. The excessively close inter-personal relations and occasional personal quarrels blurred the boundary between Chinese and North Korean interests. Chinese and North Korean leaders directly intervened in the domestic affairs of the other side. For example, China directly stepped into the *"August faction"* event, whereas Kim Il Sung requested to take part in the Chinese Communist Party's "criticism and struggle" meetings against Peng Dehuai and Deng Xiaoping. After regaining power, Deng Xiaoping made drastic adjustments to China's policy towards North Korea, reducing China's assistance to the country by a large margin. During Jiang Zemin and Hu Jintao's administrations, China-North Korea relations were kept on the level of *"maintaining the face,"* which meant that China would not intervene in North Korea's internal affairs and would pursue balance between the two Koreas, so long as North Korea did not make trouble. Nevertheless, North Korea took advantage of China's passivity and relentlessly carried forward its programs of developing nuclear weapons, creating major challenges to the situation on the Korean Peninsula.

Xi Jinping has a distinctive personality. When he took into office, he appeared to be even more averse to North Korea's unrestrained demands and inconsiderate provocations to the U.S. Particularly, after Jang Song Taek was executed by Kim Jung Un, Xi Jinping resolutely demanded that China's policy towards North Korea should be readjusted and their bilateral relations be reshaped. In July 2014, Xi Jinping broke the precedent that Chinese supreme leader should visit Pyongyang before visiting Seoul, which almost brought China-North Korea relations to a stalemate. Even worse was the "Moranbong Aktan Event" in December 2015 which once again brought the bilateral relationship to the bottom. At the time, North Korea conducted nuclear and missile tests constantly, and the Korea nuclear issue further deteriorated. In response to this deterioration, China intensified its embargos and sanctions on North Korea and demonstrated an intention to confront these changes with military means. North Korea expressed its dissatisfaction with China through open criticisms on Chinese media. Nevertheless, owing to a concern about being dragged into military conflict and economic collapse, North Korea was forced to declare on January 1, 2018 that it "has already completed the construction of nuclear strength" and would turn to economic development. It also proposed to realize complete denuclearization on the Korean Peninsula. This change means that China achieved the objectives of its sanctions and the ultimate barrier to China-North Korea relations was removed. In the following 10 months, Kim Jong Un visited China four times, restoring his country's relationship with China to some degree.

China's top priority: stabilize the peninsula

Pursuit of stability has always been the priority of China's policy towards the Korean Peninsula, which forms the utmost difference between China's policy in this region and its foreign policy dealing with other regions and countries. Based on the complex and fluid history of China's relations with its peripheral areas, it can be concluded that changes in peripheral areas are closely connected to China's security. China has learned many miserable lessons from its past. Particularly, the nearer the source of disturbances and instability was located, the more severe the loss China suffered. Gaining profit through meddling in risks and chaos has never been an option in China's policymaking towards its peripheral areas. In other words, China has drawn lessons from its miserable historical experiences and determined that a pursuit of peripheral stability shall be the foundation of its foreign policy. It is for this reason that China is always deeply concerned with any potential chaos or disturbances agitated by any external forces in its peripheral areas.

Historical experiences

From China's perspective, the term "stability" contains a broader and more profound meaning in the Korean Peninsula, due to the complex and turbulent history in this region.

History has revealed that any internal unrest within the Korean Peninsula, such as domestic disorder, rebellion, coup d'état, or even factional fight, would inevitably spread some sort of shockwaves into China and drag China into the dispute or instability. For fear of unanticipated instability occurring in their own region, the monarchs of Chinese dynasties found it necessary to maintain a buffer zone on the Korean Peninsula. But they also found it unnecessary, unprofitable, and burdensome to directly control, or even occupy, this historically poor and barren peninsula. Therefore, Chinese dynasties made efforts to ensure that the Korean Peninsula remained unified and independent, so that China was able to maintain a good relationship with this peninsula, while also being free from entanglement in Korea's local troubles.

This subtle position is the so-called "*non-involvement, non-extrication*" policy implemented by Chinese dynasties for much of history. Specifically, Chinese emperors adopted a policy as benevolent as possible and gave lavish gifts to Korea's kings after they paid homage and tributes to China. Chinese emperors also mediated Korea's internal disputes to some degree, and sometimes sent troops to help Korean kings put down local rebellions or insurgences. Generally speaking, Chinese dynasties conducted a practice of *"more giving than taking"* and maintained their friendships with Korean kings by providing extravagant gifts and benefits to them through the system of *"paying tribute in return for being conferred with titles."*

Since 1949, the situation in Northeast Asia has reached a new level of complexity. The long-term division between the two Koreas is largely consolidated, while the U.S., Japan, and Russia regularly involve themselves in the region, further complicating the situation. A multilevel complex system of deterrence has been established around the Korean Peninsula. Shaped by the two Koreas, the U.S., and China, this system can extend its power to all relevant players in the region. Viewed from the military perspective, both sides of the military demarcation line on the Korean Peninsula have the capacity for fundamental defense and have substantial military strength. An unstable balance has formed along this line, based on the pursuit of mutual deterrence between the North and South Koreas. On the other hand, due to the presence of China and the United States, a stabilized balance of power has formed on this peninsula through a double-stalemate, between China and the U.S. on one level and the two Koreas on another level. This balanced structure has been able to prevent the sudden eruption of crisis. Also, it provides maneuvering space for China and the U.S. to mediate as stakeholders and defuse any tension that might lead to military conflict.

North Korea's programs to develop nuclear weapons increased the complexity of the Korean Peninsula, seriously worsening the security situations in this area. The tensions on this peninsula were gradually escalated as both sides along the military demarcation line became more and more hostile through verbal fights and intensive military vigilance. The risk of war remained on a high level as there was a lack of substantial communication between the two Koreas within the fragile security environment. The U.S.-ROK joint military exercises were continuously uplifted to higher levels in response to the constant nuclear and missile tests conducted by North Korea. These threatening exercises in turn compelled North Korea to pursue its nuclear capacity to protect itself. Frequently escalated confrontations in this process pulled the Korean Peninsula into a spiral of hostility.

The contents of stability

Within this complex situation, China has its own interests and demands. China's policy towards the Korean Peninsula can be summarized in three terms: "*No War*," "*No Chaos*," and "*Denuclearization*." These three terms are the extension and deepening of the concept of "*stability*." More specifically, stability on the Korean Peninsula can be explained by three pursuits and four major interests.

The three pursuits include mutual respect for each other's concerns, mutual assistance to each other's development, and mutual protection of each other's security. These three pursuits are three principles of mutuality that can define China's good-willed position for its relations with the Korean Peninsula. First, China hopes the concerns of both China and the Korean Peninsula will be given basic mutual recognition and respect. In other words, either side should be friendly towards the other side and care about the interests of the other side. Particularly, China shares a common historical heritage with the Korean Peninsula and has maintained its presence on the Peninsula for several thousand years. This point should never be neglected. Second, a stabilized environment, based on mutual respect, should be built for normal social and economic activities that may integrate the Korean Peninsula with its neighboring land in China's northeast region and Shandong Province. The Korean Peninsula's situation should not form a barrier to the economic development of its neighboring land. Third, the Korean Peninsula is located near China's heartland, so this peninsula should act as a positive strength that may push forward the common development of both itself and China's heartland. This peninsula cannot be allowed to develop into a paramount trouble that harms or even threatens the security and prosperity of China's northern borderland.

Building from these three principles, China's pursuits of stability can be further clarified into four major areas of interest:

1. Maintenance of Stability and Predictability. Internal unrest and chaos has continuously occurred throughout Korea's history. Disputes, confrontations, and conflicts between various states or regimes within the Korean Peninsula always transmitted troubles or even brought destruction to China. On the other hand, only when the Korean Peninsula returned to order and realized stability could it be possible for China to exercise good governance over its own land, achieving tranquility on China's frontiers and borderland, a prosperous economy, or effective defense against external enemies. Whenever the Korean Peninsula fell into chaos or turbulence, China would suffer unavoidable damage to its interests and security due to the huge unpredictability occurring on the Korean Peninsula. A stable Korean Peninsula would bring predictability, which would help China gain substantial benefits.

2. Creation of buffer area. At the strategic level, China has always been an introspective and defensive country, with a focus on its domestic affairs. In other words, normally China was more willing to preserve its existing territory and interests without an ambition to expand its sphere of influence. It was because of this inward disposition that China built the Great Wall repeatedly in history and regarded this method as a preferred tactic to defend itself. Viewed from history, the peripheral areas, including the Korean Peninsula, have always been counted as the first line of defense to obstruct any external invasion. In this sense, China hopes that the Korean Peninsula may become a blocking valve for China's security, so any domestic unrest or disorder on the Peninsula will always make China seriously worried. China does not want to

see any chaos occurring in either of the two Koreas. It has always been likely that some inconspicuous unrest or chaos on this peninsula would become uncontrollable like a wild fire and extend its destructive force into China. If that is the case, it is very likely that China would be dragged into a state of internal turmoil.

3. Continuation of friendly relations. History reveals that it is in China's long-term interest to remain friendly with the Korean Peninsula. This historically-formed perception shapes China's attitude towards the two Koreas. Any unfriendliness or even hostility from either of the two Koreas will make China feel extremely uncomfortable, like a fish bone stuck in one's throat. It was for this reason that China was determined to establish formal diplomatic relations with South Korea despite strong opposition from North Korea. Therefore, China will definitely oppose any buildup of military strength on the Korean Peninsula, or any increase in strategic assets, or development of nuclear weapons, which will surely be interpreted as unfriendliness by China. For example, after his inauguration as the paramount leader of North Korea in 2012, Kim Jong Un conducted nuclear and missile tests repeatedly for the purpose of developing nuclear weapons. His extreme activities kept China-North Korea relations in tension. In 2014, when China-North Korea relations were in their most strained state, Xi Jinping made the decision to visit Seoul first, sending a signal to North Korea that its reckless nuclear tests would be punished. In December 2015, the *Moranbong Aktan* band was suddenly called back when it was visiting China, which was another display of the China-North Korea tension due to China's resolute demonstration of its tough attitude and prohibitive strength on the Korea nuclear issues.

4. Preservation of a balance of power on the Korean Peninsula. From China's perspective, a delicate balance

on the Korean Peninsula will benefit China and help to promote peace and stability. The balance relies on three things: First, no external power should be allowed to interfere in this balance. Any external interference into the domestic affairs of the Korean Peninsula, such as the intensive intervention by the U.S.-led UN troops during the Korea War or the deployment in the ROK of the THAAD system and other strategic assets by the United States, is regarded as unacceptable by China and will face blocking measures. Second, no subversive event should happen on the Korean Peninsula. The current balance between the two sides would be subverted by some drastic measures such as a quick development of nuclear weapons or weapons of mass destruction that overwhelm the system. North Korea's nuclear weapon programs already crossed a redline, so China decided to take tough measures to block North Korea's nuclear development. Third, it is unwise and unnecessary to adopt a double-standard to deal with the two Koreas. This means that it is not correct to treat either side more favorably than the other side. China's diplomatic trustworthiness would be destroyed by such partiality, and the overall stability of the Korean Peninsula would also be disrupted.

"No War," "No Chaos," and "Denuclearization" are connected to the concept of stability. They should be viewed as three basic means to realize stability. First, war means a complete overthrow of the current state of peace. Any attempt to resolve disputes through violence would deal a serious havoc on China's interests and breach the above-mentioned principles to keep the Korean Peninsula safe. Second, no chaos means that any radical transition or dramatic overthrow of the status quo should not be allowed in the domestic political development of either side of the two Koreas, because unpredictability occurring from fierce fights, or even collapse, of the current regimes will destroy stakeholders' interests and violate the principle of mutual respect. Third, development of nuclear weapons may lead to nuclear proliferation and pollution, which will seriously disrupt or ruin the environment and social stability of China's northern borderland. China's security will be severely challenged and the above-mentioned principles will be breached.

Within China's overall effort to protect its own interests and promote general peace on the Korean Peninsula, the three principles of "No War," "No Chaos," and "Denuclearization" are closely interconnected with each other and may be mutually transformed. They hold parallel positions and are each of the same priority. Another meaning implied by these three principles is that North Korea should be encouraged to build an environment beneficial to its economic development. For North Korea, economic development can be used to maintain its stability and ensure its security. This is a more rational and widely accepted way to protect its state security than programs to develop nuclear weapons.

China's policy toward North Korea

At present, the Korean Peninsula is encountering its fourth historically important wave of transformation; the previous three waves were caused by the First Chinese-Japanese War, the Korea War, and the end of cold war. This fourth wave is brought about by the Korean nuclear issues. In considering history and present realities, and navigating the potential gains and loss, China's policy toward North Korea can be divided into operational paths and specific measures.

The path for China to formulate and implement its policy toward North Korea

The general aim behind China's policy toward North Korea is to find a new path for North Korea that is guided by the historic realities.

First, China seeks to establish a "commonwealth of interests and destiny" with North Korea, so as to dispel the North Korean regime's fears regarding security. North Korea is located at a crucial juncture in East Asia. If it is connected to the external world, the Korean Peninsula and all of Northeast Asia will be interconnected and globally integrated. The connectivity of finance and logistics will initiate a transport system that may create some sort of *"arctic silk road."* Furthermore, risk of war in Northeast Asia will be largely reduced once the situation on the Korean Peninsula is defused. Under these circumstances, various issues related to the Peninsula will be much easier to solve. North Korea should be encouraged to step forward along the path of denuclearization and full-fledged economic development.

At the same time, it should be integrated into the international community and connected to China's Belt and Road initiative. In this way, a relaxed and benevolent external environment may be created so that it can receive external assistance and realize sustained economic development. If everything goes well, a virtuous cycle will be formed in which the idea of "nuclear weapons for peace" will be replaced by "development for peace." When North Korea gains substantial benefits from economic development, it will be glad to construct a commonwealth of interests with Northeast Asian countries and integrate itself into this region through common perceptions of history, security, and development. A commonwealth of destiny of Northeast Asia will be established.

Second, China should employ the method of "pressing," "promoting," and "inducing," in a parallel and interchangeable way, the process of carrying forward its policy toward North Korea.

"Pressing" should be used to punish North Korea's misbehavior. Kim Jong Un has ordered scores of nuclear and missile tests ever since his inauguration in 2012, in hopes of improving North Korea's security. These tests worsened the situation of the whole Korean Peninsula. The UN Security Council passed over 10 resolutions to impose sanctions and embargos on North Korea; the U.S., ROK, and Japan also enforced their own sanctions. North Korea paid a huge price for its recklessness. Facing the serious threats to China's security posed by North Korea's tests, and considering China's obligations toward the UN, China strictly implemented the UN resolutions. In the meantime, China also focused on the common people in North

Korea, who were not the target of UN sanctions, and offered some humanitarian assistance.

"Promoting" should be employed to encourage North Korea to better understand the external world and become integrated with other countries. In this way, it may gain self-confidence to deal with the external world and its trustworthiness may be increased. In late 2017 and early 2018, North Korea declared that it had "completed nuclear capacity building and decided to take an all-out effort to develop economy." China responded positively to this change, offering fertilizer and other material as an aid and mediating between various stakeholders of the Korean Peninsula so as to promote further exchanges between North Korea and the international community. In particular, China created an environment that may deepen North Korea's contact with South Korea and the U.S. China's help was effective and contributed to the realization of the U.S.-North Korea summit in Singapore. China also called for the rollback of UN resolutions putting sanctions on North Korea, and responded favorably to North Korea's measures to abandon its experimental sites for nuclear and missile engine tests.

Inducing. In addition to punishment and assistance, China has tried "inducing" North Korea onto a correct path. China took continuous, substantial measures in pace with North Korea's constant good-willed signals of denuclearization. Endeavoring to maintain the authority of the UN Security Council and international law, China took actions to bring North Korea into the international community, guiding it to the "policy line of new simultaneousness" for both continuing the process of denuclearization and pushing forward its extensive effort to develop the economy. China hopes that the new approach may create a virtuous cycle for North Korea and promote its positive interactions with the external world. In other words, denuclearization can push forward economic development, while economic and social development may ensure early denuclearization.

Third, China preserves its concerns on five core issues in its policy toward North Korea.

North Korean-U.S. relations are the core of all issues related to North Korea, while the nuclear issue is the core challenge facing North Korean-U.S. relations. China will actively guide North Korea to make contact and dialogue with the United States so that the positions and attitudes of both sides may become more aligned. Of course, denuclearization should be firmly upheld. At the same time, some proposals should be launched at the UN to urge the UN to adopt some benign measures when North Korea's behavior is good. Also, China should explain to the U.S. and ROK that the current round of interactions on the Korean Peninsula might be the last "window" for resolving the Korean nuclear issues. Generally, North Korea will wait for some other country to raise a proposal in the UN and then it will offer some revisions on the proposal. Therefore, China could initiate a clear direction and formulate a relevant roadmap. On the preliminary condition that North Korea will abandon nuclear weapons, China may help it deal with the United States and establish itself in the international community. In this way, China's own interests may be guaranteed.

Leadership contacts. China could intensify its interaction with North Korea's highest levels of leadership to become more familiar with the top-down style of North Korea's policy process. The system of paramount leadership control has been practiced in North Korea for a very long time; everything must be approved by the paramount leader Kim Jong Unbefore it can be implemented. All bureaucrats have to wait for directives from the highest leadership before they can engage in anything. As the current paramount leader, Kim Jong Un is striving for more involvement in the global big power game. He is willing to resolve complex issues once and for all through some bold measures. It is said that "there is nothing that cannot be resolved once the highest leader gives his order." Therefore, China should take advantage of the current warm atmosphere that helps to improve China-North Korea relations and intensify its contacts with North Korea's highest leadership. China should be sure to raise the requests made by the international community during these contacts.

Upgraded security assurances. China should upgrade its security relations with North Korea to some extent. China understands North

Korea's security concerns. The most difficult task facing North Korea is whether and how to integrate itself into the international community. It is excessively concerned with the security of its regime, particularly worrying about U.S.-ROK economic cooperation and their mutual assistance. In addition to its active assistance and support to North Korea's infrastructure construction, China should upgrade the level of its security cooperation with North Korea. China may exhibit its military cooperation with North Korea in some appropriate way and make timely explanations of the Treaty of China-North Korea Friendly Cooperation and Mutual Assistance. Also, China may come up with some proposal for safe denuclearization on the Korean Peninsula.

Upgraded skills and practices. China should help North Korea to strengthen its construction of "soft environment." For a long time in the past, China emphasized direct exchanges with North Korea without sufficient care for management, sustainability, and outcomes. In the future, such insufficiencies should be rectified. China already obtained some experience from the success of its cooperation with North Korea in the Raseon Special Economic Zone. China should draw from these experiences to provide intensified training to employees at North Korean companies and convert them into seasoned professionals who understand international practices. China should especially offer training to North Koreans on international business law, technologies, and health care. In this way, North Korea may be able to integrate their business firms with the international economy and accumulate expertise for doing business with foreigners. These measures may offer substantial support to North Korea's "policy line of new simultaneousness" (simultaneously improving the economy and security).

Proper sequencing. China's approach to North Korea should follow a sequence "from easy issues to difficult ones, from small measures to big ones, and from rudimentary ability to extensive capacity." The current sanctions imposed by the UN Security Council form the redline for any investment into North Korea. China should take initiatives to push the international community to relax sanctions on

North Korea. Also, sanctions do not require absolutely forbidding any business with North Korea. China may consider pushing for North Korea's cooperation with the international community in the fields of culture, tourism, education, and legal affairs.

China's policy

Currently, China's policy toward North Korea should be built around two aspects:

First, China should turn the process of resolving the Korean Peninsula's issues into a unique platform on which China can play an outstanding role as a major player in international affairs.

Closer relations. China should draw from the traditional China-North Korea friendship and inject new meaning into the China-North Korea shared historic destiny. China shares a borderline of 1343 kilometers with North Korea. Furthermore, China has already made immeasurable strategic investments into North Korea. In this sense, China has an obligation to help North Korea become integrated into the international community. China also has a responsibility to strengthen and deepen strategic consensus between the two countries. This is very natural and normal. As a party that signed the armistice agreement of the Korea War and the treaty of China-North Korea Friendly Cooperation and Mutual Assistance, China has a solid political foundation for its cooperation with North Korea and maintains a tacit understanding with it on major strategic issues. In this new age, China should carry forward and expand these areas of bilateral consensus and common understanding, so as to further promote and deepen China-North Korea relations.

More balanced relations. China should upgrade its relations with North Korea and seek a balance among obligations, rights, and interests within this set of bilateral relations. For most of history, China engaged in "non-interference" diplomacy on the Korean Peninsula, focusing on practical measures to resolve specific issues, such as the principles of "No War," "No Chaos," "Denuclearization," "Double-Suspension," and "Double-Track Operation." These measures did solve some problems, but China gradually fell into a problem posed by "being burdened with hard and dirty work but alienated from good and beneficial matters." China seldom had the occasion to raise its own requests and demands. This pulled China-North Korea relations into a vicious cycle of "unlimited protection" and "confrontation." China should do more work on top-level design and clarify its interests, strategic positions, and pursuits on the Korean Peninsula. To be more specific, China should pursue its rational and righteous interests and resume a reasonable balance between its obligations, rights, and interests.

Chinese model. The Chinese path, Chinese system, and Chinese style of social governance should offer a model from which North Korea can learn. The two countries have shared many similarities during their respective development and have handled issues of social governance against the background of changing domestic and international conditions. In the future, as the international environment and social conditions develop, North Korea will face many political and economic problems that China has already encountered during its past experience of reform and opening. China's expertise and experiences gained from this past high-speed economic development will offer new opportunities to North Korea. China is now building momentum to invest in North Korea, so there is great potential for bilateral cooperation in trade and culture.

Second, China must ensure that it will not lose focus on the Korean Peninsula's denuclearization. It should develop "new cuisines," offer new ideas, and break new paths.

Focus on Denuclearization. Nuclear issues have formed the core of all the problems of the Korean Peninsula, and the issue of denuclearization is the core of the nuclear issues. The international requests for denuclearization of the Korean Peninsula and nuclear non-proliferation should be completely and faithfully implemented. In the past, on several occasions the international community was distracted by other issues of the Korean Peninsula and did not sufficiently focus its attention on the nuclear issues. These distractions on other less important issues, such as financial sanctions and kidnappings, led to sustained deterioration of the Korea nuclear issue. This is a lesson from which the international community should learn. The success or failure of denuclearization directly determines the future trend of the Korean Peninsula, so it should be viewed as the central issue related to the Korean Peninsula. All stakeholders, including China, should concentrate on the nuclear issues of the Korean Peninsula and should not be distracted by any other minor issues, otherwise a historical opportunity will be missed again. The various multi-party talks on Korea nuclear issues have been evolving along a very long process; from original "four-party talks" and "six-party talks," then later to "double suspension" and "double-track operation." The present talks are the extension and realization of six-party talks. Faced with new circumstances, all the participating parties in the negotiations of Korea nuclear issues should recalibrate their perspectives, concentrate their attention, and retain flexibility. They should open small-scaled bilateral or multilateral talks within the framework of six-party talks, so as to push forward the situational changes in a more pragmatic way.

New approaches. China should propose new approaches and new roadmaps, striving to be a new driving force in promoting resolution of the Korea issues. At present, "double-suspension" is continuing and the "double-track operation" will enter the visions of stakeholders. Measures are going to be taken to transform the present armistice mechanism into a peace mechanism. This transformation is connected to the technological issues of denuclearization, so a correct direction is what the Korean Peninsula really needs in future. Also, the existing achievements of "double-suspension" and "double-track operation" need to be consolidated. Particularly, the promise of denuclearization needs to be fulfilled, and the past situation of "going back by two steps after marching forward by one step" should be absolutely avoided. China should maintain pressure to keep the Korean Peninsula on track toward relaxation and détente, and encourage North Korea and the United States to step toward peace continuously, using new kinds of contact so that the North Korea-U.S. talks can be successful as early as possible. China should further clarify the technological work of supervising the process of denuclearization, including those diverse tasks related to a return to NPT, the War Termination Declaration,

CVID, and CVIA. China should intervene in all these tasks as early and actively as possible so as to ensure that denuclearization will not lose its momentum. Also, the mutual-respect mechanism between the two Koreas deserves praise. This is a new promise in the new era and also a new guarantee toward security of the North Korean regime. China should push forward the actual realization of this mechanism.

Big power collaboration. China should play the role of a big power and advance big-power cooperation. China, the U.S., Japan, and Russia have different historical memories and traditions on the Korean Peninsula, which have been reflected in the international politics of Northeast Asia from time to time. The roles of the two Koreas have also changed over time. Generally speaking, the role of the Korean Peninsula has been strengthened while the roles of big powers have been weakened. However, the complexity of the Korean Peninsula's issues would have increased sharply had no compromises or coordination been made among big powers. Faced with new conditions and situations, big powers in this region should first avoid reenacting destructive power politics that might introduce hostile stalemates between big powers on the Korean Peninsula. Big powers should advance mutual cooperation and collaboration so as to offer new ideas to the issues of the Korean Peninsula. The logic for Korean Peninsula's denuclearization and nuclear non-proliferation still exists, and big powers, such as China, U.S., and Russia, maintain a highly uniformed consensus on the question of denuclearization. Now a "window of opportunity" for realizing the denuclearization has appeared, but unreasonable conflicts between big powers may destroy this rare opportunity forever. Now it is very urgent to advance big-power collaborations to support the Korean Peninsula's denucle-arization. Second, only a full collaboration between big powers can finally realize denuclearization and nuclear non-proliferation on the Korean Peninsula. As important stakeholders in Northeast Asia, China, the U.S., and Russia are not only permanent members of the Security Council of the UN, but also big powers in international mili-tary affairs and the global economy. They are all also nuclear powers. Therefore, they have natural obligations to maintain the authority of international rules and the prestige of UN. As matter of fact, non-nuclear powers are not able to intervene when the non-nuclearization process of the Korean Peninsula evolves to the stage of technological work. Only big powers such as China, U.S., and Russia have the technological capacity and expertise to fulfill their obligations to supervise and examine the destruction of nuclear weapons and prevention of nuclear proliferation. Because of this, these three countries should prioritize profound and effective cooperation on the technological work related to denuclearization.

Is China concerned with denuclearization, and why?

China is seriously concerned with the Korean Peninsula's denuclearization process. As is known to all, North Korea's *Punggye-ri* nuclear test site is only 80 kilometers away from the border of China. When North Korea was conducting nuclear tests repeatedly, earthquakes happened in some parts of China's northern borderland adjacent to North Korea, such as the *Yanbian* region, and many cracks appeared on the walls of some public buildings in this region. In other words, China's borderland has been constantly and severely impacted by North Korea's nuclear tests. Furthermore, in recent years North Korea has smuggled or secretly purchased radiation-proof materials and relevant medicines from the international market many times, and reports of nuclear leaks in North Korea have also appeared frequently on media. These reports made China even more seriously worried about the threats posed by North Korea's nuclear tests on China's safety. Therefore, China is not only strategically concerned with the pace and direction of the denuclearization process of the Korean Peninsula, but also worried about the safety of its own citizens and the threats towards its own security.

Denuclearization of the Korean Peninsula is at a crossroads and requires some crucial decisions. This situation aggravates China's worries.

North Korea's nuclear and missile capacity

North Korea is at the precipice of some critical breakthroughs in its nuclear and missile capacity, particularly in three specific dimensions: thermo-nuclearization, miniaturization, and the combination of a nuclear warhead and missile. Even more seriously, North Korea is nearly able to deploy its strategic nuclear missiles with actual combatant capacity. So the "window of opportunity" for resolving the Korean nuclear issue is gradually closing.

Data and reports regarding North Korea's six nuclear tests and scores of missile tests reveal that its development of thermo-nuclear technology is advancing forward very quickly. It is estimated by various relevant parties that, in the high-equivalent test conducted on September 3, 2017, the actual equivalent was no less than 200,000 tons; it is very likely that a hydrogen bomb was tested on that day. In addition it seems that North Korea is on the threshold of making breakthroughs on ablation experiments and the technology of re-entry into the atmosphere. If North Korea is allowed to upgrade its nuclear and missile technology even further, it will make substantial breakthroughs in critical applied technologies sometime between 2022 and 2025. This period will also be a critical time for North Korea to take a leap forward with ICBM technologies. An assessment by the United States also predicts that North Korea will develop the capacity to install nuclear warheads on long-range ballistic missiles no later than 2023. At that time, it is likely that North Korea will have the strategic ability to combine nuclear weapons with missiles.

North Korea has also made rapid progress on the miniaturization of nuclear warheads. From 2016 to 2017, North Korea publicized photos of a variety of nuclear warheads and missiles, including its Mars 12 to 14 type missiles. The payloads of these types have reached the level of 600-1000 kilograms. Photos of its nuclear warheads reveal that their mass is between 650-1000 kilograms. Technically speaking, the payloads of North Korea's missiles of "Mars series" and some other types are already large enough to carry nuclear warheads. Evaluated from the perspective of range-payload combination, it seems that North Korea's medium-range missiles, with flight ranges between

2000-2500 kilometers, are already capable of carrying nuclear warheads. Their capacities far exceed the previous assessments made by external parties and form very substantial threats towards Japan, Guam, and even Hawaii.

North Korea's ambition is not limited to this achievement. It has been said that North Korea already conducted static experiments to adapt medium-range missile load bins to nuclear warheads, and that they have obtained relevant data from these experiments. It is likely that short-range dynamic flight experiments have also been conducted. After the experiment on September 3, 2017, North Korea declared it would again conduct atmospheric tests. As a matter of fact, an atmospheric test is a comprehensive method of testing, in which a nuclear warhead is placed into a missile's load bin so as to conduct more experiments and tests on the rocket, flight, condition adjustment, remote control, and detonation. Although China, the U.S., and ROK disagree with each other over the actual progress of North Korea's nuclear and missile capacity, they share a common judgment that North Korea is closing in on the nuclear threshold and that necessary measures must be taken to block North Korea's advance, or at least postpone the day on which it steps into the top nuclear threshold.

Five major detriments brought by North Korea's nuclear tests

Ever since 2012, the bizarre and extreme actions taken by North Korea have dragged China into endless embarrassment and dilemmas. The paramount leader of North Korea constantly adopted harsh measures that shocked the whole world. First, he executed his uncle Jang Song Taek, the vice chairman of North Korea's national defense committee. Later he ordered the assassination of his elder brother Kim Jong-nam, which pulled China-North Korea economic cooperation into a predicament. Since then, repeated nuclear tests and missile launches from North Korea directly shook the existing strategic framework within Northeast Asia and deteriorated China's peripheral security environment. For China, North Korea's development of nuclear and missile capacity is absolutely not a blessing, but a catastrophe. Some part of this catastrophe is already apparent, and some part will cast its horrible spell on China in future.

Serious confrontations between China and North Korea. Due to North Korea's extremist activities, very severe setbacks have appeared in China-North Korea relations. Actually, this set of bilateral relations have been in frigid stalemate since 2014. In order to press or even "tame" China's political and diplomatic leadership, North Korea adopted measures of cold confrontation and cut off its political, diplomatic, and military exchanges with China. It forced China to remove the Air Force Maintenance facility within North Korea and broke off bilateral exchanges with cadres above bureau level. It forbade any positive report about China in its media, initiated negative propaganda to attack China, and even spread slander and rumors to shift the blame onto China for the worsening of China-North Korea relations. At that time, many grassroots branches of the North Korea's Workers' Party and its military even defined China as an "enemy" or "an enemy in the north." From the beginning of 2017, North Korea's central news agency and its official newspaper *Rodong Sinmun* criticized China's policy toward North Korea and China's stance in the UN both overtly and covertly.

For many years North Korea was overconfident in its capacity to handle international situations, and its ambition became inflated dramatically, which led to its excessive expression of military strength in its diplomacy. It should be pointed out that North Korea made very precise judgments regarding the fluctuations of the international order after Kim Jong Un came into power. Particularly, its leadership was very skillful and sophisticated at manipulating the mutual animosities and grudges between China, the U.S., Japan, Russia, and ROK. Taking advantage of displeasures and discord between these countries, North Korea gained many tactical victories. Driven by complacency from these victories, North Korea sought to accelerate the pace of change in the international order. In this way, it attempted to force America and the international community to accept North Korea's ownership of nuclear weapons as a status quo. During this process, North Korea deliberately cut off its connections with the Chinese government and made an effort to develop non-official relations with common folks in China. Employing this trick, it tried to create an illusion that international sanctions could not reduce its nuclear and missile capacity, but rather that these sanctions would destroy the daily life of common people in both North Korea and China. Furthermore, it aimed at creating disparities and cleavages between the Chinese government and its population and to disconnect nuclear issues from economic issues, which would open some space for its survival.

Based on this consideration, North Korea purposefully conducted nuclear or missile tests at important times for China, so as to demonstrate that North Korea did not care about China's sentiment and that China did not have influence on North Korea. In this way, it hoped to force the U.S. to abandon its intent to press North Korea via China, and to create mutual displeasure and dissatisfaction between China, the U.S., and ROK. As China intensified sanctions and punishments even further, North Korea's banking, trade, and labor contracting activities in China shrank abruptly and its cash flow gradually dried up. However, in the short term, it is true that sanctions may not be able to substantially influence North Korea's development of nuclear weapons and that North Korea's hostility toward China quickly developed. Confrontations occurred, however, between China and North Korea only for a short time.

China-ROK setbacks. The trouble created by North Korea's nuclear tests should not be regarded as the fundamental cause for South Korea to deploy the THAAD anti-missile system. Rather, the troubles are a secondary and derivative excuse for this deployment. In fact, South Korea deliberately brought its relations with China onto a collision course under the pretext of North Korea's nuclear issue. South Korea purposefully took on the nuclear issue as a preliminary condition for considering and handling its relations with China, linking it with South Korea's deployment of THAAD. When South Korea was contemplating whether it should increase the deployment of its own missiles, North Korea intervened with an attempt to create mutual animosities between China and South Korea. North Korea hoped that South Korean conservatives could gain an advantage and complete the deployment of THAAD system. Actually, THAAD was a link that the U.S. established to weaken China's capacity to launch a strategic counterattack. South Korea was either unable or unwilling to prevent the U.S. from setting up this link, and it even assisted the U.S. in the process. When China launched countermeasures that dealt heavy blows to South Korea's institutions responsible for handling its relations with China, South Korea did not express remorse for its actions and attempted to cover up its true purpose and intention through dishonest and empty words. For some time in the future, it will not be possible for South Korea to come up with better approaches or solutions to the nuclear issue, because it is restricted by the general power structure of the Korean Peninsula and the intentions of the U.S. Therefore, China-ROK relations might continue to suffer for a substantial amount of time.

The Domino Effect in Northeast Asia. North Korea carried forward its nuclear and missile tests constantly, and even conducted a "hydrogen bomb test," seriously disrupting the international mechanism of nuclear non-proliferation and breaking the existing balance of military power on the Korean Peninsula. Its reckless actions directly stirred up those voices within South Korea and Japan that advocate a buildup of these two countries' own nuclear capacities, and even posed a bad influence on Taiwan. Currently, voices are rising in South Korea that advocate for a re-deployment of tactical nuclear weapons and even for a self-controlled program of developing South Korea's own nuclear weapons. Since the end of 2016, ROK's defense ministry and some South Korean scholars have begun to get in touch with the U.S., and some ultra-right scholars even established a "South Korean Research Institute for Nuclear Weapons" to discuss the possibility of South Korea's ownership of nuclear weapons. Some U.S. scholars from well-known American think tanks gave a positive response to these South Korean scholars and argued that "it is not impossible to envision a prospect of South Korea's ownership of Nuclear weapons" and "this option may not be a worst choice." At the same time, compared to the radical idea of South Korea's independent ownership of nuclear weapons, many pragmatic South Koreans hope that the

U.S. may redeploy tactical nuclear weapons on the Korean Peninsula so that a strategic balance may be restored. Many hawkish policymakers in the U.S., including President Trump, also regard this idea as a practicable and pragmatic approach.

The domino effect extends to Japan, which is accelerating its process of becoming a "normal" country with a normal military. North Korea conducted several tests that shot missiles over Japan's sky, inspiring a tougher attitude among the Japanese citizens that advocate for Japan's ownership of nuclear weapons. Nevertheless, Japan is relatively more pragmatic than South Korea and did not deeply consider this kind of option, which may seriously breach the intentions of the U.S. In contrast, Japan can become the largest beneficiary of turbulence emerging from North Korea's nuclear issue by making steady progress through a series of diplomatic and security measures. When North Korea's nuclear issue first appeared, Japan took advantage of this opportunity and unleash the initiative to transform Japan into a normal state and a military power. Its effort to revise its peace constitution followed very quickly. After North Korea conducted several rounds of nuclear tests, Japan used momentum created by these tests to initiate many strategic transformations and become the stakeholder that gained the largest benefits.

Accelerated U.S. deployment of anti-missile systems. The anti-missile systems that the U.S. deployed in East Asia contain in-born defects, because South Korea and Japan have been deadlocked in territorial disputes and tension over the historical issue of "comfort women." Taking advantage of the tension and pressure posed by North Korea's nuclear issue, the U.S. managed to remove the barriers to U.S.-Japan-ROK military cooperation and pressed the ROK to accept Japan's approach to permanently resolve the issue of "comfort women" through financial compensation. The U.S. made continuous efforts to connect the ROK and Japan to a common and integrated framework of military cooperation through some specific arrangements, such as the ROK-Japan agreement of military intelligence protection and the ROK-Japan mutual inspections of military exercises. In addition to the THAAD system, the U.S. shares with the

ROK its data from the Aegis Combat System; has deployed advanced stealth warships, together with ROK, in Jeju Island; and shares with the ROK its anti-missile data. Through these measures, U.S.-ROK and U.S.-ROK-Japan military cooperation has become more and more substantial. At the same time, the U.S. prepares to synchronize its THAAD system in South Korea with its various anti-missile systems stationed in Japan through a space-based (military satellite), sea-based (warships with Aegis combat system), and land-based (on-land Aegis system and THAAD) network of data chains, so as to promote the process of transforming its telescope installations of its anti-missile systems from traditional telescope mode to the "telescope + microscope" mode. In this way, the "remote vision" of its anti-missile system can be upgraded to the "precision vision." U.S.-Japan-ROK military cooperation has developed rapidly, catalyzed by North Korea's nuclear issue, creating irreversible momentum.

The U.S.-Japan-ROK military cooperation may be regarded as a small structure within the macro framework of its anti-missile systems, whereas the immense interconnections of anti-missile systems between U.S., Japan, ROK, Philippines, Australia, and Taiwan may be regarded as a much bigger structure of anti-missile collaborations and military cooperation across the whole Asia-Pacific. The U.S. is taking radical measures to develop new collaborative frameworks, create strategic pivots through bilateral military alliances or cooperation, and steadily advance the construction of macro chains of anti-missile systems.

Interactions between the "Five Seas" are leading to a seriously deteriorated situation on China's Peripheral Areas. Another consequence brought by the Korea nuclear issue is that the sources of chaos around China are gradually integrated into a whole, seriously deteriorating security environment on China's periphery. What is different from the issues regarding the South China Sea, East China Sea, and Taiwan Strait is that North Korea's nuclear issue is a high political issue; it does not bring substantial damages to China's trade and cultural exchanges with neighboring countries of North Korea, although the Korean nuclear issue always retains some heat. Even the China-North Korea border remains stable and quiet. However, North Korea's nuclear issue has been largely internationalized in recent years. ROK, Japan, and the U.S. have been continuously publicizing this issue and the activities of North Korea's regime, and North Korea itself is taking more radical and extreme steps to attract international attention. Under such circumstances, the shockwaves of North Korea's nuclear issue have spilled into the South China Sea, East China Sea and the Taiwan Strait. Even China-Russia relations have been seriously impacted by this issue. As a result, challenges around the "five seas" (South China Sea, East China Sea, the Yellow Sea, the Taiwan Sea, and the seas in Arctic region) have integrated. The physical and psychological shocks brought by North Korea's nuclear tests are also destabilizing the social lives on China's border with North Korea. The United States military leadership even claims that warships and military airplanes will be sent to China's regions in the South China Sea regularly and that its military presence in East Asia and West Pacific will increase. These intentions seriously weaken the security situation in China's neighboring areas.

In addition to the abovementioned concerns, compared to other big powers, China has the largest number of neighboring countries that own or claim to own nuclear weapons. This means the current security environment in China is already very tense. Therefore, it is absolutely a nightmare for China to see another nuclear country emerging in its neighborhood, because nuclear capacity itself poses an enormous security risk, no matter how friendly this new nuclear country seems to be. Of course, if North Korea's nuclear issue is solved and the Korean Peninsula is completely de-nuclearized, China will find it much easier to carry forward its policy and realize its strategic objectives, and China's pursuit of its interests on the Korean Peninsula will be far less difficult. Therefore, China is very resolute in its position of not wanting to see and not tolerating North Korea's ownership of nuclear weapons. China will use all means to realize a complete denuclearization on the Korean Peninsula.

To what degree are China and the United States cooperating on issues related to North Korea?

Strategic judgments in Northeast Asia

In the East Asia strategy of the United States, the priorities include: control of Japan and the ROK, and the containment and suppression of the momentum behind China's rise and its overtaking of the United States. North Korea's nuclear issue becomes a means and way for the United States to advance its East Asia strategy. The U.S. uses the North Korean nuclear issue to consolidate its alliances with Japan and South Korea and to introduce measures intended to hamper China's rise. The United States has multiple purposes behind this issue. It aims to extend deterrence and prevent North Korea from threatening its allies, but it also denies China any leading role in relevant affairs regarding the nuclear issue.

This consideration becomes its strategic objective. The United States plans to use North Korea's nuclear issue as strategic leverage to push, manipulate, and even control the two Koreas, Japan, and China, so that its own strategic interests can be maximized. It hopes that this issue could be pushed and manipulated to the optimum point so that sufficient tension and fear could be created without igniting a war. On the one hand, it is attempting to control Japan and the ROK and to establish a virtuous cycle of strategic feedback between North Korea's nuclear issue and Japan-ROK relations. On the other hand, it hopes to maximize its obstruction of China's development so as to contain China. In the United States' strategic planning, as long as North Korea's nuclear issue is under control, neither peace nor large-scale war would appear on the Korean Peninsula. In this way, a chaotic state of "no war, no peace, and denuclearization" will be created, which is fit for the triple purpose of the United States: manipulating Japan and the ROK, controlling developments in North Korea, and containing China.

China-U.S. relations will surely influence the trends of issues related to the Korean Peninsula. When there is convergence of Chinese and American objectives, the issues of the Korean Peninsula will be handled and resolved smoothly. When there is divergence, chaos will inevitably appear. To some degree, the past tensions and deteriorations on some issues pertaining to the Korean Peninsula are a direct or indirect result of the failure of China and the United States to achieve good bilateral cooperation. Sometimes one side viewed these issues as "problems of the other side" and was reluctant to take responsibility. This attitude left maneuvering room for North Korea, which took enormous advantage of the discord and lack of coordination between China and the United States, and escaped real penalty several times after it had conducted shocking nuclear tests. Only after North Korea's nuclear issue became extremely serious did the United States and China come to realize they were faced with a common threat and begin to cooperate sincerely. Since Donald Trump's inauguration, China-U.S. relations have been evolving toward long-term strategic competition and there appears to be a more heated rivalry between the development models of the two countries. Trump thinks that China has adopted a cheating trick of "Janus (double-faced man)," but he also manages to strengthen cooperation with China, dragging China into a secondary boycott of North Korea and compelling China to become concerned with situational changes. Nonetheless it is obvious that China and the United States are sharing more and more common points on issues related to the Korean Peninsula.

On the other hand, the United States may not tolerate any trends of excessively accelerated détente or drastically escalated violence on the Korean Peninsula, because these trends would be out of its control. There once appeared many dramatic solutions or approaches to tackle the issues of the Korean Peninsula, but they have never been implemented because they may impact some of the above-mentioned strategic objectives of the U.S. In the history of the Korean Peninsula, the phenomenon of "seeing the destination on the horizon but never reaching it" appeared many times. In fact, North Korea attempts to establish direct negotiation with the United States through the development of nuclear weapons and ICBMs, but it does not want to realize "mutual destruction." The United States controls the largest and most powerful arsenal in the world; grave threats of North Korea's nuclear weapons may be just an imagined terror and an excuse. Viewed from a cost-benefit calculation, a military strike on North Korea may not be unacceptable to the United States. However, in consideration of the status quo of U.S. military presence in Japan and South Korea, and the possible human loss in such strike, the United States has not decided to launch a military strike against North Korea. According to its calculation, by taking advantage of the repeated shocks brought by North Korea's nuclear tests, the U.S. can optimize its strategic deployment in East Asia, force North Korea to suffer loss in its economy and diplomacy, and create mutual dissatisfaction and displeasure between China, Japan, and the two Koreas. In this way, the U.S.'s control in East Asia may be further optimized. Nevertheless, it is undeniable that the domino effect has not appeared in Northeast Asia because the U.S. worries about the possibility that the ROK and Japan may break off from the U.S. if they have nuclear weapons themselves. It is more effective for the U.S. to manipulate the North Korean nuclear issue.

Naturally, China wants "no war," "no chaos," and "denuclearization" on the Korean Peninsula. This situation is the best in China's strategic expectations, and secures China's interests. In other words, there is an overlap between China's strategic expectations and the U.S. strategic objectives of "no war," "moderate and controllable chaos," and "denuclearization." The biggest difference between the Chinese and American attitude toward the Korean nuclear issue is a divergence of perspectives, not a fundamental disagreement. The U.S. may be more concerned with the long-term consequences. It worries about the process and pace of the resolution of Korean nuclear issue. Particularly, it fears that it will be forced to make a strategic retreat from East Asia if the Korean War is declared over or a peace treaty is signed by various parties of the Korean Peninsula.

On the other hand, China is more anxious about the present situation and fears that the status quo of the Korean Peninsula may be drastically changed. It is concerned with the stability of this region. All the countries surrounding the Korean Peninsula, including China and the U.S., show enormous care regarding the general trend that may emerge in this region if denuclearization is achieved and a "unified Korean Peninsula" is created. Both of the two Koreas have already indicated a strong nationalist emotion and focused attention on "one nation" in the initiation of the process of denuclearization. This tendency may synchronize with the rise of nationalist moods in East Asia and form a destabilizing force in this region.

The distinctive personalities of the leaders of these countries should also be taken into consideration as preliminary conditions for handling a strategic transformation of the Korean Peninsula. It is expected that the current paramount leader of North Korea will remain in office for a very long time because there is no term limit in that country. As for the ROK and U.S., a successful reelection has always been the ultimate concern of any incumbent leader. This situation may offer some rational anticipation and calculation on the Korean nuclear issue. Xi Jinping's long-term control of China's highest office is also guaranteed. In this sense, political expectations in each of these countries are relatively clarified. The distinctive and changing personalities of these leaders has created a "window of opportunity" for resolving the issues on the Korean Peninsula. Although there seem to be more opposers than supporters of the current official stances regarding nuclear issues within ROK and the United States, the leaders of these countries are still pushing forward their policies and measures. Presidents of the ROK and the U.S. have insisted on a summit meeting with North Korea and have persistently pushed forward substantial measures, despite opposition from their respective congresses and other governmental institutions. As for China, Xi Jinping hopes that China's rejuvenation can be realized within a given timetable. From his perspective, a resolution of the issues regarding the Korean Peninsula may offer new strategic opportunity and provide a good example for Mainland China to tackle important issues related to Taiwan. For this reason, he hopes to maintain good cooperation with the United States so as to create a more stable and predictable strategic environment. Therefore, leaders of all these countries have established a consensus that multilateral cooperation on the Korean Peninsula's issues should be sustained and should not be obstructed. Donald Trump might be the only one of all the presidents of the U.S. who is willing to make a substantial and meaningful deal with North Korea, so North Korea has no other options but to socialize with him. To Trump, the Korean nuclear issue can be used to create diplomatic leverage, so he is more concerned with the sustainability of it.

All these changes have led to enormous transformation of the environment of the Korean Peninsula, which means that traditional perceptions and behaviors may not be appropriate to tackle the current issues of this peninsula. On the one hand, the traditional perspectives of geopolitics and big power games have gradually lost their effect. For example, the six-party talks were abandoned. On the other hand, some non-traditional forms and methods, such as multi-round summits of top leaders, direct contacts between North Korea and U.S., more flexible "dialogues," and the ways and means of "operating on the limit" are playing a more outstanding role. Particularly, the methods of traditional working-level contacts and top-level strategic assessments have been overthrown, while a new communication model of "top leader plus intelligence agency" based on a "top-down" structure has removed many barriers on the working level. The past method of integrating the Korean nuclear issue with the missile issue and human rights problems is finished, because Donald Trump is emphasizing the resolution of each problem one by one. The prospect of realizing complete denuclearization will be determined by actual situations in the future. It is still uncertain to what extent the leaders of the neighboring big powers are committed to materializing their plans and visions for eliminating nuclear weapons on the Korean Peninsula. Despite this uncertainty, the will of the leaders of all these countries to resolve the Korean nuclear issue is strong and real to some degree, and they are willing to exchange opportunities for North Korea's actual abandonment of nuclear weapons. For the first time in history, the Korean Peninsula is greeting the "Kim Jong Un opportunity" and "Trump opportunity."

China-U.S. cooperation

Both China and the U.S. have a strong influence on the Korean Peninsula. These two countries have brought certainty and tremendous uncertainty. The problems of the Korean Peninsula are outcomes and consequences of the game between big powers. The continuously deepening partition of the Korean Peninsula was caused by the U.S.-Soviet confrontation in the Cold War, while the military stalemate between the two Koreas was an outcome of the U.S. containment of China after the Cold War. On normal occasions, cooperation between big powers contributes to the progress of the resolution of issues on the Korean Peninsula, whereas competition and rivalries between big powers will bring setbacks and reversions to the regional situation. However, even though all-round strategic rivalries have already occurred between China and the U.S., and between Russia and the U.S., substantial progress is now appearing on the Korean Peninsula.

North Korea conducted scores of nuclear and missile tests, breaking the security barrier to its regime after 2012. These actions aggravated the tensions on the Korean Peninsula. The UN Security Council passed more than ten resolutions and imposed severe sanctions on North Korea. At the same time the U.S., Japan, and South Korea also conducted separate sanctions and embargos on North Korea. In consideration of the serious threats posed by North Korea's nuclear tests to China's security, and China's international obligations to fulfill UN Security resolutions, China faithfully implemented the UN resolutions and put penalties on North Korea. On the other hand, China also offered some humanitarian assistance to North Korea, since aid to support the lives of North Korean civilians is not connected to UN sanctions. When China took part in the UN sanctions, North Korea lost its most important external supporter. Infuriated with China's stand, North Korea launched several rounds of confrontations against China. However, Kim Jong Un finally agreed to abandon nuclear weapons and take part in the Korean Peninsula's denuclearization process in late 2017 and early 2018. It is obvious that China's resolute stand and tough sanctions created the heaviest pressure on North Korea and forced Kim Jong Un to give up his extreme policy of military confrontation and agree to fundamentally transform his nuclear policy, although the military pressure from the U.S. also made a contribution. During Kim Jong Un's four visits to Beijing since early 2018, Chinese leader Xi Jinping had sincere talks with him and persuaded him to carry forward the denuclearization process and uphold dialogues with the U.S. At the same time, China also strengthened its communication with the U.S. on the Korean nuclear issue.

Joint pressure from China and the U.S. had an effect. Judged from Kim Jong Un's meetings with leaders of China, ROK, and U.S. and his subsequent actions, it may be concluded that North Korea will not give up its current stand of promoting denuclearization abruptly, because Kim repeatedly mentioned his vision of "complete denuclearization on the Korean Peninsula" and said that "there is no need to keep nuclear weapons if North Korea is given a relaxed environment." Although it is still hard to anticipate whether denuclearization will be finally achieved on the Korean Peninsula, a "window of opportunity" has indeed opened due to cooperation and mutual support between China and the U.S. on this issue. Therefore, as long as China and the U.S. continue to push forward the momentum of cooperation, there should be no drastic twists and turns on the issues of the Korean Peninsula. In other words, the China-U.S. divergence on these issues is much smaller and relatively insignificant than their convergence and cooperation. Cooperation will still be the mainstream of China-U.S. relations on the issues related to the denuclearization.

Observing good cooperation between China and U.S. on the issues of Korean Peninsula also creates good expectations for North Korea. As long as North Korea maintains good relations with both China and the U.S., the two biggest powers on the Korean Peninsula, a stable external environment for North Korea will naturally emerge. In this way, the vicious cycle of "creating trouble-settling the trouble-asking for a price-creating trouble again" on the Korean Peninsula was broken since early 2018. Despite its continued gaming on the nuclear issue, North Korea thinks that "fighting without a complete break-off" will become the keynote of its relations with the U.S. It is confident that it has the ability to stabilize North Korea-U.S. relations and that it will face less demanding tasks for dealing with foreign relations, so long as it is skillful at playing the cards it has gained from China and U.S. in the international community. North Korea regards Trump's presidency as a rare "window of opportunity" and is willing to satisfy Trump's requests on some specific issues, to some degree, at some critical moments.

From China's perspective, North Korea plays a critical role in East Asian cooperation. If North Korea is successfully connected to the external world, the Korean Peninsula and even the whole Northeast Asia can be entirely integrated. Once the hot issues regarding the Korean Peninsula are cooled down, the risk of war in the Northeast Asia will be largely reduced, and it will be much easier to resolve existing problems and troubles. Therefore, on the one hand it should be ensured that North Korea is guided onto the path of its "parallel strategy of combining denuclearization with an all-out effort to develop its economy." On the other hand, it should be encouraged to integrate with the international community and to connect itself to China's Belt and Road Initiative. In this way, a benign and relaxed external environment can be created for North Korea to absorb useful economic development experience and obtain substantial benefits from its growth and prosperity. If everything is getting on well, North Korea's economic development and denuclearization will turn into a virtuous cycle and the logic of "development for security" will replace the old logic of "owning nuclear weapons for security." After obtaining substantial benefits from its economic development, North Korea will integrate itself into the East Asian commonwealth of interests and share a common view of history, security, and development with the rest of East Asia. Finally, it may actively integrate itself into the Northeast Asian community of common destiny.

The preliminary condition for achieving these objectives is to create an active and positive interaction between North Korea and the U.S. China supports such an interaction. When North Korea declared that it would "take an all-out effort to develop national economy" in late 2017 and early 2018, China quickly gave a positive response. In addition to more assistance to North Korean civilians,

China also actively contacted various parties involved on the Korean Peninsula and mediated between them. Furthermore, China encouraged North Korea to get in touch with the international community and exchange with different countries. China created benign conditions and a good environment for summit meetings between the two Koreas and the U.S., contributing substantially to the North Korea-U.S. summit in Singapore. China also urged the UN to initiate the reversible articles of its resolutions on North Korea as soon as possible, and gave quick and positive feedback in response to North Korea's progress in destroying its nuclear test site and abandoning its missile engine experiment site.

On the one hand, China supports the U.S. position on the nuclear issue and continues to protect the authority of UN Security Council and international law, pushing North Korea to integrate itself to the international community. On the other hand, China also adopts active measures to guide North Korea to carry forward its "new policy line of simultaneousness" that combines the policy of realizing a complete denuclearization with an all-round effort to develop the economy. In other words, China works hard to ensure that North Korea is promoting economic growth through its denuclearization policy, and also making an effort to push forward the denuclearization progress by means of economic and social development. China hopes that in this way, a virtuous cycle may be established.

The prospect and possibility of North Korea's abandonment of nuclear weapons

North Korea's internal factors and external environment should be evaluated when considering the possibility of North Korea abandoning its nuclear weapons.

The international changes of North Korea
First, new challenges and transformations are occurring in North Korea's society:

1. Some dimensions of a market economy are growing and spreading their influence, which is transforming North Korea's social structure. Now there are over 3.8 million mobile phones, over 600 "free markets," and an even larger number of spontaneously-gathered bazaars. Several hundred thousand civilians are doing contracted work. North Korea's internal trade is flourishing. The spread of market factors and the change of information flow has changed the daily lives of many North Koreans and nurtured a relatively affluent class. These changes have also transformed the beliefs of North Koreans with regard to the internal and external politics to an almost irreversible degree. It is unavoidable that economic changes will ultimately reshape the political structure.

2. There are now intensive clashes between new ideas and old thoughts in North Korea. North Korea's younger and brighter generation are using their sharper mentalities to propose a diversity of new ideas and approaches to tackle the world. These ideas keep up with new trends in the international community. However, North Korean society as a whole is less receptive to these new ideas and perceptions, because most of the older generation who were raised through the 70-year-old traditional North Korean education cannot understand them. And the existing social and institutional structure of North Korea determines that it is not possible to convert many of these new ideas into actual actions or practices. However, the young paramount leader Kim Jong Un seems to be impatient with the speed of progress in economic and social development. That is the reason he has rebuked the leaders of many North Korean enterprises.

3. Changes and transformations will bring enormous political opportunities and risks. So far, it is not possible to achieve dramatic economic development if no breakthrough is made with regard to the normal practices of

North Korea's politics dominated by the elderly genera-tion. So North Korea is faced with a new dilemma: how to break loose from the old restrictions of development while maintaining the legitimacy of its regime at the same time.

What is more important is that Kim Jong Un has connected North Korea's economic development to the denuclearization process to some degree. These three issues should be taken into careful consideration:

1. How to ensure that economic development acts as a driving force that can guarantee North Korea's state security. The international community should prove to North Korea that there is a positive relationship between "denuclearization" and "all-out economic development." This is perhaps the most urgent task that the interna-tional community has to fulfill right now. In other words, it should be shown that denuclearization benefits North Korea's all-out effort to develop its economy, and that the social stability guaranteed by good economic develop-ment can replace a security ensured by weapons. All in all, it should be shown that denuclearization is beneficial to North Korea's state security and economic development.

2. How to guarantee that North Korea has enough incen-tive to integrate itself in the international community. It should be demonstrated to North Korea that some rewarding and substantial benefits have indeed been brought about by its effort to integrate into the world and the multiple rounds of summit meeting between its para-mount leader and the leaders of other countries. It should be proved to North Korea that it is a normal country welcomed by the international community, just like any other country, and that its normal demands for its own security and development are respected by the interna-tional community.

3. How to ensure the legitimacy of the rulers of North Korea. The present top leadership of North Korea is practicing a ruling style that is different from the past. The real conditions of North Korean society at present do not offer much room for its younger generation of top leadership to follow the old ways of operating political power. Only social progress and economic takeoff will provide its top leadership with new political legitimacy, which will be vastly different from the old legitimacy enjoyed by their fathers.

At the present, North Korea's requests are rather simple: a security guarantee and economic assistance. The security guarantee requested by North Korea includes three points: establishment of formal diplomatic relations between North Korea and the U.S., the signing of a memorandum of security guarantee, and recognition from the U.S. of the armistice agreement and peace treaty. The last point is the most important one. It seems that Donald Trump is trying to achieve all these three points. North Korea has realized that the current U.S. president may offer an opportunity and that the denuclearization process cannot be reversed once it is initiated, because the price for stepping back and reversing the situation will be extremely high. North Korea has come to understand that, if it breaks its commitments and reverts the situation, it will not only lose all the favorable conditions that it now enjoys in politics and diplomacy, but also destroy a benign external environment that its economic development urgently requires. Therefore, North Korea has to faithfully carry forward its commitment on the denuclearization of the Korean Peninsula so as to obtain the necessary conditions for its economic development and its integration with the external world.

It is under these circumstances that North Korea has not only altered its previous strategic direction determined by the "*Songun* (military-first) Policy" and "objective of building North Korea into a strong and big power" which had been established as national strategy in Kim Jong Il's time, but also changed the tough stand of confrontation and struggle that had been practiced at the beginning of Kim Jong Un's rule (2012-2017). In fact, Kim Jong Un has a fairly precise and detailed mastery of North Korea's internal and external situations. He understands very well that an effective resolution to the nuclear issue is the preliminary condition for North Korea's survival and development, no matter which development path or whatever political model it adopts.

Changes in North Korea's external environment

The transformation of the external conditions has also brought the denuclearization process into a state of irreversibility for North Korea.

First, the attitudes of big powers have changed, because the patience of the whole world toward North Korea's nuclear issue has been exhausted. U.S. President Donald Trump and China's paramount leader Xi Jinping have reached a consensus that they should not be cheated or played by Kim Jong Un again. Their distinctive personalities determine that they will not tolerate another swindle from North Korea on the nuclear issue. If Kim Jong Un plays tricks once again and breaks his commitments made before top leaders of important countries such as Xi Jinping, Donald Trump, and Moon Jae-in, or before the whole world, he will destroy the unwritten bottom-line tacitly agreed by the leaders of major stakeholders in the Korean Peninsula that the North Korean regime should be preserved. If he breaks his promise for denuclearization once again, the leaders of these countries will conclude that "all the moderate and peaceful measures for tackling the Korean nuclear issue have already lost effect, and only the option of military action is left." If that is the case, there will be no stopping an external military attack on North Korea.

Second, the basis for considering and evaluating the issues of Korean Peninsula has changed. All the approaches and plans for arms control of the Korean Peninsula have been proposed and clarified. Almost all the possible approaches and plans for denuclearization have already been raised, and all the possible principles for tackling this issue, such as "synchronized move," "stepping forward in stages," and "action-to-action," have been proposed and road-shown many times. Under such circumstances, the requests and bottom lines of each stakeholder in the Korean nuclear issue have been clarified to an extraordinary degree. For example, the concept of denucleariza- tion demands that not only should clear-cut definitions and confir- mations be made of North Korea's abandonment of nuclear weapons and the process of denuclearization on the Korean Peninsula, but that detailed descriptions should also be made regarding the treatment of nuclear weapons, nuclear materials, and potential nuclear capacity. Clear regulations should be formulated on how to handle the details relevant to the production, storage, shooting, and materials related to long-range missiles. On the issue of peace mechanisms, accurate requests have been drawn on the specific conditions of the war termi- nation declaration, peace declaration, and peace treaty, which should be differentiated and refined beyond a level of obscure principles. Of course, the proceeding of the issues of Korean Peninsula will also touch the core of ROK-U.S. military relations and their strategic alliance. Now various stakeholders are gradually getting out of those conceptual traps that put one-way pressure on North Korea, such as "Complete, verifiable and irreversible dismantlement" (CVID) and "Final, fully verified denuclearization" (FFVD), and accepting the practices of reciprocity, dividing into stages, and parallel resolu- tion. There remains a need to locate a viable and pragmatic way for the U.S. to make a security guarantee toward North Korea and for a good-willed response from North Korea. Particularly, a practicable way should be found to break the deadlock between North Korea and the U.S. through a conditional, reciprocal, and incremental denuclearization.

Third, the future institutional arrangements, including the peace mechanism, will be extended to China-U.S. relations and will contribute to a new mechanism for China-U.S. big power relations. If the peace mechanism for the Korean Peninsula can be constructed smoothly, in accordance with the wishes and visions of various stakeholders, discussions on the security of the Korean Peninsula will include issues regarding a multilateral security guarantee on the Korean Peninsula, establishment of a no-nuclear zone, and arms control in Northeast Asia. On the contrary, if the construction of the peace mechanism cannot be pushed forward as scheduled, military threats will become more and more outstanding and will inevitably create abrupt changes that may reshape the balance of power in Northeast Asia. Once the Korean Peninsula's neighboring countries fall into rivalries and conflicts, not only will the traditional security problems become exacerbated, the non-traditional security issues will also become more and more intensified. At present, the two Koreas have already reached some consensus and established some degree of mutual trust through a series of measures, such as military meetings, removal of armed forces, and the demolishing of some frontline posts. Also, the two Koreas are attempting to lead and promote the processes of tackling issues related to mutual military power reductions, missile deployment, and the Northern Limit Line (NLL). If these measures for building mutual trust can be carried forward and deepened, a real mutual trust may be constructed and sustained on the Korean Peninsula. However, the U.S. military presence in South Korea is a key issue. The United States worries that the turnover of the security situations on Korean Peninsula may negatively impact the USFK and the U.S.-ROK alliance. Therefore, more consultation and compromises need to be made to separate strategic issues from tactical ones, such as the THAAD system and INF.

Now there is a need to manage the issues on the Korean Peninsula in a more refined way. More efforts should especially be made to intensify pragmatic exchanges, understand the real demands and needs of various stakeholders, clarify a positive and negative list, and clearly define the directions, fields, and key points of cooperation in the short, medium, and long term. The concepts and process of denuclearization need to be well-managed. This process should be carried forward though different stages, with the buildup of mutual trust. Only in this way are the achievements of denuclearization likely to consolidate.

Of course, despite the positive progress on the Korean Peninsula, there still exists a need to strengthen intra-region communication for risk-prevention. The United States is playing a crucial role through its guidance on the issues of denuclearization, but its approach and path should not be regarded as the only ones. The past deadlock between U.S. actions and the advance of denuclearization should be broken and a new and virtuous cycle should be established. An approach of "de-Americanization" should be formulated for the denuclearization so that the sources of security guarantee to North Korea will be more diversified. North Korea should get rid of its past, extreme idea of ensuring security through nuclear weapons, and should try to secure the dividends of development by abandoning nuclear weapons and concentrating on economic development. Its mentality should be transformed towards a logic that only social progress and economic development can guarantee its state security.

Now some still-fragile mechanism of mutual trust has appeared on the Korean Peninsula. Its fragility and relevant risks are increasing, which may be explained by the theory of marginal progressive decrease of expectations. South Korea's expectation is decreasing, while North Korea's enthusiasm is also cooling down because it finds no substantial growth in its economy. In order to handle this difficulty, there is a need to make some new approach that may bring quick and good effect. For example, big powers in Northeast Asia should clearly confirm their commitment to the security of the Korean Peninsula, and pragmatic measures should be taken to encourage North Korea to break itself from its old and extreme mentality of protecting security through the development of nuclear weapons. All in all, North Korea should be guided to concentrate on economic development and get the real benefits of prosperity. In this way, it should be directed to establish a new logic that only social progress and economic takeoff will provide a reliable guarantee to its state security.

11

Japan's View of Nuclear North Korea: What Could Possibly Go Wrong?

Eric Heginbotham and Richard J. Samuels

Despite occasional efforts to nudge the North Korea-Japan relationship toward normalization – as in 1990 when LDP power broker Kanemaru Shin led a supra-partisan delegation of Japanese political leaders to Pyongyang – Japan and the DPRK have long danced on knife's edge. In 1991, normalization talks that followed Japan's formal apology for its colonial rule of Korea were stillborn. A subsequent nuclear crisis in 1993-4 that brought Washington to the edge of preemptive war did little to slow the North Korean nuclear weapons program. North Korea's 1998 test of a Taepodong-1 ballistic missile through Japanese airspace did little to allay Japan's concerns. Once it was confirmed by Kim Jong Il that North Korean agents had abducted Japanese youth, Japanese public opinion gyrated into paroxysms of rage, despite an October 2002 "Pyongyang Declaration" designed to restart normalization talks.[1] The Kim dynasty has had little reason to trust Tokyo, and Japanese leaders – most notably Abe Shinz – have derived great benefit from demonizing North Korea.

Now that North Korea is a demonstrated nuclear weapons state with real delivery capability – and now that there is an ROK government that favors unification over sanctions and isolation – Japanese leaders fear that the multinational consensus for "maximum pressure" to limit WMD on the peninsula may be slipping away. Tokyo is anxious about what it deems are risky unilateral efforts by the United States and the ROK to engage the North with

---

[1] For more on this issue see Chapter 4 in Richard J. Samuels, *Special Duty: A History of the Japanese Intelligence Community*. Ithaca, NY: Cornell University Press, 2019 forthcoming.

dramatic overtures from which it believes it has little to gain, and much to lose.

In Tokyo's view, failure of the uncoordinated efforts by Donald Trump and by Moon Jae-in that are designed to appeal to their respective domestic audiences could undermine sanctions and leave North Korea with a far more robust and threatening nuclear and missile capability.[2] Moreover, even success in these efforts, though preferable, could also produce outcomes unfavorable to Japan. "Success" could, for example, prompt the withdrawal of U.S. forces from the peninsula, much as it did in Syria. It could also drive a wedge between Tokyo and Washington, and/or produce an untethered and reunified Korea at a time when many Japanese increasingly view the ROK itself as a competitor. Japan has direct interests in the outcome of events on the peninsula, including, first and foremost, the threat posed by North Korean weapons, but some of its larger interests are also subject to influence by events there.

Below, we examine the wider interests and objectives that shape Japan's views of events on the peninsula and then explore how a constrained Japan is confronting its limited alternatives in this dynamic and dangerous security environment.

Japan's international interests and the peninsula

Japan has abiding interests in a non-nuclear North Korea. Second only to those threats directed at the United States, Pyongyang's rhetorical flourishes target Japan. In September 2017, for example, North Korea's Asia-Pacific Peace Committee declared that "the four islands of the [Japanese] archipelago should be sunken into the sea by the nuclear bomb of Juche," and "Japan is no longer needed to exist near us."[3] Nor is there good cause to entirely discount Pyongyang's threats. In a conflict, North Korean weapons might logically be aimed

---

2 *Sankei*, June 15, 2018, *Japan Times*, August 28, 2018.
3 *Financial Times*, September 14, 2017.

at U.S. and UN support bases in Japan – or Pyongyang might simply aim its fire in Japan's direction to energize its public or beautify its cause.

Given the stakes, Tokyo has supported a series of efforts to purchase, pressure, contain or eliminate the nuclear threat from the North. Together with South Korea, it financed most of the assistance given Pyongyang under the 1994 Agreed Framework. It deployed substantial diplomatic resources to back initiatives taken under the Six Party Talks. It is one of the most active participants in the Proliferation Security Initiative (PSI); Japan is on the PSI Operational Experts Group, and has hosted many of the group's exercises, including most recently the PSI Maritime Interdiction Exercise Pacific Shield 18 off the Boso and Izu peninsulas in July 2018.[4] Despite the risks that would accompany a preventive war and concerns raised by the Japanese media, the government of Japan – alone among the world's major powers – supported President Trump's confrontational rhetoric in 2017.

Tokyo is, however, more skeptical of the recent overtures of President Moon and President Trump. The government has provided public assurances of support, but not without caveats attached. Japanese diplomats do not entirely dismiss the possibility of reaching some sort of acceptable agreement, such as a freeze of critical components of North Korean capability. But they suspect North Korean intentions, doubt the likelihood of success, and fear the negative secondary effects of either failure or success. To understand why, it is useful to consider the other international interests at stake for Japan and how those have evolved as the balance of power has shifted over the last decade – specifically with regard to the alliance, Chinese power, and nascent competition with the ROK.

Centrality of Japan-U.S. Alliance

Nothing is presently more central to Japanese equities than the stability and credibility of its alliance with the United States. All criti-

---

4   https://www.mofa.go.jp/press/release/press4e_002104.html

cal questions of national security – including whether Japan should possess nuclear weapons – are framed in terms of the alliance.[5] While the centrality of the U.S.-Japan alliance has been an enduring feature of Japanese foreign and security policy for almost sixty years, the end of the Cold War and the rise of China have produced profound shifts in how Japanese leaders view traditional alliance dilemmas.

During the Cold War, when Japanese leaders believed that the structure of U.S.-Soviet competition effectively locked in American commitment, Tokyo was far more concerned by the possibility of entanglement – that the United States might drag Japan into conflicts against Tokyo's own interests – than of abandonment by Washington. Today, with China posing a regional threat that Japan cannot ignore but the United States protected by ocean barriers, Japan is more vulnerable to abandonment – a concern that has led Tokyo to hug its U.S. ally more tightly while opening some discussion of its own latent nuclear weapons potential.

Given that the ROK hosts the third largest number of U.S. troops in the world and that one of the most important missions assigned to many U.S. elements in Japan is the defense of Korea, events on the peninsula can easily influence both the U.S. commitment to Japan, as well as Japan's confidence in it.

Balancing China's rise

Relations with China are just as complex. China is, by a large margin, Japan's largest trading partner. At the same time, it is, by the same measure, seen as the most serious potential military threat. For decades, as China rose to prominence in the region and beyond, Japanese leaders used North Korea, an international pariah, to justify controversial defense programs. Japanese strategic planning docu-

---

5   On that issue, the answer has been and remains that acquiring nuclear weapons would be constitutional, but that so long as the alliance remains healthy and extended nuclear deterrence is credible, would do more harm than good to Japan's national interests. See Richard J. Samuels and James Schoff, "Japan's Nuclear Hedge: Beyond 'Allergy' and 'Breakout.'" Chapter in Demetrios James Caraley and Robert Jervis, eds. *The Proliferation of Nuclear weapons: Extending the U.S. Umbrella and Increasing Chances of War.* New York: The Academy of Political Science, 2018.

ments placed the discussion of the North Korean threat above that of China as late as 2013.[6] That Japanese planners were actually far more concerned about the rise of China was one of Japan's worst kept secrets. Unlike North Korean WMD – a one-dimensional, if highly lethal, threat – China's rise challenges Japan's broader political and economic position in Asia and beyond.

Tokyo has therefore juggled a variety of military, as well as trade and investment, initiatives to contest China's bid for regional preeminence, while simultaneously engaging with it in selective ways. Prime Minister Abe unveiled the Free and Open Indo-Pacific (FOIP) strategy in August 2016, pairing Japanese support for regional connectivity – establishing an alternative vision to China's Belt and Road. The strategy is supported by a variety of policy tools, from ODA (now openly deployed for military advantage), to strategic dialogues and security assistance. In the hard-power domain, the new National Defense Program Guidelines (NDPG), published in December 2018 – five years ahead of schedule – finally placed the discussion of potential challenges from China above the discussion of North Korea.

Yet absent a firm and stable regional commitment by the United States, Japan is not capable of balancing China alone. Indeed, as Washington's decision to forgo the Trans-Pacific Partnership and refusal to grant Japan blanket waivers to steel and aluminum tariffs have introduced doubts about its direction, Tokyo shows signs of returning to its Cold War "dual hedge" posture. Abe and President Xi Jin Ping agreed in Beijing in October 2018 on a long list ways to boost bilateral economic cooperation and free trade.[7] This was accompanied by a secret visit to Tokyo from China's top intelligence official, State Security Minister Chen Wenqing, to discuss antiterrorism cooperation ahead of the 2020 Tokyo Olympics.[8]

Even more than its *pas de deux* with North Korea, Japan's dual hedge with China is a delicate (often awkward) balancing act.[9]

---

6   Defense of Japan 2013: http://www.mod.go.jp/e/publ/w_paper/2013.html.
7   *Asahi Shimbun*, October 27, 2018.
8   *Yomiuri Shimbun*, December 23, 2018.
9   We introduced the concept of the "dual hedge" in Eric Heginbotham and Richard J.

Regardless of whether Tokyo seeks accommodation with China sufficient to benefit from the latter's rise, it has no desire to cede political
leadership within the region – or to compromise its own security. And
Tokyo fears that several outcomes on the peninsula could enhance
Beijing's position.

Competition with South Korea

The emerging sense in Tokyo is that rivalry with South Korea –
the third most disliked country in the world among Japanese after
China and North Korea – has become more prominent than its
shared status as a military dependent of Washington.[10] To be sure,
with strong U.S. encouragement, the two have engaged in cooperative security ventures. The Japanese and Korean militaries have
conducted biennial bilateral search operations since 1998, and have
held four trilateral Pacific Dragon exercises with the United States,
starting in 2012. Japan and the ROK also concluded a bilateral
General Security of Military Information Agreement (GSOMIA)
in November 2016.[11]

But different visions of Japan's imperial history, one version lever-
aged for political gain in South Korea and a different one employed by
Japanese nationalists to build their own domestic and international
agendas, have consistently driven the two countries apart. Strategic
cooperation remains weak at best. Intelligence sharing is restricted
and does not include, for example, real time sharing of sensor data.
The ROK has refused to discuss an Acquisition and Cross-Servicing
Agreement (ACSA), which would allow logistical cooperation during
an emergency. It has declared it will "never" take its F-35 aircraft
to Japan for maintenance, despite Japan's designation as the fighter's
regional maintenance hub. And it has said that, in the event of war
on the peninsula, it would not approve the dispatch of Japanese mili-

---

Samuels, "Japan's Dual Hedge," *Foreign Affairs*. Vol. 81, September/October 2002, pp. 110-121.
    10   Poll conducted by *Jiji Press*, 1 November 2018.
    11   See Eric Heginbotham and Richard J. Samuels, "With Friends Like These: Japan-ROK
Cooperation and U.S. Policy," *The Asan Forum*, 1 March 2018. For more on the GSOMIA, see
Samuels, 2019 forthcoming, op.cit.

tary units to facilitate a non-combatant evacuation operation (NEO) of the roughly 60,000 Japanese citizens in South Korea.

Beyond the thin veneer of strategic cooperation, there are many signs of a deeply troubled relationship – and Japanese angst that a more powerful South Korea – or a reunited Korea – could emerge as another challenge to Japan or its regional position. As Japanese economists and diplomats observe, the two countries' economic structures are inherently competitive, rather than complementary, and South Korean electronics and automobile companies frequently best their Japanese rivals in global markets. In 1998, the ROK's GDP was 9 percent as large as Japan's; it is now 33 percent the size (calculated according to exchange rate).

In late 2018, the South Korean Supreme Court ruled against two Japanese firms in a lawsuit over wartime forced labor, a move that led the Japanese government to contemplate economic retaliation for what it views as a violation of their 1965 treaty. At the same time, the Moon administration unilaterally abrogated a December 2015 agreement that had been touted as the final word ending the difficult "comfort women" issue. Symbolic of the fraught relationship, an ROK warship illuminated a Japanese P-1 maritime patrol aircraft with its fire control radar – a hostile act, but made perhaps somewhat understandable by the low altitude of the flyby conducted by the MSDF aircraft. Each side blamed the other in very public ways.

Given the possible eruption of an openly confrontational relationship, anything that could dramatically enhance South Korea's power in the long run (e.g., reunification) or unshackle it from the U.S. alliance will be viewed in Tokyo as problematic from the standpoint of Japanese national interests. It did not escape notice in Japan that a 1994 South Korean novel, which posited a nuclear demonstration shot south of Tokyo by a reunified Korea (together with the threat to destroy five Japanese cities), sold over a million copies, won numerous awards, and was made into an equally popular film.[12]

---

12   The nuclear blast is the metaphorical blooming of the Hibiscus syriacus, the national flower of Korea. The English title of the novel is *The Rose of Sharon Blooms Again.*

North Korea's wedge strategy?

Given these three complicated bilateral relationships, Japan has a strong preference for continued UN sanctions on North Korea. At an SDF troop review in November 2018 Prime Minister Abe reiterated his determination ". . . to ensure the complete implementation of the United Nations Security Council resolutions related to North Korea . . ."[13] These sorts of statements – combined with a public insistence that this position is supported by the United States, China and the ROK – receive considerable attention in the Japanese media.[14]

But the Japanese media – and Japanese strategic thinkers – are also openly concerned that North Korea understands the differences between the other parties and that Pyongyang will use those frictions to undermine opposition. As one wire service reported after the Singapore summit between Donald Trump and Kim Jong Un: "[North Korea] is "aiming to drive a wedge into cooperation between the United States and South Korea to realize relaxation and release of sanctions."[15] A popular weekly magazine placed this possibility in an even broader context, suggesting "North Korea has been inserting wedges between Japan, the United States, China and South Korea by selectively adopting pressure and dialogue for each country."[16] The article sees fertile ground for Kim's plans to succeed, observing, "The United States may aim only to invalidate threats to its own territory." However worrisome, Japan's means to safeguard itself against falling victim to U.S. abandonment are limited.

Japan's own military options are even more constrained. Indeed, Tokyo has no independent capability to deal with North Korea, and recognizes that no country, including the United States, has high-confidence military options against North Korea. Even U.S. preemptive or preventive war runs the risk that some nuclear weapons (and certainly

13   http://japan.kantei.go.jp/98_abe/statement/201810/_00005.html
14   See, for example *Jiji Press*, 19 October 2018.
15   *Jiji Press*, 2 August 2018.
16   *Gendai*. 27 June 2018. This echoed a regional newspaper, which argued in January 2018 that the Abe Administration sees Kim Jong Un's as managing "a clever detachment strategy to drive wedges into cooperation among Japan, the United States, and South Korea."

chemical and biological weapons) would be missed and might be employed in retaliation. For targets close at hand, North Korea has an array of entrenched long-range artillery that might inflict significant civilian casualties before they are destroyed. Nevertheless, there is significant disparity in terms of both the range of damage-limiting military options available to different countries and the likely magnitude of damage that might be sustained in retaliation. Despite two North Korean ICBM test flights in July 2017, the threat to Japan remains far greater than that to the United States.

Japan is in range of somewhere between one hundred and several hundred North Korean medium range ballistic missiles (and possibly, some short range ballistic missiles, SRBMs), but North Korea likely has only a relative handful of inadequately tested ICBMs.[17] To be sure, Japan has some of the world's best missile defense technology, including Patriot PAC-3 batteries for point defense and several varieties of SM-3 interceptors with wider coverage. The latter are currently employed on Japan's six Aegis-equipped warships, soon to be joined by two more Aegis ships as well two additional Aegis Ashore systems. But Japan's defenses, despite their high profile and cost, are of relatively modest scale and only provide two-tiered defenses in a few select locations. They would be of limited utility against an attack of any scale, especially if that attack came in organized salvos and assisted by decoys or other penetration aids.

Nor can Japan afford to develop a significant independent damage-limiting offensive capability. Before the new NDPG and accompanying Mid-Term Defense Buildup Plan were approved in December 2018, there was considerable discussion in of acquiring a "base attack" or "long-range strike" capability, framed primarily in terms an option to disarm North Korea immediately before or during an attack. But while the SDF is moving ahead with the acquisition of long-range missiles (specifically JSM, JASSM-ER, LRASM, and a boost glide hypersonic system), most strategists no longer talk of

---

17   For estimates of status of North Korean missile systems, see "Ballistic and Cruise Missile Threat," Defense Intelligence Ballistic Missile Analysis Committee, National Air and Space Intelligence Center, June 2017, especially p. 25; and IISS, *Military Balance*, 2018, p. 275.

these as an answer to North Korea's missile threat.[18] The DPRK's deployment of new classes of solid-fueled road mobile missiles effectively puts the DPRKs delivery systems beyond Japan's reach, except perhaps for one-off attacks against targets of opportunity.[19]

Not having an independent military capability and facing the prospect of determined North Korean efforts to unwind America's regional alliances, Tokyo faces a number of worrying scenarios. The first is that the United States might, in the words of Yoichi Funabashi, the chairman of Japan's Asia Pacific Initiative, "obtain North Korea's agreement to freeze its intercontinental ballistic missile program without obtaining guarantees that North Korea will also curtail its development of short- and mid-range missiles. Such an arrangement might," he continued, "protect the United States, but it would leave Japan (as well as South Korea) in the immediate danger zone, as well as open to nuclear coercion by North Korea."[20] In a similar vein, an April 2018 editorial in the *Asahi Shimbun* noted the U.S. interest in ICBMs and suggested that "for the neighboring countries," Trump's summit with Kim "serves as nothing more than a starting point for full scale negotiations on serious disarmament."[21]

In principle, limiting the development of the DPRK's ICBMs might strengthen extended deterrence, since the North's development of a robust and survivable ICBM force might call into question U.S. extended deterrence.[22] But successful negotiations over ICBMs, together with a peace treaty that would officially end the Korean War, might hasten the diminution of U.S. security commitments to Northeast Asia.[23] Indeed, gaps are already evident in the alliance with the United States. During the June 2018 summit in Singapore,

18   See, for example, *Reuters* (Japan), September 10, 2014 and *Sankei Shinbun*, February 17, 2017.
19   Former Defense Minister Ishiba Shigeru touched on the difficulty of finding mobile missiles and launching an attack after the threat of DPRK attack becomes evident but before the actual launch of enemy missiles in an interview in *Abema Times*, July 10, 2017.
20   *New York Times*, June 11, 2018.
21   *Asahi Shinbun*, April 22, 2018.
22   *The Defense of Japan* 2018 (English Digest) p.66. http://www.mod.go.jp/e/publ/w_paper/2018.html
23   Security expert, Michishita Narushige, quoted in *Yomiuri Shimbun*, June 21, 2018.

President Trump announced the suspension or scaling back of U.S.-ROK military exercises.

This drew quick – and negative – responses in Japan. Speaking of Trump's concessions to Kim Jong Un in Singapore, Japan's leading conservative daily reported that "President Trump announced the suspension of joint U.S.-ROK military exercises and is considering a withdrawal of the U.S. forces in Korea. Both are in China's national interest." The *Sankei* went on to list "other concerns" that bridge the economic-military divide, including that "by improving the environment for easing the UN sanctions against North Korea," the Singapore talks would "draw North Korea to China's side."[24]

The prospect that an agreement could lead to U.S. withdrawal is hardly implausible in Japan, even among mainstream strategists. With Trump having ordered the rapid withdrawal of troops from Syria in the face of staunch opposition by then Secretary of Defense James Mattis, Japan must take seriously the possibility that an agreement between the United States and North Korea could lead to a significant and sudden drawdown of U.S. forces deployed on the peninsula. Victory over ISIS was, after all, the unjustified justification for Trump's December 2018 decision on Syria, and he could just as easily declare victory in Korea and bring U.S. troops home.

The implications for Japan would be uncertain. One could imagine circumstances in which a withdrawal from Korea might give the U.S. presence in Japan greater importance in U.S. strategic circles. But in an era of flux and uncertainty, particularly with regard to the U.S. commitment and America's relative decline vis-à-vis China, Japanese speculation runs strongly towards darker scenarios. Clearly sensing the possibility of U.S. abandonment, a leading Japanese weekly has suggested that "Japan must increase its own national strength to defend itself based on the relationship with the United States."[25] That, the article suggested, might encourage the United States to maintain its interest in alliance.

---

24   *Sankei Shimbun*, 15 June 2018.
25   *Daiyamondo*, January 16, 2018.

There is even greater unanimity of views in Japan regarding how a weakened U.S.-ROK alliance would affect the broader regional balance of power. In the words of national security expert Michishita Narushige, such a development would be "compatible with China's goal of strengthening its power and expanding its sphere of influence in the region." Michishita, who advocates keeping the two Koreas divided, added that:

> the manner in which Japan builds its defense capabilities must change as ROK takes up greater responsibility for its own security, and as the Japan-US division of labor shifts regarding alliance response to China. Japan should resist manipulation by Trump and proceed with the defense buildup through working-level talks with U.S. defense authorities. In addition to reinforcing missile defense Japan should develop the capability to attack enemy bases.[26]

Conclusion

Despite adopting its historically muscular National Defense Program Guidelines in late 2018, Japan has no realistic military options beyond mitigating the threat somewhat with missile defense and buttressing U.S. extended deterrence. Diplomatically, it could look to close ranks with South Korea and strengthen military-to-military cooperation with it, though current trends run powerfully in the opposite direction. Tokyo could also further deepen engagement with other regional security partners, especially Australia and India, but it is unclear how these partners, useful as they may be in soft balancing against China, could assist materially vis-à-vis North Korea.

---

26 Michishita quoted in *Yomiuri Shimbun*, June 21, 2018. Michishita justifies his preference for a divided peninsula by suggesting that if and when sanctions against the North are eased or lifted, the South can tap the North's abundant natural resources and labor pool while the North can benefit from South Korean capital and technology. See *The Straits Times* September 14, 2018.

In military terms Japan has begun to enhance its autonomous military capacities in bold ways – including committing itself to stand off missile systems and carrier borne stealth fighters. But Japan still has a very long way to go politically, diplomatically, and fiscally before it can achieve truly "autonomous defense (*jishu bōei*)." Realistically, then, Japan is presently most likely to hold tight to the U.S. mane as Washington twists and rears, while reminding the world of the dangers of a North Korea unbound. And if that appears to be failing, it may, out of necessity, turn to an indigenous nuclear deterrent.

12

Alliance Management and Tension: Between "Fire and Fury" and Protecting Alliance Equities

VICTOR CHA

Donald J. Trump's unique approach to North Korea has created both opportunities and tension in the longstanding alliance relationship with South Korea. While others in this volume have written of the opportunities, I will address the tensions. 2017 saw the United States headed in the direction of a possible conflict with North Korea, so the first part of this chapter will address the flaws in a military strike option in the event Trump's summit diplomacy fails and the president reverts back to "fire and fury" rhetoric. The second part of this chapter will highlight the importance of preserving alliance equities in Trump's negotiations with North Korea. Even bad deals at the negotiation table are more tolerable if core alliance equities are not sacrificed. Thus, it is important to caution about the potential dangers of an overly transactional view of the alliances.

Fire and fury

In 2017, the Trump administration considered the use of a limited military strike to prevent North Korea's development of a long-range nuclear missile capacity.

Though the Trump administration has walked back its language about a military strike in 2018, even denying that it was ever under consideration,[1] the trail of statements left by the President, who talked

---

1   Matthew Pennington, "US denies plan for 'bloody nose' strike on North Korea," The Associated Press, February 15, 2018, https://apnews.com/c17f304b54e942fc90321b2603b336f8

about raining "fire and fury" on the North; by his (then) National Security Advisor Lt. Gen. H.R. McMaster, who said publicly "[the potential for war] is increasing every day," lead one to believe the option always remains under serious consideration; and by John Bolton who outlined a legal case for striking North Korea shortly before he replaced McMaster.[2]

The rationale is that a military strike on North Korea's nuclear and missile facilities, will "bloody the nose" of the North Korean leader enough to convince him to begin the process of denuclearization but not so large as to start a wider war on the peninsula.[3] Indeed, in thirty years of experience on this problem in Washington, D.C., never before have I witnessed more discussion about military options, possible North Korean reactions, and non-combatant evacuation operations than during this administration.[4]

The limited strike option may be appealing as a tactic to some, but it is fatally flawed in the context of an overall strategy. It would be ineffective in halting the North's WMD programs. It would likely escalate into an all-out conventional and possibly nuclear war. And it would work to the detriment of our overall U.S. strategy in Asia.

2 See "fire and fury" in Donald J. Trump, "Remarks by President Trump Before a Briefing on the Opioid Crisis," The White House, August 8, 2017, https://www.whitehouse.gov/briefings-statements/remarks-president-trump-briefing-opioid-crisis/; and "Luncheon with National Security Advisor Lt. General H.R. McMaster – 2017 Reagan National Defense Forum," December 2, 2017, https://www.youtube.com/watch?v=VwBrGNiZljY&feature=youtu.be "preventive war" in "National Security Advisor General H.R. McMaster on MSNBC with Hugh," MSNBC, August 5, 2017, http://www.hughhewitt.com/national-security-advisor-general-h-r-mcmaster-msnbc-hugh/; potential of war with North Korea is "increasing every day"; Mike Pompeo, "Intelligence Beyond 2018: A Conversation with CIA Director Mike Pompeo," (speech, American Enterprise Institute, Washington, D.C., January 23, 2018), https://www.aei.org/wp-content/uploads/2018/01/180123-AEI-Intelligence-Beyond-2018.pdf. Also see John Bolton, outlined "The Legal Case for Striking North Korea First" https://www.wsj.com/articles/the-legal-case-for-striking-north-korea-first-1519862374
3 Ben Riley-Smith, "Exclusive: U.S. making plans for 'bloody nose' military attack on North Korea," The Telegraph, December 20, 2017, http://www.telegraph.co.uk/news/2017/12/20/exclusive-us-making-plans-bloody-nose-military-attack-north/; and Gerald F. Seib, "Amid Signs of a Thaw in North Korea, Tensions Bubble Up," The Wall Street Journal, January 9, 2018, https://www.wsj.com/articles/amid-signs-of-a-thaw-in-north-korea-tensions-bubble-up-1515427541
4 Jung H. Pak, Sue Mi Terry and Bruce Klingner, "Bloody nose policy on North Korea would backfire: Ex-CIA analysts," USA Today, February 9, 2018, https://www.usatoday.com/story/opinion/2018/02/09/korea-olympics-close-war-first-strike-disaster-jung-pak-sue-terry-bruce-klingner-column/319072002/

The limited strike option rests on the assumption that North Korea will be undeterrable once it acquires these weapons because it is "not like the USSR during the Cold War" – in other words, it is less predictable, more economically desperate, has a smaller nuclear arsenal, and has already proliferated and used weapons of mass destruction on a family member in the VX nerve agent attack that killed Kim's half-brother, Kim Jong-nam, in February 2017.[5] Once Kim Jung Un attains these weapons, as the argument goes, the United States will not be able to prevent WMD proliferation, nuclear blackmail, or destabilizing demonstration effects around the world.[6]

The window to prevent these threats from materializing is therefore extremely small; North Korea is believed to be only a few tests away from demonstrating this capability. According to this rationale, the United States needs to act quickly and decisively to prevent the irreversible alteration of post-World War II regional and global orders that the U.S. worked hard to shape and that have generated unprecedented peace and prosperity for several decades.

The limited military strike strategy, while not without potential advantages, involves unfounded and heroic assumptions and unacceptable costs. On the positive side of the cost-benefit ledger, this strategy takes the United States out of the ineffective crisis management mode it has been in for the past several years, which essentially involved ignoring the problem until a North Korean test or another form of provocation forced the U.S. to muster a response from a set of feeble options. A limited strike would constitute immediate, decisive action not attempted before. It also would demonstrate the capability and willingness of the United States to employ "all options" to stop North Korea's nuclear program. This message would resonate beyond the region, possibly preventing the emergence of similar threats elsewhere in the world.

5 Richard C. Paddock and Choe Sang-hun, "Kim Jong-nam Was Killed by VX Nerve Agent, Malaysians Say," The New York Times, February 23, 2017, https://www.nytimes.com/2017/02/23/world/asia/kim-jong-nam-vx-nerve-agent-.html

6 David Allan Adams,, "Limited Strikes on North Korea Are Past Due," Proceedings Magazine, December 2017, Vol 143/12/1, 378, U.S. Naval Institute, https://www.usni.org/magazines/proceedings/2017-12/limited-strikes-north-korea-are-past-due

Yet, the rationale for pursuing this option rests on flawed logic likely to have devastating and irreversible consequences. If we believe that Kim Jung Un would be undeterrable with these weapons, then how can we also believe that a military strike will deter him from responding in kind? And if Kim does respond militarily, then how can the United States control the escalation ladder, which is premised on a military strategy that assumes the adversary's clear and rational understanding of signals and deterrence?

Some have argued the risks are worth taking because it's better that people die "over there" than "here."[7] On any given day, there are 230,000 Americans living in South Korea and another 90,000 or so living in Japan. These lives would be at risk, and would be impossible to evacuate. The largest American evacuation in history was 60,000 in Saigon in 1975 and South Korea would be infinitely more difficult. Even if the Department of State tripled the number of consular officers in Korea, it would take 100 days to evacuate these citizens. Moreover, the normal evacuation points south and east of the peninsula would no longer be feasible in a war scenario because they would be under threat of North Korean missiles. This leaves the only viable evacuation option to be China, but the waterways would be clogged with one million Chinese seeking to evacuate from the peninsula.[8]

Given that an evacuation of these citizens would be virtually impossible under a rain of North Korean artillery and missiles potentially laced with bio-chemical weapons, they would most likely have to hunker down in place until the war is over. While our population in Japan might be protected by U.S. missile defenses, the American

7 President Donald J. Trump reportedly said this to Senator Lindsey Graham, who revealed it on NBC's Today Show in "Sen. Lindsey Graham: Trump Says War With North Korea an Option," August 2, 2017," "If there's going to be a war to stop [Kim Jong Un], it will be over there. If thousands die, they're going to die over there. They're not going to die here. And [Trump] has told me that to my face." https://www.nbcnews.com/news/north-korea/sen-lindsey-graham-trump-says-war-north-korea-option-n788396

8 There are 1,018,074 Chinese nationals in South Korea according to the Republic of Korea Ministry of Justice. 2018. 2017nyeon chul-ibgugja / chelyuoegug-in su yeogdae choeda "2017 년 출입국자 / 체류외국인 수 역대 최다" [Highest Number of Immigrants and Foreign Residents To-date]. http://www.moj.go.kr/doc_html/viewer/skin/doc.html?fn=3c5f5afec1c8603989598bd61e8473fe&rs=/doc_html/viewer/result/201801/.

population in South Korea has no similar active defenses (aside from counterfire artillery) against thousands of artillery shells within a 30-second range of the border. The only active defense we have then is for citizens not to be where the artillery shells land. Not a comforting solution. To be clear: The President would be putting at risk an American population the size of a medium-sized U.S. city – Pittsburgh, Cleveland, Tampa, St. Louis, or Cincinnati, just to name a few, and not to mention potentially millions of Koreans and Japanese – all based on the unproven assumption that an undeterrable and unpredictable dictator will be rationally cowed into submission by a demonstration of U.S. kinetic power.

Others may argue that U.S. casualties and even a wider war on the peninsula are worth risking if this strategy enables us to prevent the threats listed above and thereby preserve post-World War II regional and international orders over the long term. But a military strike would only delay temporarily and not stop the North Korea's missile and nuclear programs because a limited strike, by definition, would not hit all of their facilities. We don't know where all of North Korea's installations are and, even if we did, many are hidden deep underground and in the side of mountains, beyond the reach of even large "bunker buster" weapons. Furthermore, a limited strike would not stem the proliferation threat but is likely to exacerbate it, turning what might be a money-making endeavor into a revengeful effort designed specifically to equip actors who are arrayed against us.

This assessment is not mine alone, but appears to be shared across the expert community by former members of the intelligence community, National Security Council, Department of State, and Department of Defense who served in both Democrat and Republican administrations, including notables like former secretary of defense Chuck Hagel and former Trump advisor Steve Bannon.[9] The former

9   See Abraham M. Denmark, "The Myth of the Limited Strike on North Korea," Foreign Affairs, January 9, 2018, https://www.foreignaffairs.com/articles/north-korea/2018-01-09/myth-limited-strike-north-korea; Victor Cha, "Victor Cha: Giving North Korea a 'bloody nose' carries a huge risk to Americans," The Washington Post, January 30, 2018, https://www.washingtonpost.com/opinions/victor-cha-giving-north-korea-a-bloody-nose-carries-a-huge-risk-to-americans/2018/01/30/43981c94-05f7-11e8-8777-2a059f168dd2_story.html?utm_

stated that he believed a unilateral first strike, despite its potential benefits, was too large a gamble for the United States to take.[10] The latter stated famously, "There's no military solution [to North Korea's nuclear threats], forget it. . . . Until somebody solves the part of the equation that shows me that ten million people in Seoul don't die in the first 30 minutes from conventional weapons, I don't know what you're talking about, there's no military solution here, they got us." [11]

This strategy also risks fracturing the rather impressive coalition of actors the Trump administration has brought together for its "maximum pressure" campaign of sanctions against the North Korean regime. These sanctions have reportedly tripled North Korean gas prices and increased rice prices.[12] They have cut over 2.7 billion (USD) in exports from North Korea that has created hard currency and material shortages in the country, including the supply of paper such that the state-run newspaper has decreased distribution. A unilateral military attack would undercut what has been to-date a successful campaign to deplete North Korean currency reserves used to build its programs.

---

term=.7c2dbf7350b3; Jung H. Pak, Sue Mi Terry and Bruce Klingner, "Bloody nose policy on North Korea would backfire: Ex-CIA analysts," USA Today, February 9, 2018, https://www .usatoday.com/story/opinion/2018/02/09/korea-olympics-close-war-first-strike-disaster-jung -pak-sue-terry-bruce-klingner-column/319072002/; Van Jackson, "Want to Strike North Korea? It's Not Going to Go the Way You Think." Politico Magazine, January 12, 2018, https://www .politico.com/magazine/story/2018/01/12/north-korea-strike-nuclear-strategist-216306; Kelly Magsamen and Ely Ratner, "An American attack on North Korea will come with epic consequences," The Hill, December 1, 2017, http://thehill.com/opinion/national-security/362736 -an-american-attack-on-north-korea-will-come-with-epic-consequences; and Christopher R. Hill, "How to Respond to North Korea's Treatment of Otto Warmbier," The New York Times, June 21, 2017, https://www.nytimes.com/2017/06/21/opinion/how-to-respond-to-north-koreas -treatment-of-otto-warmbier.html

10   Chuck Hagel, interview by Aaron Mehta, "Interview: Former Pentagon chief Chuck Hagel on Trump, Syria and NKorea." Defense News, February 2, 2018, https:// www.defensenews.com/interviews/2018/02/02/interview-former-pentagon-chief-chuck -hagel-on-trump-syria-and-korea/;

11   Aric Jenkins, "Steve Bannon: There's No Military Solution to North Korea," Time, August 17, 2017 http://time.com/4904066/steve-bannon-north-korea-military-solution/

12   Lee Chi-dong, "(Lead) Gas prices in N. Korea treble amid tougher sanctions: ministry," Yonhap News, September 26, 2017, http://english.yonhapnews.co.kr/northkorea/2017/09/26/0 401000000AEN20170926006151315.html; an earlier report of increased rice prices, Seol Song Ah, "Rice price exceeds 6,000 KPW and continues to rise," Daily NK, July 6, 2017, http://www .dailynk.com/english/read.php?num=14602&cataId=nk01500

Finally, a strike could risk equities in the alliance system, thereby weakening our position in the region and emboldening China. South Korea and Japan insist they must be consulted before the United States considers a military option, and the progressive government in Seoul, as well as conservative opposition party members have reiterated that Seoul considers any military option unacceptable. "Going it alone" is always an option for the United States, but this would involve accepting a deep fracturing if not end to the very alliances the Trump administration has declared it seeks to protect and strengthen in the face of a rising China.[13]

Preserving alliance assets

Going forward, President Trump has chosen to invest in summit diplomacy as the way to solve this problem. Despite a flimsy joint declaration out of the June 2018 Singapore summit and modest steps from the second summit, North Korea has suspended nuclear and missile testing, returned three American hostages, and dismantled some test sites with the promise of more steps toward denuclearization. [14]

Diplomacy should continue if for no other reason than negotiations are better than a devastating war, and negotiators must continue to push for more concrete commitments to denuclearization than what has been presented by the North Koreans thus far. However, with each piecemeal action taken by the North, the administration will feel compelled to offer likewise concessions in return. There

13   The White House, "National Security Strategy of the United States of America, December 2017, https://www.whitehouse.gov/wp-content/uploads/2017/12/NSS-Final-12-18-2017-0905.pdf

14   On suspension of nuclear and missile testing, see Anna Fifield, "North Korea says it will suspend nuclear and missile tests, shut down test site," The Washington Post, April 20, 2018, https://www.washingtonpost.com/world/north-korean-leader-suspends-nuclear-and-missile-tests-shuts-down-test-site/2018/04/20/71ff2eea-44e7-11e8-baaf-8b3c5a3da888_story.html?utm_term=.9221bba13215; on American hostages, seeon missile test launch site, see Choe Sang-Hun, "North Korea Starts Dismantling Key Missile Facilities, Report Says," The New York Times, July 23, 2018, https://www.nytimes.com/2018/07/23/world/asia/north-korea-dismantling-missile-facilities.html

is nothing wrong with this in principle. Indeed, this is the meat of diplomacy.

Nevertheless, the most important aspect of any strategy going forward vis-à-vis North Korea and China is adherence to the principle of not sacrificing our alliance equities as part of the negotiation. Other concessions may be available to the U.S. to employ if North Korea abandons fully and finally its weapon including the lifting of sanctions, energy assistance, economic assistance, security assurances, and a peace treaty. But we should never weaken the alliance as a price to pay for denuclearization. This not only undervalues the role of the alliance in accreting U.S. power, but would also undercut our longer-term strategy as an Asia-Pacific power in the face of a rising China.

I mention this as a concern because Donald Trump demonstrates a history of negative views on the U.S. military presence in Asia and in South Korea specifically. Dating back to an interview in *Playboy* in 1990 through to the 2016 U.S. presidential campaign, Trump has drawn a direct causal link between U.S. trade deficits with allies like South Korea, and the expense borne by the United States to maintain defense commitments to these countries. He has stated that "Our allies are making billions screwing us" and with reference to South Korea, he has said, "They're making a fortune. Let's call it hundreds of billions of dollars of profit on us. We have 25,000 soldiers over there protecting them. They don't pay us. Why don't they pay us?"[15] When asked by a *New York Times* reporter whether he would pull the troops out of Korea, Trump in March 2016 responded,

> Yes, I would. I would not do so happily, but I would be willing to do it. Not happily. David actually asked me that question before, this morning before we sort of finalized out. The answer is not happily but the answer is yes. We cannot afford

15   Glenn Plaskin, "The 1990 Playboy Interview with Donald Trump," *Playboy*, March 1, 1990, https://www.playboy.com/read/playboy-interview-donald-trump-1990; Louis Jacobson, "Donald Trump says South Korea doesn't United States for troop presence," Politifact, April 1, 2011, https://www.politifact.com/truth-o-meter/statements/2011/apr/01/donald-trump/donald-trump-says-south-korea-doesnt-pay-us-troop-/

to be losing vast amounts of billions of dollars on all of this. We just can't do it anymore.[16]

The appendix lists all of the statements by President Trump on troop commitments to Korea, many of which are factually inaccurate, but nevertheless must be taken seriously because they represent the reality for the President. Advisers around him, as well as South Korean and Japanese leaders must guard against these worst instincts to trade alliance assets for a bad deal on denuclearization. In the end, this would make the United States and its allies less, nor more secure.

Appendix I: Donald Trump's statements on troop commitments related to South Korea

1. March 1, 1990, interview with *Playboy* magazine:
   We Americans are laughed at around the world for losing a hundred and fifty billion dollars year after year, for defending wealthy nations for nothing, nations that would be wiped off the face of the earth in about fifteen minutes if it weren't for us. Our "allies" are making billions screwing us.[17]

2. March 23, 2011, interview on ABC's The View:
   If you look at North Korea, South Korea, we're protecting South Korea," Trump said. "They're making a fortune. Let's call it hundreds of billions of dollars of profit on us. We have 25,000 soldiers over there protecting them. They don't pay us. Why don't they pay us?[18]

---

16 "Transcript: Donald Trump Expounds on His Foreign Policy Views," *The New York Times*, March 26, 2016, https://www.nytimes.com/2016/03/27/us/politics/donald-trump-transcript.html

17 Glenn Plaskin, "The 1990 Playboy Interview with Donald Trump," *Playboy*, March 1, 1990, https://www.playboy.com/read/playboy-interview-donald-trump-1990

18 Louis Jacobson, "Donald Trump says South Korea doesn't United States for troop presence," Politifact, April 1, 2011, https://www.politifact.com/truth-o-meter/statements/2011/apr/01/donald-trump/donald-trump-says-south-korea-doesnt-pay-us-troop-/

3. April 5, 2013, interview with Fox News' Greta Van Susteren:

> But the big culprits are other countries and what they are doing to us . . . You look as an example, South Korea. We are spending tremendous. We spend billions and billions of dollars to protect them from North Korea. They are not giving us anything. What are we doing? You know they are a competitor of ours. Hey they are wonderful people. We have had partners from South Korea. But why are we doing this all free? We are not in that position as a country. They should be paying us for this. We send all those aircraft carriers over. All those ships, the planes, the bombers. And we get nothing out of it. Except in all fairness, they take most of our business. They have made some unbelievable deals with our government. You know they are just taking our business. So why aren't they paying for this kind of protection?[19]

4. January 7, 2016, interview with CNN's Wolf Blitzer:

> And we have 28,000 soldiers in the middle of it. And we get paid nothing, we get paid peanuts . . . Well, I would want South Korea to pay us a lot of money. We're doing a lot of – what are we doing? I just ordered 4,000 television sets. They come from South Korea. South Korea is a money machine. They pay us peanuts. We're defending them, and I have many friends from South Korea, they buy my apartments, I do business with them. But South Korea should pay us and pay us very substantially for protecting them.[20]

19   "Trump on the slowing economy, unemployment rate," Fox News, April 5, 2013, http://video.foxnews.com/v/2280557079001/?playlist_id=930909814001#sp=show-clips

20   Tim Hains, "Donald Trump on North Korea: 'Without China They Wouldn't Be Able to Eat,' 'We Have Great Power Over China,'" RealClearPolitics, January 7, 2016, https://www.realclearpolitics.com/video/2016/01/07/donald_trump_on_north_korea_china_has_total_control_of_them_south_korea_should_pay_us.html

5. January 10, 2016, interview with NBC's Chuck Todd: 'We have 28,000 soldiers on the line in South Korea between the madman and them,' Trump said, referring to Kim. 'We get practically nothing compared to the cost of this.'[21]

6. March 26, 2016, interview with *The New York Times*' Maggie Haberman and David E. Sanger:

HABERMAN: Would you be willing to withdraw U.S. forces from places like Japan and South Korea if they don't increase their contribution significantly?

TRUMP: Yes, I would. I would not do so happily, but I would be willing to do it. Not happily. David actually asked me that question before, this morning before we sort of finalized out. The answer is not happily but the answer is yes. We cannot afford to be losing vast amounts of billions of dollars on all of this. We just can't do it anymore. Now there was a time when we could have done it. When we started doing it. But we can't do it anymore. And I have a feeling that they'd up the ante very much. I think they would, and if they wouldn't I would really have to say yes.

. . . Later in the interview describing "America First:"

TRUMP: From China to Japan to South Korea to the Middle East, many states in the Middle East, for instance, protecting Saudi Arabia and not being properly reimbursed for every penny that we spend, when they're sitting with trillions of dollars, I mean they were making a billion dollars a day before the oil went down, now they're still making a fortune, you know, their oil is very high and very easy to get

21   "Is Donald Trump the P. T. Barnum of 2016? Chuck Asked Him." *NBC Meet The Press*, January 10, 2016, https://www.nbcnews.com/meet-the-press/video/is-donald-trump-the-p-t-barnum-of -2016-chuck-asked-him-599134787947

it, very inexpensive, but they're still making a lot of money, but they were making a billion dollars a day and we were paying leases for bases? We're paying leases, we're paying rent? O.K.? To have bases over there? The whole thing is preposterous. So we had, so America first, yes, we will not be ripped off anymore. We're going to be friendly with everybody, but we're not going to be taken advantage of by anybody. We won't be isolationists – I don't want to go there because I don't believe in that. I think we'll be very worldview, but we're not going to be ripped off anymore by all of these countries. I mean think of it. We have $21 trillion, essentially, very shortly, we'll be up to $21 trillion in debt. O.K.? A lot of that is just all of these horrible, horrible decisions.[22]

7. May 4, 2016, interview with CNN's Wolf Blitzer:

TRUMP: . . . I have great relationships with South Korea. I have buildings in South Korea. I have great relationships with Japan and in Japan.

But our government – and a lot of people don't even know this. You know, when I make speeches, I say we protect Germany, we protect Japan, we protect South Korea. You know, many, many people – sophisticated people in the audience – they didn't even know that.

They have to help us. We don't get reimbursed for what this massive amount of work and – and energy and weaponry, what it – what it's costing. We can't continue to do it. This isn't 40 years ago. This isn't when we were much different as a country. They have to take care of us.

22 "Transcript: Donald Trump Expounds on His Foreign Policy Views," *The New York Times*, March 26, 2016, https://www.nytimes.com/2016/03/27/us/politics/donald-trump-transcript.html

Now, I think they will. If they don't, you have to be prepared to walk. You always have to be prepared to walk from a deal, including the Iran deal, which is a disaster. They should have walked.

BLITZER: But – but you're ready to let Japan and South Korea become nuclear powers?

TRUMP: I am prepared to – if they're not going to take care of us properly, we cannot afford to be the military and the police for the world. We are, right now, the police for the entire world. We are policing the entire world.

You know, when people look at our military and they say, "Oh, wow, that's fantastic," they have many, many times – you know, we spend many times what any other country spends on the military. But it's not really for us. We're defending other countries.

So all I'm saying is this: they have to pay.

And you know what? I'm prepared to walk, and if they have to defend themselves against North Korea, where you have a maniac over there, in my opinion, if they don't – if they don't take care of us properly, if they don't respect us enough to take care of us properly, then you know what's going to have to happen, Wolf?

[17:45:10] It's very simple. They're going to have to defend themselves.

BLITZER: Because the other day, the U.S. military commander in South Korea, General Vincent Brooks, he testified up on Capitol Hill. He said South Korea pays for 50 percent of the personnel costs for U.S. troops –

TRUMP: How much – how much percent?

BLITZER: Fifty percent.

TRUMP: Fifty. Why not 100 percent?

BLITZER: But he also says that it's – it would be more

expensive to keep U.S. troops here in the U.S. than to keep them on bases in South Korea.

TRUMP: OK, well, I mean maybe you don't need them, OK? Maybe you don't need them. Look, we're policing all of these countries. They're not paying us. We're policing Saudi Arabia. We are protecting Saudi Arabia. Saudi Arabia – I have many friends in Saudi Arabia.

Saudi Arabia would not be there, Wolf. It wouldn't be there, maybe for a month, if we took our military out. The only reason they're sort of protected and they're totally protected is because we're protecting them. Saudi Arabia was making a billion dollars a day when the oil price was high. Now they're still making a fortune. Why aren't they paying us –

BLITZER: So basically what I hear you saying is, if the U.S. is going to keep troops in Japan – and there's thousands of them, tens of thousands in Korea, 28,000 in –

TRUMP: We've got to be reimbursed.

BLITZER: Korea or Germany, for that matter.

TRUMP: Yes.

BLITZER: You want the host countries to pick up all the expense.

TRUMP: Of course they should pick up all the expense. Why are we paying for this? I mean we are paying to protect them. And I think it's wonderful. I think it's good. I'd rather do it rather than have them armed. I would rather do it. And, you know, it was covered, actually, accurately in "The New York Times," very accurately. And they covered – they covered it because they talked the cost.

A lot of people like to say, oh, Trump wants Japan to arm. I don't want them to arm. I want them to reimburse us for at least the costs. Now you could say it's worth more than that. But at least reimburse us for the cost.

When you say we pay 50 percent, well, if we say we pay 50 percent, that means we pay less, OK. But we're losing a tremendous amount of money. And we have a military that's not in good shape anymore. You know that. Everybody knows that. And we have to do something about it.[23]

8. September 26, 2016, First 2016 U.S. presidential debate, Hofstra University:

TRUMP: It's not an accurate one at all. It's not an accurate one. So I just want to give a lot of things – and just to respond. I agree with her on one thing. The single greatest problem the world has is nuclear armament, nuclear weapons, not global warming, like you think and your – your president thinks.

Nuclear is the single greatest threat. Just to go down the list, we defend Japan, we defend Germany, we defend South Korea, we defend Saudi Arabia, we defend countries. They do not pay us. But they should be paying us, because we are providing tremendous service and we're losing a fortune. That's why we're losing – we're losing – we lose on everything. I say, who makes these – we lose on everything. All I said, that it's very possible that if they don't pay a fair share, because this isn't 40 years ago where we could do what we're doing. We can't defend Japan, a behemoth, selling us cars by the million . . .

HOLT: We need to move on.

TRUMP: Well, wait, but it's very important. All I said was, they may have to defend themselves or they

23 Transcript, CNN's *The Situation Room*, May 4, 2016, http://transcripts.cnn.com/TRANSCRIPTS/1605/04/sitroom.01.html

have to help us out. We're a country that owes $20 trillion. They have to help us out.[24]

9. April 27, 2017, interview with Reuters on THAAD payment:

I informed South Korea it would be appropriate if they paid. It's a billion-dollar system. It's phenomenal, shoots missiles right out of the sky.[25]

10. June 30, 2017, press conference with South Korean president Moon Jae-in at The White House:

Our goal is peace, stability and prosperity for the region. But the United States will defend itself, always will defend itself, always, and we will always defend our allies. As part of that commitment, we are working together to ensure fair burden sharing and support of the United States military presence in South Korea.

Burden sharing is a very important factor. A factor that's becoming more and more prevalent certainly in this administration. We're also working to create a fair and reciprocal economic relationship. From the when the U.S.-Korea trade deal was signed in 2011, to 2016, you know who signed it, you know who wanted it.[26]

11. February 13, 2018, remarks at The White House:

Look, we have rebuilt China. We have rebuilt a lot of – with the money they've taken out of the United States. We're like the piggybank that had people running it

24   Aaron Blake, "The First Trump-Clinton presidential debate transcript, annotated," *The Washington Post*, September 26, 2016, https://www.washingtonpost.com/news/the-fix/wp/2016/09/26/the-first-trump-clinton-presidential-debate-transcript-annotated/?noredirect=on&utm_term=.ed4ef1f51103

25   Stephen J. Adler, Jeff Mason, and Steven Holland, "Exclusive: Trump vows to fix or scrap South Korea trade deal, wants missile system payment," *Reuters*, April 27, 2017, https://in.reuters.com/article/usa-trump-southkorea-idINKBN17U0B2

26   "President Trump and South Korean President Joint Statement," *C-SPAN*, June 30, 2017, https://www.c-span.org/video/?430753-1/president-trump-patience-north-korea

that didn't know what the hell they were doing. And we have rebuilt countries, like, massively. You look at some of these countries – look at South Korea, look at Japan, look at so many countries. And then we defend them, on top of everything else.

So we defend Saudi Arabia. They pay us a fraction of what it costs. We defend Japan. We defend South Korea. They pay us a fraction of what it costs. And we're talking to all of those countries about that because it's not fair that we defend them, and they pay us a fraction of the cost of that defense. Separate argument, but a real problem.[27]

12. May 4, 2018, press gaggle at Joint Base Andrews, Maryland:

At some point in the future, I would like to save the money. We have 32,000 troops there . . . But troops are not on the table...we haven't been asked to.[28]

Appendix II: Donald Trump's tweets on troop commitments related to South Korea

1. "How much is South Korea paying the U.S. for protection against North Korea???? NOTHING!", March 9, 2013[29]
2. "What do we get from our economic competitor South Korea for the tremendous cost of protecting them from North Korea? – NOTHING!", March 30, 2013[30]

27 The White House, "Remarks by President Trump, Vice President Pence, Members of Congress, and Members of the Cabinet in Meeting on Trade," February 13, 2018, https://www.whitehouse.gov/briefings-statements/remarks-president-trump-vice-president-pence-members-congress-members-cabinet-meeting-trade/

28 "Trump: No U.S. troop withdrawal from South Korea," USA Today, May 4, 2018, https://www.usatoday.com/videos/news/world/2018/05/04/trump-no-u.s.-troop-withdrawal-south-korea/34549735/

29 https://twitter.com/realDonaldTrump/status/310338394922295296

30 https://twitter.com/realdonaldtrump/status/317965135283093504

3. "I ask again, how much is very wealthy South Korea paying the United States for protecting it against North Korea?," April 2, 2013[31]

4. "When is South Korea going to start paying us for the massive amounts of money we are spending to protect them from the North?," April 6, 2013[32]

5. "I can't believe we are not asking South Korea for anything. They make a fortune on us while we spend a fortune defending them-how stupid!," April 12, 2013[33]

6. "South Korea must in some form pay for our help-the U.S. must stop being stupid!," April 13, 2013[34]

7. "South Korea is absolutely killing us on trade deals. Their surplus vs U.S. is massive - and we pay for their protection. WHO NEGOTIATES?," April 24, 2014[35]

31   https://twitter.com/realdonaldtrump/status/319189584573497344
32   https://twitter.com/realdonaldtrump/status/320672843702607872
33   https://twitter.com/realdonaldtrump/status/322672900744286208
34   https://twitter.com/realdonaldtrump/status/323216293031460865
35   https://twitter.com/realdonaldtrump/status/459289089393840128

13

The Role of Sanctions

Stephan Haggard

The role that sanctions have played in the North Korean nuclear crisis is a matter of substantial controversy. Those committed to a strategy of engagement argue that they send the wrong signals and in any case the North Korean regime is essentially immune from them. This immunity stems in the first instance from the authoritarian nature of the regime, and the ability to pass on costs to the hapless North Korean people. In addition, China's role as lender of last resort has blunted the effects of trade and financial restrictions. North Korean enterprises have also honed their sanctions-evasion skills over the years to a remarkable degree.

For those believing that sanctions play a more central role, the story line is somewhat more complicated. To be sure, the North Korean regime is relatively closed and authoritarian. But authoritarian leaders have to be attentive to mass publics as well; the fate of autocracies around the world over the last several decades bears witness to the fact that they do not necessarily last forever. The fact that the regime weathered a famine in the first half of the 1990s does not mean that Kim Jong Un wants to go down that road again. In virtually all of his New Year's speeches since taking office on the death of his father in 2011 he has spotlighted economic issues and has even admitted that sanctions constitute an important drag on economic reconstruction.

It is also almost certainly the case that the North Korean economy is more open than it was a decade ago. The evidence is to be found both in the data and in anecdote. Trade with China has almost certainly grown more rapidly than North Korean GDP. And there is ample evidence from observers in the country that traded goods play a role in everything from construction, to intermediates, to consumer goods.

Yet sanctions do not lead automatically to a negotiated settlement. Indeed, sanctions gain their ultimate political utility precisely from being lifted. The question of the efficacy of sanctions is thus intimately tied to the negotiated quid-pro-quos that will have to be made to get to make progress on the nuclear front.

Xi Jinping, Donald Trump and the changing sanctions regime.

The fraught relationship between the U.S. and China at present obscures the surprising extent to which China has cooperated with the United States on the sanctions front. Perversely, China's centrality to the sanctions regime is partly a result of sanctions themselves. In 2003 – at the time the nuclear crisis broke – China, Japan and South Korea each accounted for about 20 percent of North Korea's trade; Russia's share was actually trivial and the U.S. effectively conducted no trade. Fast forward to the present and the steady layering on of bilateral and multilateral sanctions has left China as the mainstay of the North Korean economy, accounting for somewhere around 90-95 percent of the country's total trade. And that could actually underestimate the relationship if subsidized fuel shipments are included.

Multilateral sanctions were first imposed on North Korea in 2006 in response to missile tests and the first nuclear test. A raft of additional UN Security Council resolutions made marginal additions to these measures following further tests: in 2009, 2013, 2016 and 2017. But until 2016, precisely because of the Chinese veto on the Security Council, sanctions were initially defined relatively narrowly around WMD-related matériel and major weapons systems. Even the gradual introduction of complementary multilateral sanctions on financial flows and aid was similarly tied to WMD and weapons-related activities and did not, in principle, affect the financing of commercial trade.

In 2016, however, China's posture underwent a subtle shift, largely as a result of its own interests and concerns. Crises over nuclear and missile tests were taking place on China's – indeed on Beijing's – doorstep. Even if U.S. military options appeared limited, the escalation of tensions only strengthened U.S. alliance relationships with Japan and Korea, including around sensitive issues like ballistic missile defense. Two crucial Security Council resolutions in 2016 – UNSC 2270 and 2321 – targeted commercial trade for the first time, most notably by capping major commercial exports such as coal.

Enter President Donald Trump. At the Mar-a-Lago summit in April 2017, Trump and Xi Jinping appeared to reach a tacit agreement. The Trump administration would delay its plans to impose tariffs on Chinese exports in return for cooperation on North Korea.

However, the U.S. might have misread how far Beijing was willing to go. China's declaratory policy on North Korea's nuclear program has always been unambiguous: that North Korea should shutter its nuclear weapons program and return to prior commitments under the Non-Proliferation Treaty. But Chinese policy elites are clearly divided on how far to push. While some view the Kim dynasty as a strategic liability, others believe that the continued existence of North Korea is preferable to a unified Korea and the greater proximity to the Chinese border it would allow for American and ROK forces.

Yet even short of such a view of North Korea as a strategic asset, China faces a host of other prudential concerns about applying pressure. These range from the general uncertainty such pressure might bring, to the effect on provincial economic interests and the risks of large population movements were the North Korean economy to implode.

Partly for these reasons, China's declaratory policy also includes two other components: a commitment to settling all relevant issues through negotiations; and maintaining "peace and stability" on and around the peninsula. From China's response to particular provocations, it is clear that the meaning of maintaining "peace and stability" included opposition even to deterrent and defensive reactions to North Korea's provocations and a preference for the "stability" of the Kim dynasty itself. In sum, there are clear limits – if not precisely known – in how far China will go to sanction North Korea.

Détente: sanctions relief in the summit era

The limits on China's willingness to squeeze North Korea have become more not less apparent following the détente on the peninsula in the aftermath of the Winter Olympics and the succession of summits that followed in its wake, including between Kim Jong Un and Moon Jae In, Xi Jinping and Donald Trump.

Until very recently, the Trump administration has held to the view that the pressure campaign would remain in place until Kim Jong Un not only relented on his nuclear ambitions but actually moved to dismantle the program. China, however, has long held that sanctions are a tool for reaching a settlement and certainly not an end in themselves; sanctions relief would inevitably be a part of the negotiation process itself, not just its outcome. The aggressive pursuit of secondary sanctions on the part of the U.S. under the Trump administration – an important innovation of his administration – has not been able to deter a selective relaxation of sanctions over the course of 2018, through smuggling and probably through the land ports with China as well.

The Singapore summit between Kim Jong Un and Donald Trump played an unanticipated role in putting sanctions back on the table. Both supporters and skeptics of the summit agreed that there were downside risks of Trump meeting one-on-one with Kim Jong Un with limited opportunity for prior negotiations.

The summit document was surprising not only in its brevity and lack of substance, but also in evidence that the North Korean team had subtly stage-managed the agenda. The very order of the four bullet points – improving and normalizing the DPRK-US relationship; working toward a peace regime; denuclearization; and return of soldiers' remains – demonstrated Kim Jong Un's priorities. Any discussion of denuclearization must be undertaken in the context of the first two parts of the agreement, and each of those pointed in the direction of sanctions relief.

Normalization of relations clearly meant that the United States would have to rethink its "hostile policy," of which sanctions was the central instrument. And discussion of a wider peace regime implied a broader normalization with all of North Korea's neighbors, including South Korea and perhaps even Japan. As had all presidents going back to Roh Tae-woo, President Moon Jae-in articulated his own vision of a Northeast Asia peace and security architecture in which trade, investment and aid would play a central role.

Moving forward: the role of sanctions relief

As the American intelligence community openly affirmed at the end of January 2019, the idea that the Trump administration could reach an Iran-like deal with North Korea – in which negotiated quid-pro-quos were consummated in one large package – was always an illusion. I don't know a single North Korea watcher who believes that the prospects of complete, verifiable and irreversible dismantlement of Pyongyang's nuclear-industrial complex are good. Yet neither of those facts affects the need to put in place a robust negotiating process that could make progress on some interim steps; this is likely to be the most significant outcome of a second summit.

US bargaining power in getting to a nuclear deal has not only been weakened by commitments undertaken at the Singapore summit. It is also important to understand some important geostrategic and political realities. Pyongyang continues to hold Seoul hostage to artillery attack; military options are limited. And while sanctions have clearly played a role in moving Kim Jong Un to the table, China's ongoing patronage makes maintenance of the pressure campaign an ongoing challenge.

What role will sanctions relief play in this next stage? Perhaps there will be some deals struck at the summit itself, such as an aspirational statement on replacing the armistice, destruction of this or that for the international press, or a codification of a freeze: on nuclear and missile testing (which the North Koreans have smartly suspended) or production of fissile material or missile manufacturing and deployment (which they have decidedly not suspended).

Given the difficulty of getting a credible declaration of North Korea's facilities, however, the likely path forward will probably gravitate back to Bush negotiator Christopher Hill's strategy in 2008: to focus on Yongbyon as an entry point, with some selective sanctions relief as the quid pro quo. Freezing Yongbyon with International Atomic Energy Agency inspectors on the ground would be one such interim step but we can imagine others.

In return, however, the U.S. will have to consider sanctions relief. This is not likely to occur through revision of UN Security Council resolutions or secondary sanctions; if those were unwound, the game would be up and North Korea could slow the negotiation process to a crawl as it did in 2007-8.

Rather, the obvious trade is to give the Moon administration some running room with respect to North-South economic relations. Understanding why takes us to some key features of South Korean politics. For some time, the dominant cleavage in South Korean politics has been over how to manage the North Koreans. Conservatives favor a strong alliance with the U.S. and a robust deterrence and are skeptical about engagement. The impeachment of Park Geun Hye brought a center-left president to power, however, and one who has been particularly anxious to push forward his vision of détente in North-South relations.

Sanctions are a piece of that gambit. South Korea imposed sweeping sanctions on North Korea following the sinking of a South Korean navy corvette, the Cheonan, in 2010. However they left open joint projects with the North, most notably the Kaesong Industrial complex. This too was shuttered in 2016 in the wake of yet another North Korean nuclear test. But the Moon administration has a wide array of possible projects it could advance if exceptions were granted to the multilateral sanctions regime and the U.S. and South Korea coordinated, including reopening shuttered projects and road and rail connections that would provide the infrastructural foundation for deeper integration in the future. The risks that a wide opening of North-South relations would weaken the overall sanctions effort is real. But if taken in small steps that do not commit large amount of resources prior to progress on the nuclear front, it could be a gamble worth taking.

By way of conclusion

At this writing we are still awaiting the final announcement of the second Kim-Trump summit. Yet going forward, the crafting of sanctions relief for incremental progress on the nuclear and missile front has already been acknowledged as a likely outcome by none other than perennial North Korea hawk John Bolton. Putting in place both high-level and lower-level technical talks will be the most important outcome of the summit given the limited time to negotiate a more wide-ranging agreement.

I close on one further dilemma, though, as it could further complicate these trades going forward. North Korea appears to believe that its foreign economic relations are shaped primarily by sanctions. But the steady decline in North Korea's trade with the world outside of China is also the result of perceived risks generated by its nuclear and missile program and notoriously weak protection of property rights and contract. If trade is falling because traders and investors have no confidence in the regime's economic policies, then lifting sanctions could have scant material effect. Lifting sanctions is clearly only the very first step in the much broader challenge of opening the North Korean economy.

14

The History and Meaning Of Denuclearization

Daniel Sneider

Since the signing of the armistice agreement in 1953, the central goal of U.S. security policy in Korea has been to prevent the outbreak of another war there. American military forces have been stationed continuously on the peninsula to deter another North Korean attack on the south and to signal U.S. commitment to the security of its ally, the Republic of Korea (ROK). That goal has remained the animating purpose of the alliance, at least until now.

Over a quarter of a century ago, however, U.S. policy acquired a second, and to some degree overlapping, focus – the denuclearization of the Korean peninsula. The emergence of this focus of American policy was a direct response to the North Korean effort to develop the capacity to produce fissile material for nuclear weapons. U.S. concern was greatly heightened by North Korea's 1993 declaration of its intent to withdraw from the Nuclear Non-Proliferation Treaty following International Atomic Energy Agency (IAEA) accusations that it was cheating on the agreement.[1]

The goal of preventing North Korea from acquiring nuclear weapons is consistent with the broader security policy of deterring war on the peninsula. A nuclear North Korea would pose a significantly greater military threat to South Korea. The North's leaders might also be likelier to seek again to unify the peninsula on their terms, this time under the coercive cover of a nuclear threat. But the goal also embodies a distinct U.S. policy goal of nuclear non-proliferation, one that led the U.S. in the mid-1970s to threaten to end its security

---

1 "Chronology of U.S.-North Korean Nuclear and Missile Diplomacy," Arms Control Association, https://www.armscontrol.org/factsheets/dprkchron

alliance with the ROK if it pursued its own covert nuclear weapons program. The U.S. counter proliferation goal extends to blocking any North Korean export of nuclear materials or knowhow to other countries or third parties.

While there has been some confusion on the point, U.S. policy has long accepted the idea that denuclearization refers to the denuclearization of the entire Korean peninsula. That is coherent with U.S. non-proliferation policy toward the ROK and it flows directly from the decision made by President George Bush in September, 1991 to announce the unilateral withdrawal of all naval and land-based nuclear weapons deployed abroad. This included nuclear weapons that had been deployed in South Korea for 33 years until fully withdrawn at the end of 1991.[2] For the U.S., "denuclearization of the Korean peninsula" has very specifically referred to the existence and deployment of nuclear weapons within Korea, north and south, and clearly not to its global deployment of strategic weapons, which have never been understood to be a subject of negotiation.

President Bush's announcement on tactical nuclear weapons led South Korean President Roh Tae Woo to declare in early November, 1991 that his country would not produce, possess, store, deploy or use nuclear weapons, including building its own nuclear reprocessing or uranium enrichment facilities. This was intended to encourage North Korea to allow IAEA inspections of its nuclear facilities.

With the U.S. putting such a high priority on North Korea's denuclearization, the ROK, especially under progressive administrations, has focused more on the threat of conventional war and on the eventual goal of reunification of the peninsula than on denuclearization. North Korea, for its part, usually refused to engage in any depth with South Korea on nuclear issues. Thus, for example, the North-South summits held in 2000 and 2007 notably made no direct mention of nuclear weapons. President Moon, in his meetings with Kim Jong Un, has discussed the nuclear issue but apparently only in terms of general principles.

2   Hans M. Kristensen & Robert S. Norris, "A history of US nuclear weapons in South Korea," Bulletin of the Atomic Scientists, November, 2017, 73:6, 349-357, DOI: 10.1080/00963402.2017.1388656

That was not, however, always the case. The first clear commitment of North Korea on this issue is the product of the joint North-South declaration on the "Denuclearization of the Korean Peninsula" signed on January 20, 1992.[3] In that document, the two Koreas pledged not to "manufacture, produce, receive, possess, store, deploy or use nuclear weapons," and also not to "possess nuclear reprocessing and uranium enrichment facilities." They also agreed to mutual inspections to verify this agreement. Needless to say, only South Korea has lived up to this initial agreement.

Denuclearization in the U.S. approach to DPRK negotiations

After the breakdown of the 1992 North-South declaration, the locus of denuclearization discussion shifted to U.S.-led diplomacy. The North Korean refusal to allow IAEA inspectors to access its undeclared sites to verify its account of fissile material production – a persistent feature of North Korean nuclear diplomacy – led to a crisis accompanied by clear U.S. threats to carry out military action against nuclear sites. That yielded the October 21, 1994 U.S.-DPRK Agreed Framework which remains a reference point for all subsequent agreements to freeze and eventually disable North Korea's nuclear weapons-related capacity.[4]

In that agreement, the U.S. (in cooperation with Japan, South Korea and the EU) committed to supply North Korea with modern light-water reactors to generate electricity and to supply heavy fuel oil in the interim. In return, North Korea would halt the operations of its plutonium reactor and related facilities, submit to IAEA inspection, and comply with an intrusive IAEA inspection regime. Importantly, the language of the agreement committed the parties to "work together for peace and security on a nuclear-free Korean peninsula."

3   The full text of the declaration can be found at https://peacemaker.un.org/sites/peacemaker .un.org/files/KR %20KP_920120_JointDeclarationDenuclearizationKoreanPeninsula.pdf
4   The full text of the agreement can be found at https://www.nti.org/media/pdfs/aptagframe .pdf

Issues of compliance with that agreement emerged almost from the start. The North Korean pursuit of long-range ballistic missile and rocket programs raised suspicions that work on delivery systems for nuclear warheads was ongoing, while there was also growing evidence of a clandestine program to produce highly enriched uranium (HEU) which could provide an alternative fissile material for nuclear weapons to the plutonium extracted from the spent fuel of North Korea's so-called research reactor.

The breakdown of the Agreed Framework early in the Bush administration led to the prolonged Six-Party Talks in Beijing. The most basic substantive product of that negotiation was the joint statement of the fourth round of talks, signed on September 19, 2005.[5] From a definitional point of view, the language adopted remains another essential reference point. It proclaims the shared goal of "the verifiable denuclearization of the Korean peninsula in a peaceful manner." For U.S. negotiators, the core is this North Korean pledge: "The D.P.R.K. committed to abandoning all nuclear weapons and existing nuclear programs and returning, at an early date, to the Treaty on the Nonproliferation of Nuclear Weapons and to IAEA safeguards." The U.S. also reaffirmed its willingness, first stated in the third round of the Six-Party talks, to pursue this goal through phased and coordinated steps.

From the point of view of U.S. policy, it is clear that agreements to freeze the North Korean nuclear program, including halts in operation of its reactor and other fissile material production facilities and in the testing of nuclear weapons or delivery systems are intended as interim measures on the road to complete denuclearization. This has been true even after North Korea's first nuclear test, in October 2006, which dramatically demonstrated its capacity to build a functioning nuclear weapon, as well as after North Korea acknowledged the existence of its HEU program in 2010. Those actions only served to underscore the necessity of both a declaration of facilities and stockpiles of material and weapons and the need for an intrusive inspection regime, including of non-declared sites.

---

5   The full text is available at https://www.state.gov/p/eap/regional/c15455.htm

Attempts to restore an interim freeze agreement, conceptually not fundamentally different than the 1994 Agreed Framework, failed both at the close of the Bush administration and again during the Obama administration (the so-called 2012 Leap Day agreement). Despite some changes in language – for example, the adoption of the term "complete, verifiable, and irreversible denuclearization" (CVID), now replaced in the Trump administration by the term "final, fully verified denuclearization" (FFVD) – the U.S. remains committed to the principles agreed to in 2005.

It bears reiterating that this consistency has persisted into the Trump administration, even though the President himself, and some of his senior officials, claim to have departed fundamentally from the policies of previous administrations regarding North Korea. The Trump administration's stated goal remains complete denuclearization, while accepting the necessity of phased steps toward that end. In this regard, senior administration officials (leaving aside for the moment the President himself) have sought in their talks with North Korea an agreement on a defined timetable for denuclearization and a verification process that would begin with the declaration by the North Koreans of its inventory of fissile materials, weapons, and facilities for the production and storage of nuclear materials.[6] As we will discuss below, the North Koreans have balked at holding any detailed discussion of these issues, whether by their heads of state or lower-ranking officials.

The shift in North Korea's definition

If the U.S. has been largely consistent in its understanding and approach towards denuclearization, North Korea has been much less so in its public policy. While embracing the broad notion of denuclearization, North Korea has shifted its definition of the precondi-

6   Evans J.R. Revere, "U.S. Policy and Pyongyang's Game Plan: Will We Accept a Nuclear-Armed North Korea?," Brookings Institution Policy Brief, August, 2018, https://www.brookings .edu/wp-content/uploads/2018/08/FP_20180823_pyongyang_game_plan.pdf

tion for denuclearization – namely the end of the U.S. "threat" to the DPRK. The North Korean regime sees nuclear weapons as a means of neutralizing the imbalance in conventional armed forces, particularly in the air, holding a U.S. armed intervention on the scale of the Korean War at bay, and potentially facilitating reunification of Korea on its terms.

As we discuss in more detail below, the precise definition of what constitutes that U.S. threat has been widened to include not only the presence of U.S. military forces in the ROK but even the deployment of nuclear-capable U.S. forces beyond the borders of Korea itself. The question of whether denuclearization is even possible has also been subject to changing policy declarations from Pyongyang, particularly since the 2006 and subsequent tests of nuclear devices led to the enshrinement of its nuclear status in the North Korean constitution.[7]

This has all been stated even more boldly since the elevation of Kim Jong Un to leadership in North Korea following the death of his father, Kim Jong Il. In a March 2012 meeting with a group of American experts and former officials, North Korean Foreign Minister Ri Yong Ho explained that when the U.S. "threat" is removed, the DPRK will eventually feel secure enough and "in 10 or 20 years we will be able to consider denuclearization." Until that point, he said, the two countries could deal with each as two nuclear armed states, embarking on mutual arms control negotiations.[8]

After the third test of a nuclear device in February 2013, the North Korean regime declared its intention to pursue the dual goals of economic development and building its nuclear forces simultaneously. A report issued by a plenary meeting of the Central Committee of the Workers Party of Korea on March 31, 2013 stated this:

> The nuclear weapons of Songun [military-first] Korea are not goods for getting U.S. dollars and they are neither a political bargaining chip nor a thing for economic dealings to be

7   Ibid.
8   Ibid.

presented to the place of dialogue or be put on the table of negotiations aimed at forcing the DPRK to disarm itself.

The DPRK's nuclear armed forces represent the nation's life which can never be abandoned as long as the imperialists and nuclear threats exist on earth. They are a treasure of a reunified country which can never be traded with billions of dollars.

Only when the nuclear shield for self-defence is held fast, will it be possible to shatter the U.S. imperialists' ambition for annexing the Korean Peninsula by force and making the Korean people modern slaves, firmly defend our ideology, social system and all other socialist treasures won at the cost of blood and safeguard the nation's right to existence and its time-honored history and brilliant culture.

When the party's new line is thoroughly carried out, the DPRK will emerge as a great political, military and socialist economic power and a highly-civilized country which steers the era of independence.[9]

After an accelerated program of testing both nuclear devices and ballistic missile delivery systems, Kim Jong Un declared at the end of 2017 that the "historic tasks" of the two front policy had been accomplished and the country had now acquired "a powerful trea-sured sword," namely its nuclear arsenal.

The Kim-Moon-Trump agreements and denuclearization

On that basis, the North Koreans have concertedly entered into negotiations with both the ROK and the U.S. with the immediate aim of reducing tensions, removing the pressure of economic sanc-tions, and undermining the U.S.-ROK security alliance. In that

---

9   Cited in Joshua Pollack, "Denuclearization of the Korean Peninsula: Reviewing the Precedents," Arms Control Wonk, June 10, 2018. https://www.armscontrolwonk.com/archive/1205354/denuclearization-of-the-korean-peninsula-reviewing-the-precedents/

context, denuclearization has again been embraced as the shared goal of all parties, but with some important redefinition on the part of Pyongyang. Following the opening of contacts at the Winter Olympic Games in South Korea in early 2018, senior officials from the two Koreas met and agreed to hold a summit at the end of April of that year and announced that North Korea would halt testing of missiles and nuclear devices during talks with the U.S.

The next step in this negotiation process was the inter-Korean summit between Kim and South Korean President Moon Jae-in held on April 27, 2018 at Panmunjom inside the Demilitarized Zone. The joint declaration issued at that summit included, for the first time since 1992, language referring to nuclear weapons. It stated that:

> South and North Korea confirmed the common goal of realizing, through complete denuclearization, a nuclear-free Korean Peninsula. South and North Korea shared the view that the measures initiated by North Korea are very meaningful and crucial for the denuclearization of the Korean peninsula and agreed to carry out their respective roles and responsibilities in this regard. South and North Korea agreed to actively seek the support and cooperation of the international community for the denuclearization of the Korean Peninsula.[10]

In contacts carried out mainly through intelligence channels and also mediated by the South Korean government, Pyongyang and Washington negotiated the convening of a Kim-Trump summit. As this writer learned through discussions with senior Trump administration officials, those contacts were almost entirely confined to the logistics and planning for the summit itself, not to the substance of denuclearization. Kim Jong Un, through intermediaries and in direct meetings with both South Korean and U.S. officials (Secretary of State Mike Pompeo and CIA Korea Mission

---

10   Full text of the joint declaration is available at https://en.yna.co.kr/view/AEN20180427013900315

Center director Andrew Kim) confirmed that he was prepared to
talk about nuclear issues but also sought the signing of a peace treaty
to formally end the armistice agreement, along with other measures
that the North Koreans assert would demonstrate the easing of U.S.
hostility towards his regime.[11]

Kim sweetened the pot by blowing up the entrance to the North
Korean nuclear test site at Punggye-ri in view of foreign reporters. But
he refused efforts to negotiate a summit agreement that would spell
out a clear timetable of phased steps for denuclearization and a verification regime. The U.S. negotiators were also undercut by President
Trump's determination to go ahead with the meeting, without such
preparation, thus strengthening the hand of the North Koreans.[12]

The result was a joint statement that was the weakest formulation ever reached in the quarter century of U.S.-DPRK denuclearization negotiation. Before referring to denuclearization, it listed first
the establishment of peaceful relations and the creation of a "peace
regime" to replace the current armistice – mirroring North Korea's
policy priorities and echoing the Panmunjon declaration. And when
it came to nuclear issues, it also explicitly used the Moon-Kim summit
declaration as the reference point, unprecedented in such talks.
Without further elaboration, the declaration stated:

> Reaffirming the April 27, 2018 Panmunjom Declaration, the
> DPRK commits to work toward complete denuclearization of
> the Korean Peninsula.[13]

Secretary Pompeo and his team returned to Pyongyang in early July
to attempt to again hold detailed discussions on a timetable for denuclearization, in phased steps, as well as a facilities and stockpile decla-

---

11   Daniel Sneider, "History in Singapore- Made or Remade?," Tokyo Business Today,
Toyo Keizai Online, June 11, 2018. https://toyokeizai.net/articles/-/224643
12   Daniel Sneider, "Negotiating With North Korea – Two Roads That May Not Meet,"
Tokyo Business Today, Toyo Keizai Online, July 16, 2018. https://toyokeizai.net/articles/-/229635
13   For full text, https://www.whitehouse.gov/briefings-statements/joint-statement-president
-donald-j-trump-united-states-america-chairman-kim-jong-un-democratic-peoples-republic
-korea-singapore-summit/

ration. On the latter point, South Korean officials and some American observers have suggested this was too provocative a demand – that the North Koreans would see this as handing over a 'target list' to the U.S. But as discussed above, this is a consistent issue going back to the IAEA's talks with North Korea in the early 90s, when the need for a detailed declaration was viewed as essential due to the lack of credibility of DPRK-provided declarations of facilities and fissile material stockpiles. The request for such a declaration as a starting point is therefore not new, nor is North Korea's refusal to comply.

In any case, the North Koreans rudely rejected Pompeo, refusing him a meeting with Kim and taunting him that he was out of step with his own president.[14] In a statement issued by the North Korean foreign ministry after the visit, Pompeo was assailed for pushing a "unilateral and gangster-like demand for denuclearization." The statement pointed to the need to first issue a declaration of the end of war, arguing that the U.S. had failed to respond to the steps it had already taken. "The issues the U.S. side insisted on during the talks were the same cancerous ones that the past U.S. administrations had insisted on," the ministry said.[15]

The message from North Korea is that denuclearization can only come after the relationship of the U.S. to the Korean peninsula has fundamentally changed. At the heart of that aim is the North Korean desire to separate the South from its American partner. "Pyongyang almost certainly believes that a peace regime or peace treaty will eliminate the justification for the presence of U.S. forces in the South," concludes former senior State Department official Evans Revere.[16]

After this visit, the Trump administration sought a second trip to Pyongyang in late August to try again to negotiate an agreement.

14   Daniel Sneider, "Behind the Chaos of Washington's Korea Policy," Tokyo Business Today, Toyo Keizai Online, August 27, 2018. https://toyokeizai.net/articles/-/235272
15   Gardiner Harris and Choe Sang-Hun, "North Korea Criticizes 'Gangster-Like' U.S. Attitude After Talks with Mike Pompeo," New York Times, July 7, 2018. https://www.nytimes.com/2018/07/07/world/asia/mike-pompeo-north-korea-pyongyang.html
16   Evans J.R. Revere, "U.S. Policy and Pyongyang's Game Plan: Will We Accept a Nuclear-Armed North Korea?," Brookings Institution Policy Brief, August, 2018, https://www.brookings.edu/wp-content/uploads/2018/08/FP_20180823_pyongyang_game_plan.pdf

This time the administration was prepared to offer a "declaration for declaration," that is to give the North Koreans a political declaration of the end of the state of war in exchange for a North Korean facilities declaration.[17] But the trip was called off at the last minute when it became clear the North Koreans were not prepared to make a facilities declaration.

The new version of denuclearization – U.S. withdrawal

In subsequent statements, the North Korean regime has advanced other versions of what it seeks, including especially the lifting of economic sanctions. At the second Moon-Kim summit in Pyongyang in September 2018, North Korea committed to dismantling a test site for missile engines and to take unspecific steps to dismantle nuclear facilities at its main nuclear program site in Yongbyon, provided the U.S. took "corresponding measures." Pompeo finally went to Pyongyang in October 2018 but again the agenda focused on arranging a second U.S.-DPRK summit, where Kim was apparently confident he could again get what he wanted in direct talks with President Trump.

In a revealing official commentary issued on December 20, 2018 in the name of Jong Hyon, the North Koreans came back to the issue of how they defined denuclearization. It stated:

> When we refer to the Korean peninsula, they include both the area of the DPRK and the area of south Korea where aggression troops including the nuclear weapons of the U.S. are deployed. When we refer to the denuclearization of the Korean peninsula, it, therefore, means removing all elements of nuclear threats from the areas of both the north and the south of Korea and also from surrounding areas from where the Korean peninsula is targeted.

---

17   Daniel Sneider, "Behind the Chaos of Washington's Korea Policy," Tokyo Business Today, Toyo Keizai Online, August 27, 2018. https://toyokeizai.net/articles/-/235272

> It was the U.S. misguided understanding of the denucle-
> arization of the Korean peninsula. In other words, the U.S.
> regards the big concept of the denuclearization of the Korean
> peninsula as the same as the partial concept of the 'denuclear-
> ization of north Korea.' The June 12 DPRK-U.S. joint state-
> ment signed by the top leaders of both sides and supported by
> the whole world does not contain any phrase called 'denucle-
> arization of north Korea'.[18]

Former Central Intelligence Agency and State Department Intelligence analyst Robert Carlin argues that this is not a new North Korean position nor is it entirely untrue. In a larger sense, that is accurate, as we have discussed above. The poorly worded nature of the Singapore Statement, along with the President's decision to suspend joint U.S.-ROK military exercises, left itself open to precisely this formulation, thereby linking both to the issue of denuclearization.

What is pointedly untrue, and in some sense new, is the assertion that U.S. nuclear weapons continue to be deployed in Korea and the reference to "surrounding areas from where the Korean peninsula is targeted." The latter formulation suggests U.S. forces based else-where in the region – Japan and Guam for example – are now to be included in the process of denuclearization. This was spelled out in a less noticed statement issued on July 6, 2016, Carlin wrote. That document not only called for the 'abolishment' of all nuclear weap-ons and "their bases in South Korea" but also the "withdrawal of the U.S. forces, which hold the right to use nuclear weapons, from South Korea," as well as a ban on their introduction to surrounding areas.

The implication of the North Korean definition of how denucle-arization might proceed is that the U.S. must first accept Pyongyang's status as a nuclear weapons state, and negotiate mutual "arms control" agreements on that basis. In that formulation, denuclearization is a ultimate goal, akin to the vague aim of 'getting to zero.' To date, no

18   Robert Carlin, "DPRK Repeats Stance on Denuclearization," 38north, December 21, 2018. https://www.38north.org/2018/12/rcarlin122118/

U.S. administration has been willing to accept the nuclear status quo in Korea, and while the current South Korean government may be open to this idea, it has not stepped away publicly from the long standing ROK policy strongly opposing such a dramatic change.

Whither denuclearization

The definitional gap on denuclearization between North Korea and the United States is thus both persistent and historically rooted.

The United States has always seen denuclearization as the complete elimination of all nuclear weapons, fissile material, and the capacity to develop them, as well as to export them. Nevertheless, it has been prepared to accepted a phased process of elimination in which freezes and moratoriums on the operation of North Korean nuclear facilities were real steps toward that end. In accordance with that goal, the U.S., along with the international community (the IAEA mainly), has consistently sought a verification and inspection regime that would require full disclosure of all nuclear-related facilities and access to them, including undeclared facilities.

The establishment of a durable peace on the Korean peninsula, one which would eventually preclude the necessity of a U.S. military presence there, must, in this view, rest upon successful denuclearization.

North Korea has always defined denuclearization as a process that begins with the removal of a U.S. "threat" that justifies its development of nuclear weapons. The definition of that threat has shifted over time but it has always involved the presence of U.S. military forces on the Peninsula. This definition, however, expanded to explicitly include the deployment of strategically capable forces in the Western Pacific, if not beyond. North Korea has never been willing to allow an inspection or verification regime to have access to undeclared facilities or to put all of its most vital facilities under surveillance.

Some observers suggest that this gap is a product of failure of communication and a lack of trust. They argue this could be overcome through a process of trust building through mutual steps, albeit one that could take as long as 15 years to reach its final goal. And they point to past negotiations as evidence this trust building process will yield success if pursued consistently. [19]

While that may be a reassuring idea, the history of the last quarter century of denuclearization negotiations demonstrates that the definitional gap is unbridgeable, absent a fundamental change in the policy of either North Korea or the United States. Both may be possible, though experience suggests flexibility and change are more likely in the case of the United States than North Korea.

19   In this regard, see Siegfried S. Hecker, Robert L. Carlin, and Elliot A. Serbin, "A Comprehensive History of North Korea's Nuclear Program," Stanford Center for International Security and Cooperation. https://cisac.fsi.stanford.edu/content/cisac-north-korea

15

The Vexations of Verification

Gary Samore

Steps toward denuclearization

At their historic summit in Singapore on June 12, 2018, President Trump and DPRK Chairman Kim Jong Un agreed to a general commitment to "work toward complete denuclearization of the Korean Peninsula."[1] On September 20, 2018, at a summit in Pyongyang with South Korean President Moon Jae In, Kim Jong Un announced more specific measures to "permanently dismantle the Dongchang-ri missile engine test site and launch platform under the observation of experts from relevant countries" and "permanent dismantlement of the nuclear facilities in Yongbyon, as the United States takes corresponding measures in accordance with the spirit of the June 12 US-DPRK Joint Statement."[2] Perhaps going a step further toward offering to freeze North Korea's nuclear weapons program, Kim Jong Un proclaimed in his 2019 New Year's Address (according to the official North Korean translation) that "we declared at home and abroad that *we would neither make and test nuclear weapons any longer nor use and proliferate them* [emphasis added]."[3]

The Trump administration also seems to be seeking concrete measures towards the ultimate objective of "final fully verified denuclearization." In a speech at Stanford University on January 31, 2019, U.S. Special Representative Stephen Biegun offered a broad inter-

---

1 https://www.whitehouse.gov/briefings-statements/joint-statement-president-donald-j-trump-united-states-america-chairman-kim-jong-un-democratic-peoples-republic-korea-singapore-summit/

2 https://www.koreatimes.co.kr/www/nation/2018/09/103_255848.html

3 https://www.ncnk.org/resources/publications/kimjongun_2019_newyearaddress.pdf/file_view

pretation of Kim Jong Un's commitments. According to Biegun, "Chairman Kim also committed, in both the joint statement from the aforementioned Pyongyang summit as well as during the Secretary of State's October meetings in Pyongyang, to the dismantlement and destruction of North Korea's plutonium and uranium enrichment facilities. This complex of sites that extends beyond Yongbyon represents the totality of North Korea's plutonium reprocessing and uranium enrichment programs."[4]

Beyond the immediate step of shutting down and dismantling North Korea's facilities to produce fissile material, Biegun also outlined the U.S. requirements for "final, fully verified denuclearization." In his Stanford speech, Special Representative Biegun said, "Before the process of denuclearization can be final, we must also have a complete understanding of the full extent of the North Korean weapons of mass destruction missile programs. We will get that at some point through a comprehensive declaration. We must reach agreement on expert access and monitoring mechanisms of key sites to international standards. And ultimately, we need to ensure the removal and destruction of stockpiles of fissile material, weapons, missiles, launchers, and other weapons of mass destruction."

The challenge of verificaiton

This article evaluates the feasibility and requirements for verifying North Korean compliance with a range of agreements to freeze, reduce, and ultimately eliminate its nuclear weapons program. To be blunt, would we be able to catch North Korea cheating, as it has done on every nuclear agreement since it joined the NPT in 1985?[5]

In general, verification of arms control agreements consists of both independent capabilities and cooperative arrangements. Independent capabilities are euphemistically referred to as "national technical

4   https://www.state.gov/p/eap/rls/rm/2019/01/288702.htm
5   For a brief history of North Korea's denial and deception efforts, see https://thebulletin .org/2018/08/north-korean-verification-good-enough-for-government-work/

means" – U.S. intelligence systems for monitoring North Korean activities through space-based and other assets and traditional intelligence-collection methods – GEOINT, MASINT, HUMINT, SIGINT and so forth. Cooperative arrangements refer to the declaration, monitoring and inspection mechanisms negotiated by the U.S. and DPRK and incorporated into the nuclear agreement itself. Such cooperative arrangements normally include a mechanism for resolving ambiguities or disputes about compliance through requirements for providing additional information or access to undeclared facilities or activities.

Ideally, independent capabilities and cooperative arrangements reinforce each other to strengthen the overall verification system. For example, satellite imagery may detect suspicious activity that can be investigated further through inspections, if the cooperative arrangements permit access to undeclared facilities. Alternatively, information obtained from permitted access to facilities, personnel and records could help inform intelligence collection.

Since the effectiveness of intelligence collection by the U.S. and its allies against North Korean nuclear and missile activities is highly secret (and subject to change for better or worse), it is difficult to provide an unclassified assessment of potential verification arrangements. In theory, if one had high confidence in the reliability of "national technical means" to detect certain kinds of violations, less robust cooperative arrangements might be acceptable. Conversely, a comprehensive and intrusive system for cooperative arrangements is even more essential if intelligence collection is spotty and uncertain.

As a practical matter, no verification system is perfect. This is especially true in the case of North Korea, given its long history of lying and cheating, likely resistance to intrusive inspections and monitoring systems, and limits on intelligence collection. In the end, the adequacy of any verification system will based on a political judgment, weighing the degree of confidence in monitoring compliance verses the value of limiting or constraining North Korea's nuclear and missile capabilities. Moreover, the effectiveness of a verification system depends on timeliness – how quickly can violations be detected relative to the proscribed activity? Detecting a secret uranium enrichment plant at an initial stage of construction is preferable to detecting it after the facility is up and running.

Finally, one must consider the significance of the violation with respect to the main purpose of the agreement. An acceptable verification system could attain relatively high confidence in detecting significant violations, while allowing for lower confidence in detecting violations that are judged to be less significant. For example, verifying a halt to uranium enrichment could focus on detecting enrichment facilities of sufficient size to produce significant quantities of enriched uranium, recognizing that a few scientists experimenting with a few centrifuge machines is probably not detectable with high confidence.

With these qualifications in mind, what would be required to verify Kim Jong Un's claim not to make, test, use or proliferate nuclear weapons?

No use of nuclear weapons

Under plausible scenarios, non-use of nuclear weapons can be verified through independent capabilities. Any nuclear warhead delivered by missile or military aircraft can be reliably and immediately attributable to North Korean territory. In theory, North Korea could attempt to deliver a nuclear weapon through clandestine means (e.g., a nuclear device aboard a tramp steamer pulling into port or a nuclear device smuggled into a city), but this scenario seems highly unlikely. Whatever the dubious value of such an attack, North Korean leaders would have to contend with the risk that nuclear forensics after the explosion could determine the origin of the fissile material used in the nuclear device and therefore expose North Korea to devastating retaliation.

No testing of nuclear weapons

For the most part, verification of no nuclear testing can be completed with independent technical means that do not require the cooperation of the North Korean government. An atmospheric nuclear test would be immediately detected. For underground nuclear testing, the Comprehensive Test Ban Treaty Organization (CTBO) based in Vienna has already demonstrated that its worldwide seismic monitoring system can detect underground nuclear tests as small as 1 kiloton – the estimated yield of North Korea's first nuclear test in 2006. The CTBO monitoring system is supplemented by various national monitoring systems in the vicinity of North Korean territory.

In theory, North Korea might attempt to evade a test moratorium by conducting extremely low yield underground nuclear tests, but it is not clear that such tests would be of much scientific value to North Korea. From all available evidence, North Korea has already achieved reliable designs for both fission and fusion weapons so further nuclear testing is not required. In any event, even low yield tests would risk detection (or suspicion of violation) because of extremely sophisticated seismic monitoring systems and other intelligence collection.

It should be noted that a moratorium on nuclear tests does not prevent North Korea from making some qualitative improvements to its nuclear weapons arsenal. Various improvements in design and engineering can be achieved without full nuclear testing. The U.S. may have some independent means to monitor North Korean nuclear weapons research and development, but North Korea is unlikely to allow access to its nuclear weapons scientists and research facilities necessary to verify that North Korea is not making quantitative improvements in its nuclear arsenal.

Finally, the moratorium on nuclear testing is easily reversible. In May 2018, North Korea invited international journalists to witness a convincing display of blowing up critical parts of its Punggye-ri nuclear test site, including above ground support buildings and portals to the nuclear test tunnels.[6] During Secretary of State Pompeo's meetings

6   https://www.38north.org/2018/05/punggye052518/

in Pyongyang in October 2018, Chairman Kim committed to invite American experts to ensure the complete destruction of Punggye-ri. This is a symbolic gesture. Whether Punggye-ri is actually "destroyed" or only "damaged" is not significant because there are many other locations in North Korea's mountainous Northern provinces to construct a new nuclear test site. Even if the U.S. detected new tunneling in an area suitable for underground nuclear testing, it would be difficult to distinguish that activity from tunneling for other purposes, such as mining.

No transfer of nuclear weapons

There is no practical way to verify through cooperative means that North Korea is complying with a commitment not to transfer nuclear weapons to a foreign government or non-state actor, beyond independent monitoring by U.S. and other intelligence agencies. In theory, one could install an array of radiation detectors and other monitoring devices at North Korean seaports, airports and border crossings, but North Korea is not likely to accept such intrusive measures. In any case, such a monitoring system would not be very effective because North Korea could circumvent the system if it was aware of its location and operations.

To reinforce the credibility of a North Korean commitment not to transfer nuclear weapons, it might be desirable to clarify that its commitment includes nuclear materials, technology and equipment. While largely cosmetic, North Korea could also establish a formal legal and regulatory system controlling nuclear and dual-use exports. North Korea's credibility would be enhanced if it acknowledged and provided information on past nuclear transfers, such as its nuclear weapons-related cooperation with Pakistan and the export of a plutonium production rector and related facilities to Syria. Needless to say, Pyongyang is unlikely to be honest about its past indiscretions.

In the absence of cooperative measures, verifying non-transfer of nuclear weapons, materials and technology rests primarily on the shoulders of U.S. and allied intelligence services. Unfortunately, the failure of U.S. and other intelligence services to detect – in timely fashion – North Korean-Pakistani nuclear weapons cooperation and North Korean nuclear exports to Syria is a cautionary lesson in how onerous this task is. In truth, it is extraordinarily difficult to detect transfers of small packages (like nuclear bombs or kilograms of fissile material) or bits of technology before or during the transfer. Instead, Pyongyang must calculate the risk that a transfer of nuclear weapons would eventually be revealed, with potentially damaging consequences depending on the recipient and what the recipient does with the nuclear weapons it obtained from North Korea.

No production of nuclear weapons

Verifying that North Korea has halted production of nuclear weapons is challenging, but doable, provided that North Korea is prepared to accept adequate verification arrangements. The ideal system to verify that North Korea has ceased production of nuclear weapons would involve a means to account for North Korea's current nuclear force (types and numbers) and a means to periodically determine that this arsenal has not increased. One could imagine technical solutions to tag and monitor North Korea's nuclear weapons at production and storage facilities. However, none of these technical solutions is remotely plausible under current political conditions. For North Korea to allow foreign access to its nuclear weapons storage and production facilities sufficient to carry out verification of non-production would inevitably expose its nuclear forces to the threat of sabotage and pre-emptive attack.

As an alternative to "counting" nuclear warheads, one could try to set boundaries on North Korea's nuclear force by limiting or ending its production of special fissionable material – separated plutonium and enriched uranium. The "dismantlement and destruction" of North Korea's facilities to produce fissile material – as Special Representative Biegun has called for – is technically easier to verify and more politically plausible than directly verifying the cessation of nuclear weapons. Determining with high confidence that a nuclear facility is not operating and verifying that it has been "dismantled and destroyed" is not technically challenging through a combination of inspection and remote monitoring.

However, ending fissile material production would require North Korea to declare and allow international access to its entire nuclear fuel cycle infrastructure, including nuclear reactors, reprocessing and enrichment facilities, as well as associated facilities for uranium mining and milling, uranium conversion, fuel fabrication, centrifuge manufacture and so forth. Thus far, North Korea has shown no willingness to expose its suspected secret nuclear facilities outside Yongbyon to inspection, much less destruction. At least in public, Kim Jong Un has only offered to "permanently dismantle" nuclear facilities at Yongbyon, which have been inspected by the International Atomic Energy Agency (IAEA) numerous times over the years.

Verifying "dismantlement" of nuclear facilities at Yongbyon – as defined by U.S. and DPRK negotiators – is straightforward, but the significance for North Korea's overall nuclear weapons capabilities is much less clear. Destroying the Yongbyon reactors and reprocessing facility would remove North Korea's only known sources of plutonium production and reduce or potentially eliminate North Korea's access to tritium supplies. However, the significance of these limits on the number and type of nuclear weapons in North Korea's arsenal would require a detailed knowledge of North Korean nuclear weapons design, for example, the amounts and how plutonium and tritium are used in different types of weapons. Such information is not publicly available.

Dismantlement of the enrichment facility at Yongbyon would reduce the overall rate of weapons grade uranium production, but would not prevent North Korea from continuing to enrich uranium at undeclared facilities outside Yongbyon.[7] Without knowing the output

7   For a review of public information on suspect sites, see https://www.nti.org/learn/countries/north-korea/facilities/

capacity of the Yongbyon enrichment facility relative to the capacity of undeclared enrichment facilities outside Yongbyon, it is not possible to calculate the significance of ending enrichment at Yongbyon. If, for example, the Yongbyon enrichment facility represents a small fraction of North Korea's overall enrichment capability, then ending enrichment at Yongbyon would have relatively little effect on North Korea's ability to continue producing additional nuclear weapons.

As a result, a comprehensive agreement to cease production of fissile material for nuclear weapons would require – at a minimum – that North Korea provide a full declaration of its fissile material production facilities and agree to allow on-site inspection to verify shutdown and eventual "dismantlement and destruction" of these facilities. Given North Korea's track record of denial and deception, any declaration of previously secret facilities will be met with much skepticism. The natural assumption is that North Korea will endeavor to admit those enrichment facilities it believes U.S. intelligence has already identified, while omitting facilities that it thinks are as yet undetected. The risk of cheating is especially acute in the case of gas centrifuge enrichment technology because relatively small facilities with a few thousand centrifuge machines can still produce significant quantities of weapons grade uranium, especially if North Korea manages to conceal a stockpile of low enriched uranium feed material.

Depending on the quality of U.S. intelligence, the North Korean declaration of its enrichment and related facilities could appear credible on its face or obviously false. Most likely, the U.S. evaluation of North Korea's declaration would be ambiguous because the U.S. has probably identified "suspect facilities" that may or may not actually be associated with enrichment. As a result, an effective verification agreement would require some means to check on the accuracy and completeness of North Korea's declaration and investigate potential evidence of non-compliance. As a practical matter, a true challenge inspection system – such as the U.S. imposed on Iraq in the aftermath of the 1990 Gulf War – is not realistic because North Korea will not accept such an invasion of its sovereignty. As an alternative, there would have to be some agreement for obtaining additional information to resolve discrepancies, including "managed access" to suspect sites, such as special inspections in the IAEA safeguards system or the inspection mechanism in the Iran nuclear deal, known as the Joint Comprehensive Plan of Action (JCPOA).

Whether North Korea would agree to such an intrusive inspection system remains to be seen. It would certainly be contrary to North Korean political culture and practice. Nonetheless, Kim Jong Un might be willing to forego additional fissile material production for the right price if he calculates that North Korea's existing nuclear arsenal is sufficient for national defense and secure from elimination for the time being. If Kim Jong Un makes a genuine decision to halt fissile material production, then North Korea could accept an inspection and monitoring system to verify (within reasonable bounds of uncertainly) the cessation of fissile material production. If Kim Jong Un decides to cheat – either by hiding existing facilities or building new facilities to produce fissile material – there is a reasonable chance that the inspection system backed by intelligence services would detect and expose significant non-compliance. While not always timely, U.S. intelligence has demonstrated a capacity for eventually detecting cheating, including, for example, North Korea's pursuit of enrichment in violation of the 1994 U.S.-DPRK Agreed Framework.

Finally, it should be noted that ending fissile material production is not the same thing as ending nuclear weapons production. Even if we could verify that North Korea had actually ended all production of additional fissile material, North Korea could still manufacture additional nuclear weapons if it has already accumulated a hidden reserve of weapons-usable fissile material. As described below, it is virtually impossible to accurately account for overall North Korean fissile material production in the past. In addition, North Korea could "mine" existing nuclear weapons for fissile material to build weapons that use less fissile material. Nonetheless, ending production of additional fissile material would be a major achievement to limit the overall size of North Korea's nuclear arsenal to approximately its current inventory – whatever that is.

Reduction and elimination of nuclear weapons

Based on North Korean statements and U.S.-DPRK contacts since the Singapore Summit, the elimination of North Korea's nuclear weapons program (or even reduction of its existing nuclear arsenal) is not a near term prospect. At best, Kim Jong Un has indicated a willingness to "cap" North Korea's current forces, but not give them up. Nonetheless, over a long period of time, North Korea might be prepared to reduce and eliminate its nuclear weapons arsenal and delivery systems in the context of economic development and assistance, normalized political relations with the U.S. and establishment of a "peace regime" on the Korean Peninsula.

Compared to verifying an end to fissile material production, verifying the elimination of North Korea's nuclear force is much more challenging. While it is certainly possible to verify the dismantlement, destruction or removal of individual nuclear weapons and stocks of fissile material, it is virtually impossible to verify the total elimination of North Korea's nuclear weapons because we cannot determine with high confidence how many nuclear weapons North Korea already has in its possession.

There are four sources of uncertainty. First and foremost, it is not possible to determine with precision how much fissile material North Korea has produced over the nearly three decades since it first began separating plutonium around 1989. Access to operating records, interviews with plant personnel and program managers, and forensic measurements can help to narrow uncertainties, but will not eliminate them. Records can be incomplete, inaccurate or falsified. Key personnel may be unavailable or unwilling to sit for interviews or they may be coached to provide false information, assuming that North Korea even allows personnel to be interrogated. Forensic testing and measurements are likely to be more useful in determining the history of operations at the Yongbyon 5MW reactor and reprocessing facility than at enrichment plants, but even the most intrusive forensic tests will contain a margin of error.

A second source of uncertainty is the possibility that North Korea obtained a significant quantity of weapons grade uranium from

Pakistan in the 1990s as part of the agreement between Islamabad and Pyongyang to exchange North Korean No Dong missiles for Pakistani centrifuge technology. Unless the Pakistani government has information on this possible transfer and is prepared to share it, it would be extremely difficult to rule out the possibility that North Korea was hiding a small quantity of foreign-origin weapons grade uranium – perhaps enough for a few nuclear weapons.

A third source of uncertainty is the amount of plutonium and weapons grade uranium that North Korea has consumed in its six nuclear tests. Presumably, as part of any overall accounting of its fissile material stocks, North Korea would be required to declare how much fissile material it used in nuclear testing and perhaps provide documentary evidence to back up its claim. One scenario for deception is North Korea could declare more fissile material than was actually used in testing, which would allow it to conceal enough fissile material for a small number of nuclear weapons. Environmental samples at the nuclear test site would provide information on the quality and type of nuclear material used in nuclear tests, but not on the quantities involved.

Finally, even if one could determine within a relatively narrow range the total quantity of fissile material currently in North Korea's possession, it is not possible to translate that overall amount into exact numbers of nuclear weapons without knowing the amount and type of material that North Korea uses to manufacture individual nuclear weapons, which might consist of several different types. As discussed above, it seems implausible that North Korea would allow a level of intrusive access to its nuclear weapons research and development and production programs that would be required to obtain such information.

Despite all of these limitations on verification, of course, any agreement to eliminate North Korea's nuclear weapons would result (at a minimum) in a significant reduction of North Korea's nuclear forces. This would be well worth the effort, even if one could not rule out the possibility that North Korea managed to squirrel away a small number of nuclear weapons.

Conclusion

The U.S. and North Korea are seeking agreement on concrete measures to make progress toward the Singapore Summit's goal of "complete denuclearization of the Korean Peninsula." It appears that the negotiations are focusing on some version of "freezing" or "capping" North Korea's current nuclear weapons capabilities. Some elements of a freeze, such as prohibitions on testing and use of nuclear weapons, can largely be verified by independent intelligence means, without requiring North Korean cooperation. The biggest challenge for a freeze is verifying a halt to nuclear weapons production, which would require North Korea to accept some degree of on-site monitoring and access to nuclear-related activities, facilities, personnel, records and so forth. Verifying that nuclear weapons production has halted through direct monitoring of weapons fabrication seems implausible because North Korea is unlikely to declare and tolerate access to sensitive nuclear production and storage facilities.

As an alternative, verifying that North Korea has halted production of fissile material and has dismantled relevant fissile material production facilities would establish hard limits on the size of North Korea's nuclear force. Thus far, Kim Jong Un has publicly offered to "permanently dismantle" nuclear facilities at Yongbyon. This can be verified without serious difficulty, but would not prevent North Korea from continuing to produce fissile material for additional nuclear weapons at facilities outside Yongbyon. Accordingly, the U.S. is seeking a broader North Korean commitment to end fissile material production at all facilities throughout the country and permit access to verify that these production facilities have been shut down and dismantled. If North Korea accepts this proposal, it will need to negotiate arrangements with the U.S. to declare and permit access to a range of enrichment and enrichment-related facilities that it has built and operated in secret for many years. Given North Korea's long record of nuclear cheating and the risk that it would seek to evade a ban on fissile material production, the negotiated verification arrangements would need to include some mechanism for resolving disputes and concerns about compliance, including managed access to "suspect" facilities or activities. Such a verification system – combined with continuing intelligence collection by the U.S. and its allies – would provide a sufficient degree of confidence to verify that North Korea had halted fissile material production. In short, the main obstacle to ending fissile material production in North Korea is a political decision by Kim Jong Un, not the challenge of verification.

16

Could the Trump Administration Achieve a Breakthrough? Perspectives of an East Asianist

Ezra F. Vogel

Many authors brought together by Bill Overholt have far more knowledge of North Korea and of the relations between North Korea and the outside world than I. But for the last 60 years I have followed developments in East Asia and will try to put developments in North Korea in this broader East Asian context during these six decades.

After the Korean War, in the 1950s and early 1960s the North Korean economy was stronger than that of South Korea's. Under Japanese occupation from 1910-1945, Japanese industrialists had built up the chemical and fertilizer industries in the north taking advantage of the Yalu River, and the south had been the agricultural base.

But with the industrial breakthroughs in South Korea in the 1960s and 1970s, under Park Chung Hee, South Korea became far stronger economically than North Korea. I had the honor of working with Kim Byung Kook who was the senior co-editor of the book that he and I edited on Park Chung Hee. Park came to power in 1959 with a coup. He was a military leader who had served under the Japanese military. He was intensely disliked by many American officials who despised his ruthless authoritarian leadership. He was hated by Korean intellectuals who suffered under his authoritarian limitations on free intellectual inquiry. He was cruel in dealing with labor movements and with political opposition. Yet he was brilliant, dedicated and ultimately successful in his efforts to build a modern economy. He worked closely with Japanese industrialists to build modern industries, including textiles, steel, automobiles, and electronics.

By the time Park Chung Hee was assassinated in 1979, the South Korean economy was many times stronger than the rigid Communist economy led by the Kim Il Sung. North Korea for many years had tried to manipulate the relationship with Russia and China to maintain its independence and to gain economic aid, but the aid that Park Chung Hee received from the Japanese overwhelmed the North Korean economy.

In the tense relationship between Taiwan and mainland China, mainland China has over 50 times the population of Taiwan and by the late 20th century the size of the mainland economy overwhelmed that of Taiwan. But since the Korean War, the population of South Korea has been roughly twice that of North Korea and by 1979 the size of the south Korean economy many times that of North Korea.

Furthermore, South Korea has had the solid military support of the United States.

As a tiny country, with a weak economy, with a small population, which could not rely on the support of China and Russia after the Korean War, North Korea has felt overwhelmed by fear of its enemies in the South and the Western countries and decided that the only way to protect itself and gain leverage with the outside world is by developing nuclear weapons. By 1965 it had built a nuclear reactor and by the 1980s had made progress in developing nuclear weapons and by the early 1990s had processed enough uranium to begin building nuclear weapons.

As a small country with nothing else to protect it, North Korea, despite its very poor small economy, has continued to be dedicated to building nuclear weapons. There have been times when progress was made in bringing the North Korean nuclear program under some kind of international control. In 1994, under pressure and negotiations from the United States, North Korea signed an Agreed Framework in which it agreed to stop producing plutonium at Yongbyong and to allow inspectors from the International Atomic Energy Agency. In 1998, former Secretary of Defense William Perry was put in charge of a policy review to work with the North Koreans in a series of consultations that would have led to normalization of relations and to a gradual reduction in North Korea's nuclear program. The "Perry Process" included close discussions with Japanese and South Korean officials. He and his team were making progress in dealing with North Korea, with the possibility of normalization of relations and gaining international control of nuclear facilities in North Korea.

As specialists know, when Kim Dae Jong of South Korea met with President George W. Bush shortly after he became president in 2001, Bush announced that he was breaking off all discussions with North Korea that William Perry and his team had worked so hard on. For two years thereafter there were no contacts with North Korea, and as is well known, North Korea resumed processing plutonium at Yongbyong and stopped allowing in IAEA inspectors. The North Koreans had not fulfilled their pledge to stop nuclear developments elsewhere and the United States had not fulfilled its pledge to supply nuclear reactors to North Korea for peaceful nuclear development.

North Korea has at times shown willingness to negotiate, and Steve Bosworth, the diplomat who has played a key role in negotiations with North Korea since the mid-1990s was presented with opportunities to move forward with negotiations which were not supported by higher U.S. officials. As we all know, North Korea therefore continued its nuclear weapons development program.

In 2018 we reached a new point at which North Korea had a well-developed nuclear program with a supply of nuclear weapons and a well-developed missile program capable of striking distant targets, including those in the United States. Under these conditions, President Trump met Kim Jong Un to reduce the risk of nuclear conflict. Officials under President Trump in the United States have by now undertaken a process of serious discussions with North Korea and other concerned countries, including South Korea, Japan, and China on the question of whether we can develop an understanding that would allow North Korea to begin to open its economy to the outside world and work in steps toward normalizing relations between North Korea and the United States.

In my mind, it is practically impossible to imagine that North Korea would give up its nuclear weapons capacity until far along in the process of developing diplomatic and economic relations with the United States and South Korea. The issue now is whether the U.S.

and other Western countries can be sufficiently patient in the process of gaining control over all nuclear weapons processing in North Korea to enable North Korea to begin opening up and expanding relations between North Korea and other countries.

In the summer of 2018, I was part of a delegation that met with Chinese officials in Dandong, a city on the border with North Korea. An official from the Dandong government told us that they have discussions with the government of the North Korea city, Sinuiju, on the other side of the border. The North Koreans are frightened of being overwhelmed by outside businesses and governments if they begin to open up. Officials in Dandong and Sinuiju are discussing the possibility of expanding economic relations between North Korea and the outside world in a way that would give North Korea some assurance that they would not be overwhelmed by businesses and governments from South Korea, the United States, China, and Japan. From the perspective of North Korea, their leaders would like to begin to open their economy if they could be convinced they would not be overwhelmed by the power of outside governments and businesses. The question for the United States is whether we can accept a staged process so that steps can be made to satisfy our goal of ultimate verifiable control over nuclear programs in North Korea that would allow us to continue to expand a process by which North Korea can develop peaceful relations with its neighbors and gradually open up its economy.

17

Missed Opportunities: Years of Suspicion, Brief Viable Trust

CHRISTINE BOSWORTH

At Stanford University in 2014, my husband, Stephen "Steve" Bosworth, was asked by colleagues, students, friends and those attending his lectures why North Korea had "hedged," or as many would say, "cheated," on the "Agreed Framework of 1994" by pursuing a uranium enrichment program. He would reply by saying the answer was "fairly simple."

"They were driven by their long years of suspicion – some would say paranoia – about the United States," Steve wrote in *Parting Reflections and Observations on American Foreign Policy* in 2014 as a Payne lecturer at the Shorenstein Center at Stanford University, I became convinced by my dealings with the North Koreans while I was Executive Director at KEDO (Korean Peninsula Energy Development Organization) that the non-nuclear aspects of the Agreed Framework – movement toward a more normal, less hostile political relationship with Washington – were more important to them than the reactors we had agreed to build "for energy purposes." Steve had no illusions about results, but that was one of those brief times of "viable trust" to build on – some would say an opportunity lost.

Steve had a long Foreign Service career, and was one of the few "generalists" in the State Department working, respectively, in Europe as a young diplomat, in Washington D.C. on international energy issues, as Deputy Assistant Secretary for Economic Affairs; Assistant Secretary for Latin American Affairs; Director of Policy Planning in the State Department; Ambassador to Tunisia; and Ambassador to the Philippines. He left the State Department as Ambassador to the Philippines in 1987, and began his focus on Northeast Asia as

President of the U.S. Japan Foundation where he gave to and gained from respect by the Japanese.

Steve was a "realist." As a diplomat he treated everyone with fairness and respect while being tough-minded about American interests. He dealt with Ferdinand Marcos and Corazon Aquino calmly and respectfully, with lines of communication open, but always acted decisively in support of American interests. He was an attentive listener of ideas, especially of opposing ideas while considering the synthesis; a diplomat had to think of future ramifications from decisions. Cautious, he was rarely triggered by negative situations unless he felt he must respond to uphold his or his country's integrity. He never demonized those he was negotiating with – they were high level leaders or diplomats defending their interests with their own history, culture, and challenges. One must negotiate based on a deep appreciation of the other country's special situation and unique problems, not just impose one's own preconceptions. As George Kennan believed, effective diplomatic communication includes "maximum accuracy, imagination, tact and good sense . . . propaganda and aid, not pistols and tanks."

The question for Steve was how do you make a deal – one that is in your country's interest? One that builds on "viable trust." It's not that he didn't see the weaknesses of the other sovereign state(s) or find the atrocities committed under their governments to be repugnant, but he knew that "in order for there to be agreement, goodwill, and common ground the other guy has to win something too." Negotiators are human, their country's interests complex, and deals created are fostered by honesty and implementation. As a diplomat Steve believed one had to deal with the adversary, as they were – bad behavior, insecurities and all, not the way one wished them to be. "You're trying to stop the worst behavior at the lowest possible price," he told *Frontline*. It was his job as a diplomat to show respect "to further and protect the United States' long-term interests and policies through dialogue and negotiation." And, leaders had to follow through on commitments – in order to "avoid war." As General James Mattis responded, as Secretary of Defense, on "slashing" the

American Foreign Service, "if the State Department gets cut then I need more ammunition."

In 1995 Steve was asked by the Clinton Administration to be the first Executive Director of KEDO, a multinational organization with the U.S., Japan, and South Korea carrying out the Agreed Framework of 1994. "Under the Framework, Pyongyang agreed to first freeze and then dismantle its nuclear weapons program. In return the U.S., Japan and South Korea agreed to build two 1,000-megawat light water reactors in North Korea for energy purposes and provide heavy fuel oil." Most importantly, we – the U.S. – agreed to "the full normalization of political and economic relations with the DPRK." As he would point out, the U.S never did "normalize the diplomatic relationship and establish a diplomatic presence."

Being circumspect, Steve initially agreed to take the job part time to help the multilateral organization get off the ground. They had to find office space, build consensus, and meet with the North Korean delegation. As executive director, Steve admired those who had negotiated the agreement, but "the Framework itself was exactly and only that – a framework." The challenge was that he, and his two experienced deputy executive directors, from Japan and South Korea: Itarru Umezu and Choi Young-Jin, "had to" as Steve would say, "make it all up." "It set forth basic principles but it left open fundamental aspects of what we were going to do and how." After some time Steve decided to take the job full time. He saw KEDO's potential. Its positive impact of multilateralism and diplomacy – as he said, "I knew little about North Korea and the mission was clearly challenging, but after some reflection and discussion with my wife Chris, I agreed." The experiment was exhilarating to him and I must admit to me too.

"One of KEDO's greatest challenges was that there had been an election in 1994 where the Republicans had won both the Senate and the House and – the majority Congress was not in favor of KEDO . . . The reality was that the Clinton administration had no prospect of getting a KEDO appropriation bill through the Republican controlled Congress – the U. S. had no money for KEDO. Fortunately, South Korea and Japan were committed to providing financial support to fund the light water reactor construction," part of the agreement. So, Steve was disappointed but not surprised by the backlash from the Republicans. He did not see the Agreed Framework as a Republican or Democrat deal; he saw it as an American deal. He believed as Kennan wrote, "A political society does not live to conduct foreign policy; it would be more correct to say that it conducts foreign policy in order to live." Diplomacy is an antidote to war.

Observing the cultural barriers developing in KEDO, Steve hired a cross-cultural trainer to work with the group. He knew that in order for them to work cooperatively they had to have their own identity as a multilateral organization. In a 38 North website remembrance of Steve by Choi Young-jin, the deputy executive representative from South Korea at KEDO, he recalls that Steve wanted the group to enjoy their work. For Young-jin, who would later become Ambassador to the United States and Vice Minister of Foreign Affairs and Trade for South Korea, it "revealed a leader who is on top of the situation while maintaining perspective."

I will never forget Steve coming home one evening in 1995 to say that the North Korean delegation was coming to New York, and what did I think about having a reception in our home in Manhattan. I immediately agreed. The reception would be a time to create a sense of joint cooperation and further camaraderie – to personalize relations. The North Koreans responded positively and stated they would be at our home at exactly 6:00 and leave at exactly 8:00. Indeed, they did arrive as a group at exactly at 6:00 but fortunately after a buffet of Korean, Japanese and American food and drink – soju, beer, sake, and Scotch – they stayed until around 11:00. Within a short period of time after they arrived South and North Koreans huddled in corners talking. At the end of the evening, Ho Jung, the head of the North Korean delegation, led a toast to thank Steve and me for the evening *and*, most importantly, to toast his "South Korean cousins." My uncle, Leo, a First Lieutenant flying the China-Burma-India "Hump" during World War Two and a Captain during the Korean War, was visiting us at the time stood next to me. As the toast was given he gasped quietly – he was not only stunned, but emotional. As toasts can do at times, they brought four countries of diplomats together for a brief time of "viable trust" to build on.

Choi Young-jin continues "But managing KEDO was not always easy. At the highest point of tensions, the North Korean head of the delegation suddenly called into question Steve's integrity. According to the North Koreans, KEDO did not keep its words or promises. Upon this accusation, Steve stopped the meeting, but once it resumed, he directly addressed the accusation and said:

> The North Korean delegation has its own way of managing the negotiations by creating problems and raising questions on matters that KEDO does not need to discuss over and over. It is a waste of time, but it is your method. We have to deal with it. But if you begin to question my integrity, after having accepted me as your negotiating partner, it is quite another matter. You must take responsibility for this attack on my integrity. I don't need to continue our discussion. Even if we reach an agreement among us, what confidence can you give to it? I don't want to discuss any more KEDO matters with you.

Then, Steve ended the meeting and left the room and a surprised and puzzled North Korean delegation. Less than 30 minutes later, the North Koreans requested a separate meeting in which they apologized for their mistake and asked to continue the talks. Steve said, "I have participated in negotiations with North Koreans many times in North Korea and elsewhere, but I have never witnessed their delegations accept their mistakes in such a way."

In 1997 Steve was nominated by President Clinton and confirmed by the Senate to be Ambassador to South Korea. We were on our way to Seoul via Los Angeles for Thanksgiving with my family when Steve received a call from Secretary Albright. She asked him to arrive in Seoul as soon as possible. We cut our visit short and arrived in Seoul a few weeks before the South Korean election in December. When we first arrived in Seoul, Koreans we met were convinced that Lee Hoi-chang would be the winner. The victory of Kim Dae-jung, a progressive from the National Congress Party, ended 36 years of conservative rule.

When people asked Steve if there was another time when he was optimistic about the U.S.-DPRK relationship, his answer was yes. He said, "In late 1998, while I was ambassador, former Secretary of Defense William 'Bill' Perry, was appointed as President Clinton's special envoy to deal with the North Korea situation. Under him, we began working with Japan and South Korea to bring about a normalization of relationships with the North."

I am going to digress here to point out an article in the Atlantic Magazine in March of 2018, by Uri Friedman. He writes, "Perry had seriously considered military strikes to destroy a North Korean nuclear reactor." That is true, but upon arriving to Seoul, what is also true is that after consultations with Steve he decided to reconsider. "Secretary Albright and President Clinton agreed." . . . (North Korea could retaliate by firing artillery systems to inflict devastating damage to destroy the northern outskirts of Seoul and kill millions of people.)

Steve continues, "President Kim embarked on the so-called Sunshine Policy toward the North, a bold attempt to change fundamentally the structure of North-South relations." It was much like what South Korean President Moon is endeavoring to do today. "After careful consideration, the Clinton Administration decided to support President Kim's initiative. We needed to ensure that our strategy remained in harmony with that of our ally South Korea. We also felt cautious optimism that perhaps there was an opportunity to begin to change the half-century of confrontation on the Peninsula."

After extensive consultation, Bill Perry visited Pyongyang in the summer of 1999 to end its nuclear-weapons program. We hoped discussions there would open serious engagement with North Korea. While we initially had some difficulty interpreting the complex signals coming from Secretary Perry's North Korean interlocutors, it soon became clear that the North Koreans had their own reasons for wanting to move down a path of engagement with both Washington and Seoul. Kim Dae-jung followed Perry's trip in June of 2000 and received the Nobel Peace Prize for the first-ever inter-Korean summit and his work for democracy and human rights.

> That, in turn contributed to a visit by Kim Jong Il's senior military envoy to Washington in October and, later the same month, Secretary of State Madeleine Albright's visit to Pyongyang. Kim Jong-il invited President Clinton to visit to Pyongyang, and I know the president seriously considered going. With the American presidential election taking place the following month, however, the Clinton administration ran out of time.

Until 2001, and the aftermath of the inauguration of President George W. Bush, Steve believed

> that there has been considerable continuity in American foreign policy from administration to administration . . . As I was preparing to leave Seoul, I quoted the axiom about American interests not changing to President Kim Dae-jung, and said I expected that, after its settling-in period was over, the Bush administration would pursue roughly the same policy as Clinton. After all U.S. interests don't change just because we have a change of government.
>
> I must confess, however, that this was not always the case. My prediction of course proved to be very wrong . . . all this seemingly positive movement was short lived. The sense of optimism and promise dissipated abruptly after George W. Bush was inaugurated.

President Kim-Dae-jung visited Washington shortly after President Bush had taken office to discuss North Korea policy with the new president. He was "anxious to create a positive relationship with the new president." Steve and I were in Washington at the time; he had been invited to a luncheon for President Kim and I had been invited to attend a luncheon for Lee Hee Ho, President Kim's wife. During that time Steve talked to Secretary Colin Powell – a retired four-star General, former NSC Advisor, and Chairman of the Joint Chiefs of Staff – and it appeared to Secretary Powell that Clinton's policy of engagement would continue, but Steve soon learned that President Bush's foreign policy had become politicized and hijacked by the hawks. Continuity in U.S. foreign policy was over. "To what end?" Steve wondered.

Steve remembers "President Bush made it clear that his administration not only did not endorse the Sunshine Policy but in fact considered the Agreed Framework had been a massive mistake. President Bush believed President Kim to be hopelessly naïve in his attempts to build a different kind of relationship with the North. A series of inexorable events ensued.

From 1994, when the Geneva agreement was signed, until the end of 2002 when it fell apart during George W. Bush administration's first term, we enjoyed eight years in which North Korea produced no plutonium." At the time, Steve lamented that not only had hard liners permeated domestic policy but now foreign policy. "By the end of 2002, the Agreed Framework had collapsed, KEDO was being dismantled, and the North Koreans had restarted their nuclear weapons programs at Yongbyon. . . . It took years for the U.S.-South Korea relationship to recover and as might be expected the ongoing diplomatic effort with North Korea."

Steve "strongly argued the fact that North Korea had not manufactured those several dozens of nuclear weapons was itself well worth the cost, political and financial, of the Geneva agreement." And, yes, "North Korea had hedged/cheated on the deal and began working on enriching uranium as an alternative to producing plutonium as a source of fissile material to produce nuclear weapons." And, yes that was against the agreement. Why? Again, "viable trust" had diminished bringing out suspicion, and the worst, from the North Korean government. As Steve said in 2014, "While one has their own view of why North Korea was hedging, and why the Agreed Framework ended, after the collapse the North Koreans promptly restarted their 5-megawatt reactor at Yongbyon. . . ."

In "North Korean eyes," Steve continued to reflect,

> There was little sign that Washington saw the situation in
> broader terms. The U.S. government, on both sides of the
> isle, was neither willing nor able to move to a new phase in
> relations with Pyongyang. Indeed, a cynical but not unre-
> alistic narrative was that the United States saw the Agreed
> Framework primarily as a means of coping with the problem
> of North Korea until the Pyongyang regime collapsed, some-
> thing many regarded as almost certain at the time. There
> were even those in the Clinton administration who argued
> that KEDO's mission was not to build nuclear reactors but to
> act as though we were building nuclear reactors . . . there was
> no need to hurry with the reactor construction.

At the State of Union Address in January 2002 President Bush
designated "North Korea as one of the "Axis of Evil" countries, a fore-
warning of American Foreign Policy. Many called this declaration a
"blunder," or as President George W. Bush's father, George H.W. Bush,
who rarely criticized his son, called it, a "mistake." Steve initially saw
this edict as strong rhetoric, but within months he began to worry that
it could be a foreign policy that could lead to war, or what the administration defined as "preventive war." Luckily reasoned minds prevailed
with regards to North Korea. As George Kennan said, "War has a
momentum of its own . . . you never know where you're going to end."

"As a result," of increasing tension and nuclear development by
North Korea during the Bush administration "China became acutely
concerned about the trend of developments on the Korean Peninsula
. . . and decided to become more involved." In 2003 they led the creation
of the Six Party Talks (China, U.S., South Korea, Japan, Russia, and
North Korea), hosted and chaired by Beijing to find a diplomatic solution. In 2005 their multilateral effort drafted a Joint Statement: denuclearization of the peninsula; negotiation of a peace treaty; provision
of economic and energy and assistance to North Korea; and establishment of diplomatic relations among the parties. For a brief period of

time Steve was relieved and hopeful that "viable trust" could be recreated and that an agreement would be signed. "The Joint Statement," Steve wrote, "was a significant accomplishment and remains the only agreed agenda with North Korea for negotiations." Unfortunately, "by 2008 it was clear that the Six Party Talks had run out of momentum." Also at the same time, The New York Times reported: "American intelligence agencies believed North Korea's leader Kim Jong-il had had some form of a stroke," This would complicate future negotiations. Kim Jong-il would die in December 2011.

In January of 2009 after President Barack Obama's inauguration, Steve was asked to be Special Representative for North Korea Policy for the administration. By that time, North Korea had made steady strides in their nuclear capability, and the threat had grown substantially. Much had changed since his days at KEDO and in Seoul as Ambassador when there had been another momentary time of time of trust, albeit a tenuous one. "I was not naïve about what might be possible. Mistrust and suspicion were deeply rooted on all sides, and it was clear that progress would not come easily," but Steve believed the new American President initially had " a genuine willingness to engage with Six Party Talks and bilaterally." He thought long and hard about the decision before he accepted, and agreed to take it on while keeping his job as Dean of the Fletcher School. Larry Bacow, then President of Tufts University, encouraged him knowing he would give his all to both jobs. Secretary Clinton also agreed. Steve became U.S. Special Representative on February 20, 2009.

For all American presidents, especially with success in nuclear development, a nuclear-armed North Korea capable of striking the U.S., Seoul, or Tokyo, could precipitate an outbreak of war. Seven nuclear-armed countries were the reality since the Cold War; with North Korea it was eight. Nuclear weapons for North Korea had been their "survival," a strategic decision and a deterrent from a U.S. attack. Yet North Korea knew that if they attacked, they would be attacked. While Steve, and most in the Obama administration, did not believe that North Korea was rash enough to launch missiles to hit the U.S., it had to be considered seriously. It was a real and existential threat.

"After another long-range missile test," in April and again in May, Steve wrote, "I remain puzzled by the North Korean refusal to accept what I believe could have been the beginning of a less hostile relationship with the U.S." Yet he also knew that because of Kim Jong-il's illness, Kim Jong Un might well have needed to solidify domestic and military support in advance of his father's death for "the regime to appear strong for the leadership transition." The threat continued to grow.

After several rounds of consultations with Six Party members Steve went to Pyongyang in December 2009. "We had what we thought were fairly constructive talks, and I . . . was "hopeful" that we could start a new process of engagement and reinvigorate the Six Party talks." Then, implausibly, the North Korean Navy sank the Cheonan, a South Korean warship, in waters near disputed territory killing 46 soldiers; in November 2010 the North Koreans shelled South Korean Yeonsgeong island, the first such attack since the Korean War. Steve was frustrated by North Korean behavior, as was the administration, and it was known that President Obama had developed a close relationship with Lee Myun-bak whose conservative views may have influenced North Korea policy. However, Steve believed during Obama's second term the Iran nuclear deal negotiated by John Kerry and his team, with our allies, was a positive step in diplomacy.

In August 2011, Steve had another meeting with his counterpart Kim Kye-gwan. By this time North Koreans had seen what happened to Libya in March of that year. Yet, he found North Korean diplomats more positive about the negotiations. The New York meeting was followed by a session in Geneva in October 201; he and the administration had brought North Korea back to the table, which produced the "Leap Day Agreement." Steve was increasingly hopeful that the North Korean government saw it in their interest to normalize their country in order to open it to economic development and to recreate their image in the international community. How did the seed of "viable trust" return? It returned through common ground, personal diplomacy, and negotiation with the two countries, its neighbors, and their long-term interest to avoid war. Now came the hardest part – implementation.

In October the administration told Steve that they needed some-one full- time to lead the discussions. "Six Party" talks were about to take place, yet they did not ask Steve to work out how he could stay on. He was surprised, for him to take part in these talks would have been a privilege. Was this another time of missed opportunity? Was his long history of building relationships with North Korea as well as China discounted? Steve believed strongly that a working relationship with China was key to success in U.S. foreign policy, and particularly with North Korea. Steve had worked closely with Ambassador Wu Dawei, his Chinese counterpart at the time, who had been Ambassador in Seoul when he was Ambassador. Steve saw this collaboration a time of shared objectives; and China, a strategic partner, as a key to solving denuclearization on the Korean Peninsula. And, yes, China was, and is, a competitor to the United States; but an adversary, hopefully not.

As Steve would often say "diplomacy is a great deal about timing." 2012 was not 1994. As the political climate had changed, continuity in foreign policy that he so believed in continued to erode. He became worried that the moralists, political opportunists, and doubters who feared failure and the true believers and hawks who had encouraged the militarization of foreign policy dominated the realists. Anger had taken hold; their voices resonated on cable news. While American foreign policy had become more politicized and less diplomatic, North Korea had become more entrenched. In 2017 the editor of 38 North after an interview wrote, "Steve, nothing if not always tactful, had a very uncharacteristic moment in which he bluntly made the point that the United States likes to tell other countries what their national interests are and that, in his experience, it doesn't work. He felt this was particularly true in the case of Washington's fixation that China could solve, for us, the growing challenge posed by North Korea."

From the time Steve left the Obama administration in 2011 to his death in January 2016, he continued his efforts of engagement. He continued to take part in Track Two diplomacy ("backchannel diplo-macy"), with U.S. nongovernmental civilians (many former diplo-mats, CIA, experts and academics) with North Korean diplomats. I was on two of those trips, Berlin (2013) and Singapore (2015), albeit not in the meetings, but at the dinners. The two following encounters are not substantive to policy but show a difference in attitude and behavior over a short period of time.

In Berlin we were staying at a small hotel with the American and North Korean delegations. One morning I got into a small elevator with two men I assumed were North Korean. Steve had gone down earlier. I introduced myself and found their distant gaze became a cordial interaction portraying respect. That evening there was a long and friendly dinner with good spirits, laughter, and open conversation.

In 2015 there was another Track Two meeting between the two countries in Singapore. It was shortly after the *The Interview*, the movie/comedy produced by Sony Pictures about Kim Jung Un. That evening there was a dinner in a private room at a Chinese restaurant. Behavior was more businesslike, restrained, and cool; they said they were upset and insulted by The Interview. Kim Jung Un had been demeaned, and somehow the U.S. was responsible. They had "lost face." While everyone was respectful, the atmosphere had discernibly changed. Yet, as we all stood up ready to leave, the head of the delegation who had been sitting next to me said that he had been at our home in Manhattan in 1996 as a young North Korean foreign-service officer – he said what a good time he and the others had had.

That evening Steve and I talked about how time had continued to change the rollercoaster relationship between the U.S. and North Korea. The two countries were again at a low point. Hostility had grown. With change, years of suspicion, a fear that both countries had experienced during the Korean War, the fear of a nuclear war had grown. Would future American presidents and diplomats be able to build "viable trust" and convince North Korea to denuclearize? Could we normalize relations and sign a peace treaty? Hopefully. That would mean tough negotiations of defining what denuclearization means: their following through on their commitment to freeze the nuclear program and dismantle parts of its facilities; discontinue the production of fissile material; an inventory of weapons; better enforcement at international ports with regards to breaking sanctions; as well as

American troops continuing military exercises and troops remaining in South Korea – and importantly constant verification. It would also mean holding them accountable for their cyber attacks and money laundering. Joshua Stanton, Lee Sung-yoon, and Bruce Klinger suggest, "The only remaining hope for denuclearizing North Korea peacefully lies in convincing it that it must disarm and reform or perish."

Or, could the United States accept North Korea as a nuclear power state with IAEA inspections, end the Korean War with a Peace Treaty, and normalize relations? This would also mean many of the tough negotiations mentioned above. We don't know the answer to these questions, but we have to hope both countries choose rational and realistic diplomacy to solve issues to prevent war.

Steve believed if the United States is to have a successful foreign policy we have to "tend the garden" of diplomacy, as George Schultz would say. It means continuity – a coherent and thought through foreign policy from administration to administration. If not, our allies and our foes are left in the lurch and will not be able to anticipate consequences. Diplomats, like the military, are deterrents to war – the first prong. A strong military is essential – but the second prong.

Was Steve hopeful about future diplomatic engagement? Yes, if we are astute, perceptive and patient. While he was a realist, he was also an optimistic one. As he said, the North Koreans were driven by their long years of suspicion – some would say paranoia – about the United States. With presidential leadership and able diplomats situations change – individuals make a difference. Considering and imagining different results makes a difference. Having a "realistic end game" makes a difference. Treating those you are negotiating with dignity and respect makes a difference. Upholding your and your country's self-respect makes a difference. Human connection and chemistry make a difference. Building on trust makes a difference.

At this time "doing nothing" doesn't work. Threatening and bullying doesn't work. And, neither does cynicism.

18

Hope and History

Kathleen Stephens

It is mid-February. In Washington the transition from the old year to the new was interminable and unpleasant: The federal government, budgetless, shut down before Christmas and didn't reopen for a record-shattering 35 days. A "polar vortex" of Arctic air broke cold weather records in the Midwest. The U.S.-South Korea talks on military burden-sharing stalemated.

Happily, Lunar New Year gave us a second crack at a fresh start for 2019. We welcomed warmer weather, donned our hanbok and ate dduk-kuk, and heard President Trump in his shutdown-delayed State of the Union address announce that his long-teased second summit with Kim Jong Un will happen in Vietnam February 26-27.

This second summit won't get the same stratospheric attention in the U.S. that the first did, though interest remains high, along with skepticism. Americans uniformly express relief that war was averted on the Korean Peninsula last year, though their views on whether Trump's role was more to stoke or reduce tensions is influenced by how they view this brash, norms- shattering Commander in Chief about whom no one is neutral.

The Trump Administration has been prickly in pushing back against the notion that the Singapore summit was ill-prepared, the joint statement disastrously vague, and the follow-up a failure. The January 29 Director of National Intelligence (DNI) report to the Congress assessing that Pyongyang was "unlikely to give up all of its WMD stockpiles, delivery systems, and production capabilities" enraged Trump, who insists that Kim Jung-Un's economic ambitions for his country, combined with Trump-Kim personal chemistry, makes an historic "great deal" on denuclearization attainable.

There are lots of reasons for doubt, or at least caution, and we see it voluminously outlined in opinion pages and expert analyses in both our countries. But for all the skepticism about North Korea and for that matter Trumpian intent and capability, for all the past decades of failure, I remain convinced that diplomacy, backed by continued deterrence and defense, remains the right path forward.

It was encouraging to hear U.S. Special Representative for North Korea Stephen Biegun tell a Stanford audience recently that he was listening to and learning from those involved in past efforts, from the Agreed Framework to the Six Party Talks to the range of inter-Korean engagements. The North Koreans know this history well, as do others in the region. American negotiators need to know it, too.

A longer-term, broader perspective on what are the likely outcomes of this kind of process is also needed. I get that not just from studying the history of the nuclear issue, and of Korea itself, but in looking at other parts of the world. Every situation is different, but from my own experience in Northern Ireland and the Balkans, I think there is something to be learned – and encouraged by – looking at other troubled regions of the world with decades (or centuries) of painful attempts at ending conflict.

I was involved in the Northern Ireland peace process for much of the 1990s, first working from the State Department and the White House, and then for three years, 1995-1998, leading the U.S. official presence in Belfast.

The short version of the story is this: Paramilitary ceasefires (1994) followed by negotiations (1995-1998) followed by the Good Friday Agreement (GFA) of 1998. End of story. The Troubles over. Peace and reconciliation achieved.

In fact, at virtually every stage, and even now, decades later, progress has been fitful, often reversed, and never easy.

I was the State Department officer in charge of U.S.-UK relations in 1993 when U.S.-UK relations hit a modern low (as my colleagues sometimes teased me, "the worst since the British sacked the White House in the War of 1812"); President Clinton, over the objections of his entire Cabinet, and the British Prime Minister, approved a U.S.

visa for Sinn Fein leader Gerry Adams, whom the British – and U.S. visa law – regarded as a terrorist. Even after the IRA and other paramilitary groups declared ceasefires, the Northern Ireland Unionists and the British insisted that they declare the ceasefires "permanent." They also insisted the paramilitaries, notably the IRA, disarm before negotiations begin. The other side refused, and the peace process seemed stillborn yet again.

Ten weeks after the first-ever U.S. Presidential visit to Northern Ireland, where Clinton exhorted all to take "risks for peace" to build on the ceasefires, the IRA, angered over demands for "decommissioning," broke its ceasefire with a bomb attack in London.

Negotiations finally got going after decommissioning was put on a separate track from the political negotiations. With this, talks got underway, involving the range of Northern Ireland parties, the UK, Ireland, a panel of international chairs, the EU, and frequent interventions from the White House. Continued eruptions of sectarian protest and violence complicated and sometimes stopped the talks.

But, finally, on Good Friday, 1998, an agreement was announced and put to the vote in Northern Ireland.

Within months, a splinter IRA group bombed the Northern Ireland town of Omagh.

Still, the GFA held, though full implementation took a decade and more. Full decommissioning of paramilitary explosive and arms stockpiles was a long, slow process, tied to verification requirements, and to negotiating further police reforms and other confidence building measures in Northern Ireland.

Today, the Good Friday Agreement is again threatened, this time by the implications of Brexit for Northern Ireland.

Up close, at any time over the past twenty-plus years, the prospects for lasting peace and reconciliation in Northern Ireland seemed dim, the process fragile. Stepping back, though, it's clear that while the Good Friday Agreement is far from perfect, it worked and is working today as a bulwark against a return to the worst of the past, and it provides a framework for continuing to move forward toward peaceful reconciliation. In the meantime, the people of Northern Ireland

– from all communities – and the surrounding region have reaped economic, social, and cultural benefits.

I was often skeptical about where U.S. engagement in Northern Ireland might lead through all the years I worked on it. As a diplomat I shared the worries that President Clinton was damaging our "special relationship" with the UK in his aggressive and unconventional courting of Sinn Fein. Living in Belfast for three years, I empathized with the long-suffering working-class people of both Protestant and Catholic communities who had lived in the shadow of violence for so long, and insisted there should be "No Surrender" to those who had once espoused it.

Seamus Heaney, the 1995 Nobel Prize recipient for poetry, was from Northern Ireland. When I had my fill of press reports, political speeches, and learned analyses, I turned to his insights about his native land. He had no time for false optimism, or the professional "cautiously optimistic" bromides of politicians and diplomats. But he did believe in "a people's right at least to hope." Here's to hope – and to continued dialogue – in the year ahead.

> History says, Don't hope
> On this side of the grave,
> But then, once in a lifetime
> The longed-for tidal wave
> Of justice can rise up
> And hope and history can rhyme.
> (From "The Cure at Troy")

Contributors

WILLIAM H. OVERHOLT, a specialist on Asian development and Asian geopolitics, is Senior Research Fellow in Harvard University's Massavar-Rahmani Center for Business and Government. He has been involved with Korea since 1973, when he contributed to a joint Korean-American study published as *Korean Futures*. In 1976 he published the first book, *Asia's Nuclear Future*, on nuclear proliferation and nuclear strategy in Asia. His nine books include *The Rise of China* (1993) and *Asia, America and the Transformation of Geopolitics* (2008). His career includes 16 year in think tanks, 21 years running investment bank research teams, mainly in Hong Kong, and ten years at Harvard. He received his B.A. from Harvard and his Ph.D. from Yale.

SUNG-YOON LEE is Kim Koo-Korea Foundation Professor of Korean Studies and Assistant Professor at The Fletcher School of Law and Diplomacy, Tufts University. Dr. Lee's essays on the international politics of the Korean peninsula and Northeast Asia have been published multiple times in the *New York Times*, *Wall Street Journal*, *Washington Post*, *LA Times*, *Foreign Affairs*, *Foreign Policy*, *Christian Science Monitor*, *CNN*.com, *The Hill*, etc. His most recent publications are "Seoul's Supporting Role in North Korea's Sanctions-Busting Scheme" in *Asia Policy* (13.3, July 2018), "Forgotten Borders: Japan's Maritime Operations in the Korean War and Implications for North Korea," in Geoffrey F. Gresh, ed., *Eurasia's Maritime Rise and Global Security: From the Indian Ocean to Pacific Asia and the Arctic* (Palgrave, 2018), and "Getting Tough on North Korea: How to Hit Pyongyang Where it Hurts," in the May/June 2017 issue of *Foreign Affairs*.

CHUNG-IN MOON is special advisor to the ROK president for foreign affairs and national security. He is also a distinguished university professor at Yonsei University, Krause distinguished fellow at School of Global Policy and Strategy at the University of California, San Diego, and editor-in-chief of *Global Asia*, a quarterly journal in English. He is co-convener of APLN (Asia-Pacific Leadership Network for Nuclear Disarmament and Non-Proliferation). He was dean of the Graduate School of International Studies, Yonsei Univ. and served as Ambassador for International Security Affairs of the Korean Ministry of Foreign Affairs and Trade and Chairman of the Presidential Committee on Northeast Asian Cooperation Initiative, a cabinet-level post. Dr. Moon was a special delegate to the first (2000), second (2007), and third Korean summit (2018) held in Pyongyang. He has published over 60 books and 300 articles in edited volumes and scholarly journals.

ANDREI LANKOV was born 26 July 1963 in Leningrad (now Petersburg). He completed his undergraduate and graduate studies at Leningrad State University (PhD in 1989). In 1996-2004 he taught Korean history at the Australian National University, and since 2004 he teaches at Kookmin University in 2004, Seoul (currently a professor at the College of Social Studies), and is also director of Korearisk.com group. His major research interest is North Korean history and society. His major English language publications on North Korea include: *From Stalin to Kim Il Sung: The Formation of North Korea, 1945-1960* (Rutgers University Press, 2003); *Crisis in North Korea: The Failure of De-Stalinization, 1956* (University of Hawaii Press, 2004), *North of the DMZ: Essays on Daily Life in North Korea* (McFarland and Company, 2007), *The Real North Korea* (Oxford University Press, 2013). He contributed to *Wall Street Journal*, *The New York Times*, *Financial Times*, *Newsweek*, and published a number of academic articles, including two articles in the *Foreign Affairs* and an article in *Foreign Policy*. He also writes extensively in Korean and Russian.

JOHN DELURY is an associate professor of Chinese studies at Yonsei University Graduate School of International Studies in Seoul, South Korea. He is a historian of modern China, specializing on US-China and Sino-Korean relations, and expert on Korean Peninsula affairs. He is the author, with Orville Schell, of *Wealth and Power: China's Long March to the Twenty-first Century* (Random House, 2013), contributes regularly to *Foreign Affairs*, *Foreign Policy*, *Global Asia*, and *38 North*, and his articles have appeared in the *Journal of Asian Studies*, *Asian Perspective* and *Late Imperial China*. He is a senior fellow of the Asia Society and Pacific Century Institute and member of the Council of Foreign Relations, National Committee on US-China Relations and National Committee on North Korea. Dr. Delury offered courses at Brown, Columbia, Yale and Peking University, and served as founding associate director of the Asia Society Center on US-China Relations in New York.

DWIGHT H. PERKINS is Harold Hitchings Burbank Professor of Political Economy, Emeritus, of Harvard University. Previous positions at Harvard include Associate Director of the East Asian Research Center (now Fairbank Center for Chinese Studies), Chairman of the Department of Economics, Director of the Harvard Institute for International Development, and Director of the Harvard Asia Center. Dwight Perkins has authored, coauthored or edited 25 books and over 100 articles on economic history and development including six books on the economic history and development of the Republic of Korea. He has served as a consultant/advisor to governments in Vietnam, Republic of Korea, Indonesia, Malaysia, China, and Papua New Guinea as well as to the U.S. government, the Ford Foundation, and the World Bank.

CARTER J. ECKERT is the Yoon Se Young Professor of Korean History in the Department of East Asian Languages and Civilizations at Harvard University. For eleven years, from 1993 to 2004, Eckert served as the director of the Korea Institute at Harvard and presided over a major financial and academic expansion that transformed the Institute into one of the most active and respected international Korean studies centers. He is also currently serving again as the Institute's Interim Director. He is the author of *Offspring of Empire: The Colonial Origins of*

Korean Capitalism 1876-1945, winner of the John K. Fairbank Prize in East Asian History from the American Historical Association, as well as the John Whitney Hall Book Prize from the Association for Asian Studies. He is also a co-author of *Korea Old and New: A History*, a widely-used university textbook on Korean history. He also co-edited a book on the economic development of the Republic of Korea with Professor Lee-Jay Cho of the University of Hawaii. In 1996-97 he was a fellow at the Woodrow Wilson Center for International Scholars in Washington, D.C. At present he is engaged an historical study of Korean militarization and the rise of Korean militarism, in relation to the economic development of South Korea under Park Chung Hee (1961-1979). The first volume of this study, *Park Chung Hee and Modern Korea: The Roots of Militarism 1866-1945* was published by Harvard University Press in 2016. In recognition of this work, Eckert was designated a Walter Channing Cabot Fellow by Harvard University in 2017.

KATHARINE H.S. MOON is Professor of Political Science and the Wasserman Chair of Asian Studies at Wellesley College, where she has taught since 1993. She is also a nonresident senior fellow at The Brookings Institution Center for East Asia Policy and was the inaugural holder of the SK-Korea Foundation Chair in Korea Studies (2014-2016). She received a B.A., *magna cum laude*, from Smith College and a Ph.D. from Princeton University. Professor Moon's research encompasses the U.S.-Korea alliance, East Asian politics, inter-Korean relations, democratization, nationalisms, women and gender politics, international migration, identity politics, and comparative social movements. She is the author of *Protesting America: Democracy and the U.S.-Korea Alliance*, which discusses the impact of South Korean democracy on the U.S.-Korea alliance. She also authored *Sex Among Allies: Military Prostitution in U.S.-Korea Relations*, which explains how foreign policy decisions affect local communities hosting U.S. bases, particularly women.

ZHENG JIYONG is Professor and Director at the Center for Korean Studies, Fudan University, and Secretary-General of Shanghai

Institute of Korean Studies. Zheng Jiyong joined the army and studied at the School of Foreign Languages, the Chinese People's Liberation Army. In 1991, he was assigned to research the military and diplomacy of the Korean Peninsula. In 2009, he retired from the army and joined Fudan University. He received his Doctoral Degree at Fudan University, and had post-doctoral experiences at IFES, Kyungnam University, ROK(2009/09-2010/12), and in Kim Il Sung University, DPRK(2014/07-11), and a Visiting Scholar in Seoul National University, ROK(2016/09-2017/09). His research focuses on domestic politics in the two Koreas, and on bilateral and multilateral relations related to the Korean peninsula. He is the author and coauthor of more than 100 scholarly articles and author or editor of more than 10 books, including ROK's *Political Party Systems* (2008), ROK's *Parliamentary Politics* (2017), The *"Conflict-Reconciliation" Cycle on the Korean Peninsula: A Chinese Perspective* (2012), and *Road Map to a Korean Peninsula Peace Regime: A Chinese Perspective* (2015). He can be reached at zhengjiyong@fudan.edu.cn.

WANG XINGXING is Research Fellow of Global Security Cooperation Center of Hankuk University of Foreign Studies. Secretary-General of Korean-China Culture Exchange Association, Ph.D of International Studies in Seoul National University, jointly completed at UCLA. She was a visiting Scholar in Kim Il Sung University, DPRK, and is currently in SAIS, Johns Hopkins University. Her research focuses mainly on regional issues in Northeast Asia, the history and relations between China and Korean peninsula, and North Korean issues.

RICHARD J. SAMUELS is Ford International Professor of Political Science and Director of the Center for International Studies at the Massachusetts Institute of Technology. In 2005 he was elected to the American Academy of Arts and Sciences and in 2011 he received the Order of the Rising Sun, Gold and Silver Star, an Imperial decoration awarded by the Emperor of Japan and Japanese Prime Minister. In 2015 he was named an Albert Einstein Fellow at the Free University of Berlin, where he supervises a small research group. In 2013, Cornell

University Press published Samuels' book about the political effects of Japan's March 2011 catastrophes, *3.11: Disaster and Change in Japan*. His previous book, *Securing Japan: Tokyo's Grand Strategy and the Future of East Asia*, was one of five finalists for the 2008 Lionel Gelber Prize for the best book in international affairs. Cornell University Press will publish his *Special Duty: A History of the Japanese Intelligence Community* in 2019.

ERIC HEGINBOTHAM is a principal research scientist at MIT's Center for International Studies and a specialist in Asian security issues. Before joining MIT, he was a senior political scientist at the RAND Corporation, where he led research projects on China, Japan, and regional security issues and regularly briefed senior military, intelligence, and political leaders. He was the lead author of the *U.S.-China Military Scorecard* (RAND, 2015) and *China's Evolving Nuclear Deterrent* (RAND, 2017). He is the coauthor (with George Gilboy) of *Chinese and Indian Strategic Behavior: Growing Power and Alarm* (Cambridge University Press, 2012), and co-editor of *China Steps Out: Beijing's Major Power Engagement with the Developing World* (Routledge, 2018). He has published numerous articles in *Foreign Affairs*, *International Security*, *Washington Quarterly*, *Current History*, and elsewhere. He is fluent in Chinese and Japanese, and was a Captain in the U.S. Army Reserve.

VICTOR CHA is a senior adviser and the inaugural holder of the Korea Chair at the Center for Strategic and International Studies. He also holds the D.S. Song-KF Professorship in Government and International Affairs at Georgetown University. He served in the White House 2004-2007 as Director for Asian Affairs at the National Security Council (NSC). He was also deputy head of delegation for the United States at the Six-Party Talks in Beijing and received two Outstanding Service commendations during his tenure at the NSC. He is the author of five books, including the award-winning *Alignment Despite Antagonism: The United States-Korea-Japan Security Triangle* (winner of the 2000 Ohira Book Prize) and *The Impossible*

State: North Korea, Past and Future, which was selected by *Foreign Affairs* as a "Best Book on the Asia-Pacific for 2012." His newest book is *Powerplay: Origins of the American Alliance System in Asia* (Princeton University Press, 2016). He is writing a new book on Korean unification.

STEPHAN HAGGARD is the Lawrence and Sallye Krause Professor of Korea-Pacific Studies, director of the Korea-Pacific Program and distinguished professor of political science at the School. He has written on transitions to and from democratic rule and the political economy of economic reform, social policy and globalization. His focus on the Asia-Pacific region includes extensive work on North Korea with with Marcus Noland, including *Famine in North Korea: Markets, Aid, and Reform* (2007), *Witness to Transformation: Refugee Insights into North Korea* (2011) and *Hard Target: Sanctions., Inducements and the Case of North Korea* (2017). Haggard is the current editor of the *Journal of East Asian Studies*, maintains the "North Korea: Witness to Transformation" blog and has a regular column with the *Joongang Daily*.

DANIEL C. SNEIDER is Associate Director for Research, Freeman Spogli Institute for International Studies, Stanford University, and a Lecturer in International Policy at Stanford. His research focuses on U.S. foreign and national security policy in Asia and on the foreign policy of Japan and Korea. Sneider was named a National Asia Research Fellow by the Woodrow Wilson International Center for Scholars and the National Bureau of Asian Research in 2010. He is the co-editor, with Gi-Wook Shin, of *History Textbooks and the Wars in Asia: Divided Memories* (2011). He is the co-editor of *Cross Currents: Regionalism and Nationalism in Northeast Asia* (2007); of *First Drafts of Korea: The U.S. Media and Perceptions of the Last Cold War Frontier* (2009); as well as of *Does South Asia Exist?: Prospects for Regional Integration* (2010). Sneider's path-breaking study "The New Asianism: Japanese Foreign Policy under the Democratic Party of Japan" appeared in the July 2011 issue of *Asia Policy*.

DR. GARY SAMORE is Senior Executive Director of the Crown Center for Middle East Studies and Professor of Practice at Brandeis University. He is also a nonresident Senior Fellow at the Belfer Center for Science and International Affairs at the Kennedy School of Government at Harvard University. From 2009 to 2013, he served as President Obama's White House Coordinator for Arms Control and Weapons of Mass Destruction (WMD). He also served as President Clinton's Senior Director for Nonproliferation and Export Controls on the National Security Council from 1996 to 2001. Prior to that, Dr. Samore led the U.S. delegation of experts that negotiated the 1994 U.S.-DPRK Agreed Framework, for which he received the Secretary of Defense Medal for Meritorious Civilian Service in October 1995. Dr. Samore was a National Science Foundation Fellow at Harvard University, where he received his M.A. and Ph.D. in government in 1984.

EZRA F. VOGEL is Professor Emeritus, Harvard University. He received his Ph.D. at Harvard in 1958 in Sociology in the Department of Social Relations and was professor at Harvard from 1967-2000. In 1973, he succeeded John Fairbank to become the second Director of Harvard's East Asian Research Center. At Harvard he served as director of the US-Japan Program, director of the Fairbank Center, and as the founding director of the Asia Center. From fall 1993 to fall 1995, Vogel was the National Intelligence Officer for East Asia at the National Intelligence Council in Washington. His book **Japan As Number One** (1979), in Japanese translation, became a best seller in Japan, and his book *Deng Xiaoping and the Transformation of China* (2011), in Chinese translation, became a best seller in China. He lectures frequently in Asia, in both Chinese and Japanese. He has received numerous honors, including eleven honorary degrees.

CHRISTINE BOSWORTH is the author of a forthcoming biography of a woman who experienced the Russian Revolution, the Finnish Civil War, and migration to New York. Her article, "Can Trump and Moon Quell North Korea's Saber Rattling?" appeared in *The National*

Interest in June 2017. In Korea and elsewhere she initiated programs to bring the diplomatic community together and in Seoul to enhance understanding between Koreans and Americans. For instance, she raised funds for Korean projects during the Asian Crisis. She organized a project, based on art, to enhance understanding between Koreans and Korean-Americans Throughout, she supported her husband, Ambassador Stephen W. Bosworth, in multiple Korea-related assignments, including Ambassador to Korea, an earlier Embassy assignment in Seoul, Executive Director of the Korea Peninsula Energy Development Organization (KEDO – 1995-1997); and later Special Representative for North Korea Policy. She was President of the Sister City Program of the City of New York.

KATHLEEN STEPHENS is President and CEO of the Korea Economic Institute. A career diplomat, 1978-2015, she was U.S. Ambassador to the Republic of Korea 2008-2011. She served in rural Korea as a Peace Corps volunteer, 1975-1977. She was in Korea 1983-1989, first as a political officer at the U.S. Embassy in Seoul and later leading the U.S. Consulate in Busan. Ambassador Stephens also served as acting Under Secretary of State for Public Diplomacy and Public Affairs (2012), Principal Deputy Assistant Secretary of State for East Asian and Pacific Affairs (2005-2007), Deputy Assistant Secretary of State for European and Eurasian Affairs (2003-2005), and National Security Council Director for European Affairs. Other overseas assignments included postings to China, former Yugoslavia, Portugal, Northern Ireland (where she was U.S. Consul General in Belfast during the negotiations culminating in the 1998 Good Friday Agreement), and India (where she was U.S. Charge 'd Affaires, 2014-2015).